A Fly Fisher's Life

The Art and Mechanics of Fly Fishing

by Charles Ritz

prepared in collaboration with
John Piper

MJF Books
NEW YORK

TO ARNOLD GINGRICH
and all my fishing friends

P.S: And not because he
wrote the introduction!

Published by MJF Books
Fine Communications
Two Lincoln Square
60 West 66th Street
New York, NY 10023

A Fly Fisher's Life
Library of Congress Catalog Card Number 99-70065
ISBN 1-56731-264-0

English translation Copyright © Max Reinhardt 1959
Additional material copyright © Charles Ritz 1965, 1972
First published in Great Britain 1959. Reprinted with additional material 1965.
Reprinted 1967 and 1969. This revised edition 1972. Reprinted 1977. First reprinted
by Robert Hale 1996.

Published by arrangement with Robert Hale Limited, London.

Manufactured in the United States of America on acid-free paper

MJF Books and the MJF colophon are trademarks of Fine Creative Media, Inc.

10   9   8   7   6   5   4   3   2   1

CONTENTS

For the reader's convenience a table of comparison of metric and British measure for nylon is given below

Diameter		Breaking strain	
mm	*inch*	*kg*	*lbs*
0·08	·003	0·2	½
0·10	·004	0·55	1½
0·15	·006	1·00	2¼
0·175	·007	1·4	3
0·20	·008	1·8	4
0·225	·009	2·2	5
0·25	·010	2·7	6
0·275	·011	3·3	7
0·30	·012	4·00	9
0·35	·014	5·00	11
0·40	·016	6·3	14
0·45	·018	8·00	18
0·50	·020	10·4	23
0·60	·024	12·00	27
0·70	·027	16·00	35
0·80	·031	20·00	44
0·90	·035	30·00	66
1·00	·040	33·00	77

PLATES

THERE ARE ALSO 62 FIGURES IN THE TEXT

THIS edition of *A Fly Fisher's Life* has been completely revised and
contains much new material. I want to acknowledge the great help I have
had from my friend John Piper, without whom it would have been
difficult for me to produce the book in this form. I am not a professional
writer and have never been the best of friends with French or English
grammar. I shall long remember his kindness, patience and co-operation
as we prepared these pages for the printers. Thanks to his efforts, the book
is easier to read and better arranged than any previous edition and as a
token of my appreciation he is now a member of the International Fario
Club. – *Charles Ritz.*

FOREWORD

———

Charles Ritz is one of the very finest fishermen I know. He is not only a great fly fisherman for trout and salmon but he is an articulate writer and a splendid technician.

He is also an iconoclast who never hesitates to destroy an idol in order to deal only with true and important facts.

Because he is a charming companion he does not bore a non-technical reader with his knowledge. But it is there like a mine of true information for anyone with the desire and the intelligence to work it.

Fishing with Charles Ritz you come to know the streams of Normandy and Austria and the salmon rivers of the North.

As the world is run now few people can fish as far as Monsieur Charles fishes. No matter how it is run even fewer people could ever fish as well.

ERNEST HEMINGWAY

INTRODUCTION
By Arnold Gingrich

———

The first time I ever fished with Charles Ritz was on the Risle in Normandy in the spring of 1959. He was then nearing his sixty-eighth birthday (he was born August 1, 1891), and his movements were graceful, but deliberate, as befits a person of a certain age. I don't say he was an adagio dancer, but let's settle for an andante walker. We had driven out from the Ritz in his mother's Cadillac – his own little Lancia was left in the semi-circular cobblestone entrance of the Hotel on the Place Vendôme, as being too small for the three of us and the chauffeur and our picnic stuff and all our gear – and I noticed as we were getting in and out of the car that all his gestures and postures and stoopings and bendings were – well, not ponderous, because Charles is slight, lean and lithe, but suitable to a senior citizen. His mother, in her nineties, was still living in the Hotel, and checking up on his whereabouts as if he were a teenager, and by all objective accounts she seemed a lot livelier in those days than he did.

While we were fishing I kept noticing how measured his every motion was. He flicked his rod exactly as if it were a tack hammer, and he was just lightly nailing something to the wall, so he could step back and see how it looked and still change its position if he didn't like it. The very lightest forward motion of his thumb, as he held the rod up as you'd hold an umbrella while waiting for a tardy bus, and – whish – the line shot forward like something launched from a crossbow, and travelled a country mile in the blink of an eye, and at a difficult angle, to a spot near the other bank where he had apparently detected a dimple that nobody else had noticed. The dimple exploded into a little geyser as a fat brown trout began chinning himself on Charlie's fly and splashing water for a yard in all directions at once.

I watched this happen five more times before I'd had so much as a touch myself, and I came to the conclusion that nobody, to my knowledge and recollection, had ever exercised such economy of motion in relation to results, not only in fishing but in any other purposeful activity I had ever observed.

His example was infectious. Within minutes he had my wife imparting that same little tack-hammer flick to her rod, and the line going out with an impetus and

3

distance that I wouldn't have dreamed she could have attained without shooting it from a gun.

Wow, I thought to myself as I looked across from the other bank, this is not merely the most efficient fisher I've ever seen, but also the best teacher, by far. I decided to profit from the opportunity and try a little of this tack-hammering myself. It looked so completely effortless, as I stood there seeing them doing it, but all I managed to impart to my line was an unholy tangle, and a birdsnest of my leader.

Well, that was a dozen years ago, and I must have seen Charles Ritz at least an average of once a year since. He has gone from andante to allegretto to vivace to presto, in the interim, and I marvel at the man's seemingly infinite capacity for acceleration.

A few weeks back, as this is written, we were together in the Poconos, when Charles was taking in a Federation of Fly Fishermen's meeting by way of winding up a three-week cross-continent tour with a schedule that would have taxed the endurance of a horse, and he was bounding around under a broiling sun out on the casting green, for hours on end, with all the agility of a mountain goat from his ancestral Valais.

Along toward the mid-sixties, which were of course his own mid-seventies, Charles Ritz embraced a new religion, so to speak, and changed his casting style overnight. From Jon Tarantino, a man twice his size and half his age, and several times a world champion, Charles got the inspiration for a wholly new casting stance, which he proceeded to systematize into a technique called High Speed/High Line. With Charles to think is to act, and in no time he had spread the new gospel of HS/HL in the pages of angling publications in France, England, Switzerland and the United States. Then, to make it official, as it were, he got his friend Max Reinhardt to put out another edition of *A Fly Fisher's Life*, with a new first chapter devoted to High Speed/High Line. He got his old *copain* Pierre Creusevaut, the Professional World Champion, to take up the new technique and Pierre obligingly set a new salmon fly distance cast record with it at Scarborough in 1963. Not content with that, Charles decided that Pierre might do still better with a rod more suited to the new technique and out of their consultations there emerged that strange device – strange coming from Charles, the classicist of the split-cane rod – a new rod called *Vario-Power*, with a bamboo tip section and a glass butt section.

Those of us who had thought of Charles Ritz as Baron Bamboo of Amboise, from his long years of research and development of the Pezon et Michel rods at the factory where he was the acknowledged *genius loci*, were a bit startled by this. Not that it is so unusual for Charles to invent something – after all, he invented the *après-ski* boot when he had a shoe shop on the rue St. Honoré, behind which he maintained a more or less clandestine tackle shop for the diversion of Pierre and some other cronies – but for Charles to do anything with glass seemed about like Toscanini taking up jazz. Still, it was only a foretaste of what was to come.

For now, as this new and final edition of *A Fly Fisher's Life* will quickly make clear, Charles has once again come up with something new. It supplements HS/HL without supplanting it, and again it can be expressed in four initials, LF/LL, but this time Charles goes all the way with glass. This is the Long Flex/Long Lift rod, as conceived by Charles Ritz and embodied by Garcia, the colossus of the American tackle-making industry, and it was the object of the recent breakneck cross-country tour. There's no need for me to go into it further here, because in a new chapter Charles tells about it as only he can.

But I would like to take a shot at trying to fathom what makes Charlie run today, when a dozen years back he had already slowed down to a walk. I have several notions, none of which he may like, but all of which I'm sure he is open-minded enough to entertain.

In that last sentence is my first clue. Open-minded Charles certainly is, and it may be the simple common denominator of his many successes. The rest of us make up our minds, or have them made up for us, and it takes something practically earth-shaking to change them. Not Charles. He's as ready as a gypsy to move on to something new.

In fact, Charles *is* a gypsy. His mother couldn't nurse him, so she got a gypsy wet nurse to do it for her. And if that alone wasn't enough to instill a good deal of the gypsy into him, then the family's travel habits of the first few years of his life were enough to do the rest. The nineties were the period of Cesar Ritz's most frenzied activity, as he doubled back and forth between hotels in England and the continent, which he was in effect managing to supervise and help direct all at once. Though the Savoy, where he installed Escoffier, was then his main post, he was like a juggler keeping others in the air without dropping any, and his wife Marie-Louise and the infant Charles found themselves almost living in *wagons-lits.* The hammock-like mesh hanger alongside the berth, meant for the passenger's belongings, became the swinging cradle for Charles on these frequent travels, so it is small wonder that he grew up to be a man in motion.

These almost constant travels away from their then home in London persisted until 1898, when Charles was seven, and Cesar Ritz at last had, in the Place Vendôme, a hotel of his own, the Paris Ritz of today, in which Charles literally grew up.

Add the fact that he spent the decade between his twenty-fifth and thirty-fifth birthdays in America to the circumstance that his first at least nominal home was London, and it is easy to see why Charles is the perfect cosmopolite that he is, and why he seems so much more at home and at ease with the English and the Americans than the average Frenchman or Swiss. He is both child and man of the big cities, London and Paris, New York and Boston – yet he has had a lifelong itchy foot, to be out of doors and in the woods and at least near if not on the waters. Truly a gypsy restlessness.

Another paradox is that nobody could be either more Swiss or less Swiss than he is. The average traveller thinks of him as practically synonymous with Paris, yet the only citizenships he has ever held were Swiss and American (he got the latter after serving in the American army during World War I and gave it up when it would have occasioned his being interned, after the German occupation of Paris, in World War II) and though his birthday is the Swiss equivalent of our Fourth of July, being the date that celebrates the independence of the first three cantons of the Confederation, and though he is almost fiercely proud of being Swiss, and thus at liberty to make cracks about Frenchmen, he has spent relatively little of his long life in Switzerland.

Oddly, too, though his father's family since time out of mind were from the Valais, that mountainous canton lying between Lake Geneva and the Alps, he wasn't born there, but in Molsheim, near Strassburg, where his mother happened to be visiting her aunt and uncle. Certainly he never acquired that homing Swiss attitude that made his mother run back to Niederwald every chance she had to get away from Paris.

He hates to be called Charlie, and will always correct any such reference to him in print if he has the chance. Joseph Wechsberg wrote a piece about him in *Esquire* which he started to call *The One and Only Charlie Ritz*, and Charles made no other objection to it than to insist that the 'ie' be changed to 'es', though Wechsberg quite logically pointed out both that he had never heard him referred to, by any of his friends, any other way, and that it made it doubly hard to avoid confusing his name with that of Charles of the Ritz, the trade-marked firm style of a cosmetics manufacturer.

His mother, in her superb book about his father, frequently referred to her son as 'Charly', but Monique, whom you will meet later in these pages, never calls him anything but Charles. Neither do his friends, after the third or fourth time they forget, but speaking of him among themselves they never call him anything else.

Monique is another clue, in the mystery of what makes Charles Ritz so much more dynamic today than he was a dozen years ago. A Genevoise named Ramseier, she was once married to a man called Foy, and it is as Madame Foy that she is listed on the Board of Directors of the Paris Ritz. Though not born on their Independence Day, she is if anything and if possible an even more independent Swiss than Charles himself, and if the term 'whim of iron' were not already in established usage it would have to be coined just for her.

Charles is completely frank in discussing the circumstances that nobody, not even a fisherman, can expect to be around forever, and equally frank in telling anybody who might have any conceivable interest in the matter that he expects Monique to be around the Paris Ritz when he no longer can.

I would like to go back and niggle a little more on this matter of open-mindedness that I threw out as the first clue. In Charles I think it's not merely the mind that's open, but the entire essence of the man. He can change his mind faster and oftener than you or I can change our socks. He can and does re-think things through that you or I would consider as settled as the sum of twice two, and I believe this explains the phenomenon that is Charles Ritz as nothing else could.

About the only thing I haven't forgotten from four years of college more than four decades back is what they told us in a psychology class about those little dinguses we all have but aren't aware of that are called synapses, those little nerve endings that are distributed throughout our frames about as widely as our very marrow. In children the synapses are wide open, but they start very gradually closing from childhood on, and we are all as old or as young as this closing tendency of our synapses lets us be.

In Charles Ritz, somewhere along about his sixty-eighth birthday, for reasons quite possibly not clear to anybody including himself, the damn things must have started opening up again, and wondrous is the result to behold ever since.

Look at the change in the Paris Ritz itself, over the past dozen years, if you choose not to take at face value my appraisal of the change that has come over Charles. That, too, is a paradox. To all outward seeming, the Ritz is more fully the Ritz today than it has been at any time since the opening in 1898, when the future Edward VII told Cesar Ritz that he seemed to have a better understanding of what royalty would like than they seemed to have themselves. Yet behind all that 'instant elegance' that today seems tantamount to a veritable embalming of the past is an undetected subsurface of modernity, in the use of quick-cleanable and synthetic materials and a host of behind-the-façade labour-saving devices and gadgets that could make a Hilton blink.

Charles is a gadgeteer, beyond any other that I know, and it shows in the Paris Ritz, but only if you know where to look for it, because otherwise it would escape your notice, or anybody's. He is a tinker, as becomes a gypsy, and has been all his life. Surprising in one seemingly so impetuous and so prone to what appear to be snap judgments, he has the patience, along with the ingenuity, of the born tinker. He was tinkering with fishing tackle in a room in New York, as far back as 1916, when his father first entrusted him to come over and make a deal for the use of the name 'Ritz-Carlton', and he transformed apparent junk into splendid rods, with nothing but a knack for patient and protracted experimentation.

It was not long after that, on the Jersey shore, that he was making movies of people on the beaches, as a come-on to get them to see themselves on the screen in his theatre that night – and if you see the name Ritz in a listing of New Jersey motion picture schedules, it's not because somebody in the ensuing more than half a century decided that it would be a ritzy name on a marquee, but quite simply because Charles Ritz started it, that long ago, in his restless youth.

He started other things, too, like couplings for toy trains, that are still being made over here, decades after Charles went back to Europe, and some of them he seems actually to have forgotten.

To the annual gathering of as many as four score friends he has fished with from all over the world, who gather for dinner on a mid-to-late November night, he has often said that without his American years he couldn't have had half the success he has enjoyed in Europe. These dinners constitute the only activity, except for casting the next morning in the ponds of the Bois de Boulogne, of an extremely democratic organization known as the International Fario Club, whose members pre-empt the dining room and the tea salon of the Paris Ritz for the occasion. Two drinks are followed by at least two fishing movies, in an adjoining downstairs room on the Vendôme side of the hotel, and the members' dinner is followed by a tombola, featuring prizes of tackle and flies, an event at which no member has as yet failed to win something, while Monique presides at a table in the Espadon grill, on the rue Cambon side, for the delectation and degustation of their non-fishing consorts, and Monique sees to it that their prizes are much prettier than anything that is drawn in the dining room lottery.

There are princesses as well as princes among the membership, and personages of every size and sort, and the only thing they have in common is that they have all, at one time or another, fished with Charles Ritz. Membership is facultative, as the Swiss say of some of their railway stops. You are a member as soon as, and indeed as long as, Charles says you are, and the membership though growing, over the past decade of the organization's existence, has obvious limitations. Membership is signified by a lapel button and an emblazoned embroidered patch for the blazer pocket, and in the streets of Paris the week of the dinner peers of the realm have been seen proudly sporting both.

What do you make of a man who has all this going for him! Charles C. Ritz, 15 Place Vendôme, is all his stationery says, along with the arondissement and the phone number. The 'C' is for César, of course, and it is from him that he has his name and his innate elegance, for Cesar Ritz was one of the dandies of his time. But his abounding health he must have from his mother, and more than a little of the spark besides. Marie-Louise Ritz was very much her own woman, in the long years after 1918, when her husband died, and indeed from the century's turn onward, for she had to carry on after her brilliant mate had literally spent himself, rocket-like, doing too much too soon, in too many places, at a burning pace. In her book about him she tells it all, eschewing both false modesty and any complaint, and the account is one that does them both proud. No man ever had a more affectionate memorial, and no woman ever did a man's job better, when it was beyond him to do.

Foolish to speculate what Charles would have been without them, for he is their sum. But there will be other books, about him and about them, for they brought out of Switzerland what is sure to be a lasting contribution to an important branch of the arts. An applied art, surely, but basic none the less, the art of making people both happier and more comfortable than they would otherwise be, and it is not for nothing that their name has invaded every language as an adjective standing for unique distinction.

Meanwhile, there is this book, about which I wrote, some years ago, that 'he who would try today to lead a flyfisher's life will surely miss a few tricks if he doesn't, somewhere along the way, take time out to study the one now near sundown led by Charles Ritz, one of the most gracious as well as most graceful of its modern practitioners.'

Silly of me, that was 1965, and it's an odds-on bet that a lot of us are nearer sundown now than Charles was then, but the rest of it still stands. I picked it then as one of the thirty outstanding fishing books out of all the thousands published since 1496, and I was interested to notice, last year, that the same choice had been made by the compilers of *The Contemplative Man's Recreation*, a Bibliography of Books on Angling and Game Fish in the Library of the University of British Columbia, listing *A Fly Fisher's Life* as one of the thirty-nine Landmarks in the Evolution of the Literature of Angling: 1496–1969.

Like his master Izaak Walton before him, Charles Ritz brought out the first edition of his book in a much smaller size than subsequent editions. First published in 1953, exactly three centuries after Old Izaak's first edition, under the French title *Pris sur le Vif*, this book has been reissued with added material in 1959, 1969, and now again in 1972. This compares with the various editions of *The Compleat Angler* in Walton's lifetime between 1653 and 1676. There were five of them, so let's hope that Charles Ritz has still another one coming after this. Don't bet against it. For that matter, though there is no now-known way of collecting, don't bet that they won't both be read three hundred years hence.

ARNOLD GINGRICH

Arnold Gingrich and Charles Ritz, May 1971

Charles Ritz with Ernest Hemingway

PART I * BASIC CONSIDERATIONS

Beginnings 1912

My cousin Louis had invited me to a party to fish trout on the property of Monsieur X. near Forges-les-Eaux, on the upper reaches of the Andelle.

Until then, I had only fished lake sardines in Switzerland and had become pretty good at it. As soon as I had a rod in my hand, a line, a hook and a pellet of bread, I was the equal of anyone! I thought of myself as the king of sardine fishers, and it was not without a certain anticipatory pride that I imagined my cousin's astonishment at seeing me catch all the trout in the stream with my bread pellets.

When I told him of my intentions, he looked rather startled: 'Don't be funny! You don't fish for trout with bread pellets but with an artificial fly, a split bamboo rod and by casting!'

It was goodbye to my bread pellets! The king of sardine fishers was to be a tender-foot, as the cowboys in the Far West call people from the East who go there to ride unbroken horses.

We left at eight o'clock in the morning. Louis had lent me a splendid rod. When we reached the river, our host left us, having business to attend to, and promised to return and join us before luncheon.

The water was clear, there was much weed but not a fish in sight.

I went into the attack with a great flogging of the water, more like an omnibus driver than a sporting angler!

At half-past eleven, our host reappeared, armed with a greenheart rod. I was exhausted! The muscles of my arm were in agony, the palm of my hand covered with red blisters. I was furious! I thought my leg had been pulled and that there were no more trout in the stream than there were sardines.

'Any luck?' my host asked.

'I don't believe there are any trout in this river, anyway I haven't seen any!'

Monsieur X. smiled.

'If you like, I'll try to catch a few before luncheon. Look, can you see under the opposite bank, just by the corner at the foot of that tree? There's one lying there.'

My eyes wide with astonishment, I said 'yes', but I hadn't seen anything at all!

A few rapid casts and he placed his fly precisely on the spot. There was a violent swirl; he had caught the trout and it was soon in his creel. During the next three quarters of an hour he repeated the operation frequently and only stopped at the dozen.

Well, I had seen a brilliant performance and I thought I had understood. Clearly, Monsieur X. was a Hercules, a magician, to catch trout on a fly!

The different schools of fishing

Of the many different approaches to the sport, the English school is the most classical. It is inspired by the British temperament, the 'perfect gentleman' attitude at every hour of the day and night, even towards fish. British phlegm and dignity impose a slowness of cadence on the English which is peculiar to them. Their love of flies and their tendency to plunge into the entomology of aquatic insects, tends to make them attach great importance to the fly. They are less interested than the Americans in simplification; or in the reduction of the weight of their tackle and in the great advantages to be derived from it. The manipulation of their tackle is on the whole slow. But the British school, to the eye of the spectator, has a leisurely grace and elegance, though with the drawbacks inherent in these qualities. Great precaution in approaching the fish, a leather kneeling pad to assist in getting into position, a fight on the reel across weed, and a club for dispatching the fish with elegance are all characteristic of this school. The fact that two or three brace of trout suffice them for a day's catch is witness to their sporting instincts and their wise sense of conservation. The way they maintain their fishing and the peculiar care with which they are always trying to improve it ought to be adopted more often by fishermen of other countries. Sawyer has even changed the blood of the Mayfly on the Avon by mingling it at the moment of flight with ephemerids from neighbouring rivers. The Englishman has the gift of drawing the maximum pleasure from the by-products of fishing. He savours the smallest incident in a day's sport. We owe him eternal gratitude for having been first to invent the art of fly fishing.

The American school was based on the English school but has quickly transformed itself. Today, there is as much difference between the two schools as between cricket and baseball. Similarly with the tackle they use. Nevertheless, there is a select club in New York, The Anglers' Club, whose members continue to keep British classicism alive.

One of my good fishing friends in New York always had on his desk a notice with the following inscription: 'Time is money, please get to the point and make it easy for me'. This is an exact definition of the modern school in favour in America.

American flies are a practical and effective compromise between the fish and the fishermen. Larger, with more bushy hackles, they must above all float high, and they are therefore more visible on the surface and show a more confused outline beneath the surface. The hook, being larger, holds better. Since their flies can be made to float more easily, they require less repeated drying. Their tying is of the first order.

The English anxiety to obtain a reproduction of the insect, as close as the tying of an artificial will permit, reduces the value of their patterns.

Certain flies fashionable in America, such as the Brown Bivisible and the Fan-Wing Coachman, were invented with the major object of visibility to the fisherman.

The Americans are the inventors of the ultra-light rod and of tip-action which I cannot approve except in special circumstances: very close fishing, for example. They fish rather short and present the fly quickly. In my opinion, their lines are too heavy and too thick in the forward taper, but they bring the rod immediately into action.

As for their equipment, they take great care to make it light: a landing-net attached to the back by an elastic, for instance. Their waders and boots are of the featherweight type with felt soles. Their coats have multiple pockets of the exact dimensions for the accessories. There are even pockets on the sleeves. A light cloth cap with a long peak protects the eyes. Everything they use has been designed to avoid encumbrance, preserve the maximum freedom of movement, comfort and avoidance of loss of time. Some of their fishing waistcoats and coats have even a waterproof fish pocket, ventilated and removable, thanks to a zip fastener.

The French and the Belgians are more ardent. The French fisherman is more classical than the Belgian and fishes with elegance.

They are certainly less good at conservation and have a tendency to pay too little attention to the management of their fishing, which in general is less well maintained and organised. In England, looking after one's fishing has become both an art and a science.

The Belgians, giving way to their enthusiasm and incomparable keenness, too often become machine-gun fishermen! They are too vigorous for the number of fish the continental rivers contain. They adapt themselves very quickly to all conditions of fishing. They are always in search of the new, both in tackle and in tactics, and have the highest percentage of experts. One rarely meets a bad Belgian fisherman. The Belgian school is typical. Always avoid fishing behind a Belgian angler.

The Germans and the Swiss are now beginning to realise the advantages that modern ultra-light tackle affords; they are greatly interested in casting technique and have many admirable casting schools with first-class instructors.

The Nordics, a tall and strong race, cast forcibly and are still using big rods of 5½ to 7 oz, but are first-class casters.

In spite of these differences, I have met first-class fishermen, who were great sportsmen, in all these countries.

What I deplore most, is the comparatively small importance that the majority of anglers of all countries attach to a profound knowledge of the technique of casting. They are too rarely aware of the pleasure and satisfaction that the good caster can add to his day's fishing. The basic reason for this is that, in our sport, unlike others, there are too few qualified instructors. The beginner ought to realise once and for all that, as in golf, tennis, ski-ing, skating, riding, etc., he should begin by entrusting himself to an instructor. The result of failing to do so is that the number of fishermen who are good casters is much inferior to the number of experts in other sports.

An understanding of the mechanics of casting ensures ability to detect your own faults and a knowledge of how to remedy them. I wish to emphasise this as much as I can.

I think the English are to be envied their disciplined phlegm, their contempt for the greedy fisherman and their perfect respect for the word 'sport'; the Americans their practical sense and their natural ability to simplify; the French and Belgians their finesse, their enthusiasm, and the fact that they have been in a position to achieve a golden mean; and the Swiss, Germans and Scandinavians for their great interest in casting mechanics and for learning how to master them.

Today, thanks to the great evolution in fly casting tournaments and thanks to the I.C.A. President, Myron Gregory, tuition in casting will soon become as popular as it is in golf.

The most complete and outstanding casters I have had the privilege of watching are: Captain Tommy Edwards, Captain Terry Thomas, C. MacLaren and Lionel Sweet of Great Britain; Albert Godart of Belgium; Pierre Creusevaut of France; Al McClane, Myron Gregory, Johnny Dickman and John Tarantino (the All World Champion, I.C.A. Tournament, Kiel, 1957, and Brussels, 1958) of U.S.A.

The following may give you some idea of Tarantino's skill and knowledge. While making a trial cast for salmon fly distance from the platform, I asked him to try out one of my rods. These were double-built, with no hollow centre, whereas he used Winston hollow centre with, therefore, a completely different type of action. Besides, my line was also different. Any tournament caster knows that the very slightest change in tackle for distance casting necessitates a readaptation which is often only to be achieved after numerous casts. At his first cast, using dry fly style and not more than two false casts, Tarantino landed the fly at a distance of 200 feet.

I can assure you also that all these casters are first-class anglers. Most of us believe that Tarantino is one of the greatest casters who ever lived.

14

Tournament casting. The world Champion, Walter Kummerow of Germany, in Berlin, 1971.

*The author demonstrates the correct function of the left hand,
always keeping the line taut*

The mechanics of fly casting

In 1947, the great American magazine *Field and Stream* asked me to write an article on Parabolic rods in response to a great number of demands for information they had received from readers. Moreover, a few American manufacturers had put on the market so-called Parabolic rods. The article appeared and I received a letter from a reader asking me to show him these rods.

He arrived early one morning at the Ritz-Carlton in New York and, as soon as he was shown into my room, he rushed to my rods which were lying mounted on the bed. I stopped him and said as politely as possible:

'Before you look at the rods, may I ask you a question? This is necessary so that I should be able to give you the precise information you require and make sure there is no error. What do you do with your left hand, and in what position is it, when you cast?'

He looked at me in astonishment, placed his two hands in the casting position, moved them about, assumed a perplexed expression, appeared to be searching for the correct position for his left hand, started all over again several times and, finally, stopped in discouragement.

'Mr Ritz,' he said, 'I can't tell you what I do with my left hand when I cast . . .'

I politely begged his pardon for asking so indiscreet a question and began explaining to him, rod in hand, the importance of the left hand and why its correct use was indispensable if a rod was to give of its best. Having done so, I handed him one of my rods, but he refused to take it and, with an appalled expression, said:

'To think that I've always posed as an expert, and that most of the members of my fishing club have at one time or another asked me to help them choose fly rods, and that for more than twenty years I've never known what my left hand was doing! I'm going straight home to practise casting in the garden, in order to find out exactly what I do do. If you will allow me, I'll come back to see you and try your rod with line and leader as soon as I've organised my left hand. I thank you very much for your frankness for, in a few minutes, you've taught me more than all my twenty years of practice!'

The only reason I tell this true story, is because I have too often had similar experiences and, indeed, can no longer remember the number of fishermen, often good ones too, whom I've met on the water making useless and exaggerated efforts during casting. They often unjustly accuse their rods. And, on many occasions, I have had the privilege of showing them, after a few relatively simple explanations that, on the contrary, they had an excellent rod but did not know how to use it properly.

One last piece of advice, which is perhaps the most important: if your rod is not giving you satisfaction, consult an expert in your district before condemning it.

The rod is a spring. It can be used to a greater or lesser extent. It must be used to the maximum. The greater the flexion of the rod the more the caster economises his strength. It is possible to cast with a rigid stick, provided you use your body, shoulder, arms, hand and wrist, practically all rigid, but you suppress very nearly all the wrist action which controls the flexion, and the flexibility of the rod then becomes non-existent. The proper use of the rod depends very much on the grip of the caster's fingers on the handle.

∗ *Thumb on top.* This is the best method, but it demands a very supple wrist which can only be acquired with time and not always then.

∗ *Thumb slightly to the side.* This allows the wrist to be bent in the natural position, but limits the quality of the finish and forces the rod to work with a twist, the alignment of the rings having a tendency to depart from the vertical and turn under the rod towards the right, semi-horizontally.

∗ *Forefinger on top.* This limits the power of the cast but increases precision. A beginner may find it of value in stopping the rod at the high-point of the back-cast, but this relatively weak grip is not to be recommended. It should be used only with very short rods – nothing longer than 6½ feet.

Fig. 1 Three possible finger positions on the rod handle

To be an expert fisherman it is not essential to be an expert caster, but:

To become a reasonable fisherman and acquire the muscular strength to cast without fatigue and if necessary with ease and power, you need on an average four seasons' fishing. To begin with it is very difficult. In tennis and golf, the whole effort of concentration is directed towards hitting a ball. In fishing, there are obstacles behind you, wind, the presentation of the fly, the strike and, finally, landing your fish. In golf and tennis, specialist instructors are numerous. In fishing, the majority of beginners are content with the advice of fishing companions and, in fact, merely get on as best they can. The result is that 95 per cent of them remain only average or bad casters, and though they catch fish, they will never know the whole satisfaction and recreation that the sport can afford them.

The mechanics of casting are very little known.

On the Traun, in 1951, a woman beginner, after a fortnight's training of the muscles by the bottle method, took lessons from the head keeper, Hans Gebetsroither, with the result that she caught four grayling on a dry fly on the third day and seven on the day following. Moreover, she can herself correct the rear extension whenever it is defective. I think this is a conclusive experience!

To write a treatise on casting has only relative value. Instruction can be given only by an expert, rod in hand. I shall therefore limit my description of casting to the most important elements.

To those of us who have coached large classes in fly casting, it is well known that eight out of ten people can become proficient with quite a modest amount of instruction. This is especially noticeable among youngsters who have never held a rod before. They have no bad habits to overcome. Adults with considerable fishing experience frequently relapse into the very rod movement they are endeavouring to correct.

At one time Al McClane, Fishing Editor of *Field and Stream* magazine, conducted a Casting Clinic at the New York Sport Show every year. When I visited him some years after the 1939-1945 War, he agreed with my view that most instructors fail by not emphasising the fact that fundamental rod movements are not precisely applicable to distance casting – which is what most people want to learn. But the basic movements must be completely understood before the pupil can adapt himself to a style suited for distance. What Al had in mind was that, after learning the regulated motions of ordinary casting, his student would return for advanced instruction and find he was being taught what appeared to be a new set of rules. In fact, the motions involved in distance casting are an adaptation of fundamentals.

* *Necessity for professional instructors.* If all fly fishers' clubs had professional instructors, as there are in golf and tennis clubs, the beginner would not be compelled to ask advice of old hands who most of the time do not, unfortunately, understand the technique of the use of the line hand, and we would have a fair number of near expert casters who understood the mechanics of fly casting.

They would be able to present a fly with style, ease and dexterity, under most of the difficult conditions which are met with when fly fishing for trout.

Teaching is an art; even in golf only one professional out of ten is a good instructor, capable of preventing his pupil becoming confused. The action of fly casting must from the very start be analysed into its component parts and each part must be learnt singly and progressively. For instance, at the start, the line hand should not be used and the learner should keep it in his pocket.

Perfect casting is a combination of wrist, forearm and upper arm movements, none with definite positions, from the elbow near the waist line to the hand extended

17

higher than the shoulder, according to the type of cast required. To this must be added a progressive application of power, which requires precise timing because the muscle power has to be perfectly blended into the movements, some of which are infinitesimal and are transmitted to the rod at the optimum moment so that the power of its bend performs most of the casting. Therefore, as stated above, each movement must be learned separately and somewhat exaggerated at the start. As the pupil progresses, the movements may gradually be reduced till they attain the barely visible movements of the expert caster. It is for this reason that I recommend the learner to start with the wet cast, using only the rod hand.

To start learning the dry fly cast, using both hands and holding the rod-arm elbow close to the body, is in my opinion the surest way to make it twice as difficult to learn as well as to run the risk of remaining an indifferent caster. In Great Britain there are several excellent professional teachers available, such as Captain Thomas and Lionel Sweet, and most of the good casters I have met there have had the wisdom to take advantage of their expert advice and tuition.

To sum up, learn each movement separately, and only when they have been individually mastered try to blend them together progressively. Remember that the easiest, indeed the only, way to get the real feel of the movement of casting, is for your instructor to hold your rod hand and pass on to you the feel of the movement. Do not try to fish until casting becomes almost subconscious. Have frequent checkups with your instructor after you have begun fishing. Learn first how to cast a high back line and concentrate on it until you have drilled this cast into your system. Build up your casting muscles from the very start by the bottle method.

* *Reflexive casting.* Fly fishing is meant to give the angler pleasure and complete relaxation, but this can only be savoured when casting becomes a reflex. Reflexive casting is achieved by practice and to a great extent by learning from more experienced anglers. The printed word is only moderately valuable as a method of study, with the result that we all look for an instructor at the start. The chances are, however, that your instructor has developed his own particular style and has weak points in his technique which you may absorb along with the mechanics. Rod habits are hard to change.

It is difficult when discussing casting problems to analyse the subject into simple cause and effect. An experienced caster could, for instance, take a very badly matched rod and line and cast moderately well by compensating for the mechanical inadequacies of the tackle. This does not make for pleasant hours on the river, however, and the same tackle in the hands of a beginner would be hopelessly frustrating. Yet, I often meet people on rivers throughout the country who have handicapped themselves for years with ill-matched tackle and who are unable to distinguish between their own rod habits and the symptoms of tackle failure. Beginners often ask me why they cannot throw a straight line. Although I could offer reasons such as the line being too tight, or the rod tip too soft, in ninety-nine cases out of a hundred, the fault is with the caster. He is using all wrist and no forearm, picking up slack line with a hard pull instead of sliding it off the water, and progressively lowering his back cast. I see this going on season after season.

* *Instinctive casting.* For average fishing, up to forty feet, a good rod, or more precisely its bend, should perform most of the work. The angler simply provides the motion necessary to move the rod back and forth, thereby magnifying his line speed. Unfortunately, many beginners become so anxious to catch fish that they cast from instinct, using the wrist as a pivot, and creating a back and forth circular motion of the rod tip, whereas the back movement should be upward and only slightly circular and the forward movement, starting circular, should finish straight. Should it be a windy day, or should the trout be rising just a little further out than the normal range, the wrist tends to bend more and more while the rod goes lower and lower on the back cast. The tackle gets the blame and the angler starts a futile search for a better rod or line. This is the point at which you must put your elbow on trial as if summoning it to appear before a general court martial. You cannot make a poor back cast if you hold your wrist almost completely rigid and pivot on your elbow. A straight upward forearm movement will kick the line high and straight in the air. In one movement, elbow casting will tell you whether you are struggling with a tackle problem or a casting weakness. If there is no immediate difference then, and only then, you can evaluate the flight of your moving line.

* *Relaxation important.* When you take a rod in your hand, you must be relaxed. Proper relaxation is at least half the secret of good fly casting. Most of the adults we teach freeze as soon as their line is in motion, and this feeling of uncertainty is transmitted to the rod in quick jerky movements. People are natural wrist benders. As the wrist is bent, so the back cast is lowered. Paradoxically, the dropping back cast seems to signal that more wrist bending is necessary; and when casting becomes an effort, the student is no longer relaxed. I solve this by holding the rod just above a beginner's hand and casting back and forth very slowly, dropping the line on the water with each forward cast. This forces the pupil to keep a 'dead' wrist. I mention this because if you are ever charged with instructing anybody, you must not underestimate the value of dual demonstration. There is a feeling about fly casting which cannot be put into words but you can convey it by actually casting with your pupil. Within the first ten casts he gains confidence, and ten casts later will be completely relaxed.

* *Tournament casting.* The designing of rods intended for fly-fishermen, many of them new to the sport or far from expert, has been much influenced by tournament casters, their techniques and the rods they use. The mechanics of fly-casting were then being developed in both branches of the sport and competitors and fishermen alike faced much the same problems.

Today, August 20th, 1970, Pierre Creusevaut returned from the International Casting Federation's tournament in Kalmar, Sweden, convinced that from now on tournament casting and fly-fishing must go their separate ways. It is his opinion that tournament casting has become a totally athletic sport; that most of today's champions are essentially athletes, relying on the exceptional strength needed to wield the very stiff, very strong rods suited to their style of casting.*

By contrast, vast numbers of fly-fishermen are coming to appreciate the value of more flexible all-glass rods and the disadvantages of the tip-action rods – too weak on top, too stiff in the lower section – developed in liaison with the tournament casters of earlier days.

It is a fact that many of today's tournament casters do not know how to fish or devote very little time to fishing. Jon Tarantino, Myron Gregory and Jim Green are rare exceptions in that their casting technique is perfect for both tournament work and fishing.

To facilitate measuring, casting events are now held on land rather than water. It is thus impossible for competitors to make use of surface tension, so important to the fly-fisherman, when lifting line into the back-cast or when placing the fly on the water. Presentation of the fly plays no part in these tournaments: it has been banned for ever!

* *Indispensable conditions for achieving mastery as easily and quickly as possible.* Above all, do not begin fishing till you know how to cast.

Train the muscles and the grip of the fingers by the bottle method.

Study the mechanics of casting.

Choose an expert instructor and take twelve lessons of half an hour each. If possible, ask for advice from your local casting club. Then begin fishing, but devote half an hour to practising casting before going to fish. As soon as you lose your form, go and see your instructor again and, in any case, take more lessons after the season is over.

* *The casting machine, its mechanism, connecting rods and pivots.* Mastery is not complete till you are in a position to avoid fatigue and stiffness; to use the left hand; to achieve a back cast without touching the ground; to cast against the wind; to keep the upper part of the body still; to get the rhythm which assures synchronisation and perfect

*The point is well illustrated by the photograph of Walter Kummerow, and the rod he is using, facing page 14. *J.P.*

progression of transmission and acceleration of power at the last moment by means of the different pivots; to be able to stop the rod by a contraction of the muscles; and to execute casts from the position of elbow against the body to hand above the head. To make an absolute rule of keeping the elbow to the body and only casting with the wrist limits the caster's opportunities by more than 50 per cent.

The different positions of the rod are indicated in the diagram by the hours on a clock face between nine, extreme forward position, and two for the backward position (see figure 2), and the abbreviations BA for backwards or back cast and FO for forward. These positions on the diagram are as precise as possible, but have an element of approximation owing to certain variants of which the principal elements are: the caster, the rod and the line.

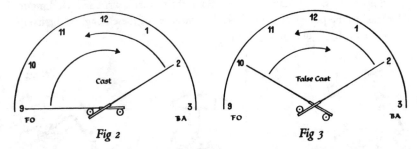

Fig 2   Fig 3

The instinctive movement of casting is a regular back and forth movement of the rod between ten and two o'clock maximum, which exercises a traction movement of the rod tip on the line, and has the defect of being circular in form (figure 3). This traction must be composed of three distinct elements, applied successively: *the start, the acceleration, and the finish* (placing for FO and blocking the rod for BA).

The rod tip must transmit the accelerating power on as horizontal a plane as possible (see figure 4), therefore, during the fraction of a second when it is nearest to the

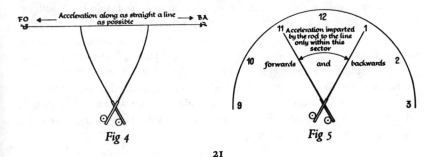

Fig 4   Fig 5

vertical between eleven and one o'clock (see figure 5) for BA traction, and from one to eleven o'clock for FO traction.

Besides the upper part of the body, the casting machine is composed of three connecting rods which create power, the upper arm, the forearm and the hand, as well as the instrument which transmits the power to the line: the rod. They are joined by the principal pivots: the wrist, the elbow and a secondary one, the shoulder. (See figure 6).

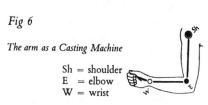

Fig 6

The arm as a Casting Machine

Sh = shoulder
E = elbow
W = wrist

A simple way of illustrating and describing the forearm, wrist and hand motions, which allow the power of the rod bend to do most of the casting, is 'the hammer stroke on a nail' (figure 7).

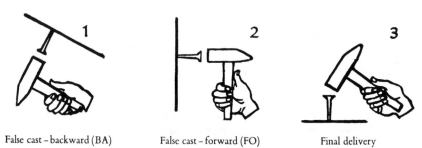

False cast – backward (BA)   False cast – forward (FO)   Final delivery

Fig 7

There are three hammer strokes. Two for the false cast, one front, one back (1 and 2) and one for the final delivery (3) to straighten out the leader and place the fly.

Mastery in casting consists of the ability to use these different factors at the opportune moment, combined with synchronisation, accurate to more than a hundredth of a second, as well as timing and THE ESSENTIAL LEFT HAND.

Timing: In FO, you can observe the extension of the line and timing is generally correct. For BA, it is much more difficult and, even if you look, you are apt to make mistakes. Timing must be instinctive. Only masters possess it completely.

The optimum traction can be obtained only with a line stretched to at least 95 per cent.

I am not a partisan of the very elegant and gentle FIGURE OF EIGHT. It lacks speed, dries the fly badly and is not effective against wind. It anticipates the moment of traction in both directions (see figure 8).

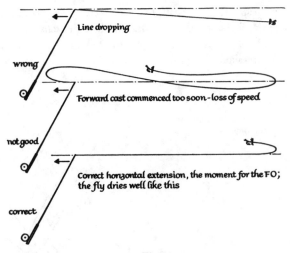

Fig 8
The end of the Extension Pause

* **The line hand.** Before you can ever become a distance caster, you must understand the role of your line hand. Let us assume that you are right-handed. In casting, the left hand always holds the line, keeping it taut at all times to provide the maximum power in delivery. Your right hand moves back and forth while your left hand follows in a parallel path, almost as though you were swinging a cricket bat, except that in casting the stroke is an upward movement instead of partly circular, as stated in *Instinctive Casting*. If your line hand remains stationary, the distance between right and left will vary, tightening the line on your back cast and throwing it slack on the forward cast. There must be tension both backwards and forwards, because with control you can add extra speed to the line whenever it is needed. Having a means of

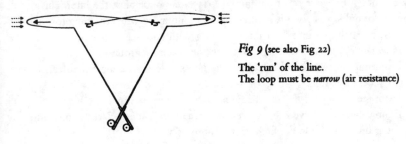

Fig 9 (see also Fig 22)
The 'run' of the line.
The loop must be *narrow* (air resistance)

adding speed, you can: (1) correct casts that are affected by the wind; (2) get greater distance because the slightest pull on the line while under tension will shoot it out much further; and (3) correct your own errors in timing. Thus, the line hand has a positive role in maintaining a tight line.

Fig 10

Observe that the line is taut between the left hand and the guide ring

S = slack line ('bag')

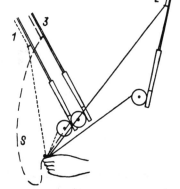

What happens if the left hand remains stationary, and why the left hand must follow the right:

1 Starting position for back cast
2 Final position of back cast
3 Taut line slackened (bag) during forward cast: the line loses speed and does not extend

* *Lifting line.* I think the best example of what your left hand can do for you is in lifting line from the water. Nearly every beginner will make his lift for the back cast by pulling line directly off the surface. If forty or fifty feet of taper is extended on the water, this direct lift is travelling at about half the speed required for an easy back cast. Yet a short pull with the left hand to start the line moving, at the same time raising the rod, is enough to send the cast high and fast to the rear. Why put an extra burden on your rod by fighting surface tension against the line? This simple motion of pulling as you lift becomes more pronounced when reaching for long distances; but first, get into the habit of casting with both hands (see figure 11).

Extension BA of the line. (Line placed FO on water or ground.)

From nine to ten o'clock: Tighten the line by slowly raising the forearm, wrist slightly bent but rigid.

From ten to eleven: *the start.* Same movement but less slow.

From eleven to twelve and twelve-thirty: *rapid acceleration.* Wrist comes into play moving upwards while the fingers grip more tightly.

At twelve: *rigidity* of all the muscles, but the rod, owing to the force of the movement and its flexibility, only stops at one. This stop should not be jerky. The wrist must act as a deadening force to avoid transmitting a quiver to the rod tip, or there will be waves in the line and a loss of speed. It is the firm grip of the hand which gives the maximum effort.

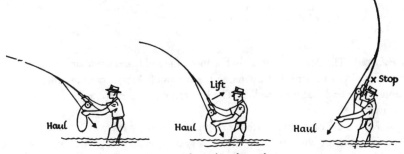

Fig 11 Single Haul, angling style

* *Sequence of movements in Back Cast and Forward Cast.* Figures 12 and 13.

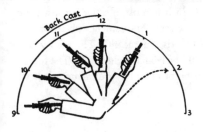

Fig 12
Normal sequence of movements in the Back Cast.
The rod comes to a dead stop between 12·30 and 2·15

  9 100% tension in line
10 10% hand, 90% forearm. Beginning of cast
11 30% hand, 70% forearm. Acceleration
12 Commencement of retardation by 100% muscular contraction
  1 STOP. Dead stop by blocking the muscles
  2 Maximum flexion of rod

The Forward Cast. *Extension FO of the line*, the lowering and dropping on the water and, over and above the start of the movement of the line and its acceleration, there is a third phase: the actual placing on the water.

From one to twelve: *the start* of movement of the forearm helped by the left hand which, by holding the line slightly taut, assists the rod tip.

From twelve to ten: *acceleration.* The coming into action of the wrist which reinforces the movements of the forearm.

From ten to nine: *the finish. The placing on the water.* Finish by increasing the movement of the wrist. It is the thumb or forefinger, according to how the rod is held, which gives the maximum effort. The finish must be smooth and without jerkiness.

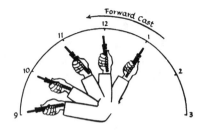

Fig 13

Normal sequence of movements in the Forward Cast.
A correct forward cast always, without exception,
results from a good back cast

1 100% forearm. Tightening (taking in the line)
12 25% hand, 75% forearm. Acceleration
11 40% hand, 60% forearm. Acceleration
10 50% hand, 50% forearm. Extension of line
 9 90% hand. Strike – force the wrist down-
    wards

* *False casts*. The same technique, but without the finish and maintaining the rod tip between eleven and one, but separating the BA and FO trajectories in order to avoid rubbing the leader against the line. The best training and exercise for false casts is as follows:

1. Make false casts with a circular movement of the wrist while standing still;

2. Do it again while walking (this is a good exercise). The circular movement should progressively grow wider. You can also increase yard by yard the length of the casts up to ten or twelve yards approximately.

To increase the power of the FO extension (which is most effective against wind), raise the elbow slightly away from the body in a circular movement upwards assisted by a rotation of the shoulder, a slight turn and rise to the FO. The elbow pivot remains rigid, the upper arm and forearm should be bent at right angles. The forearm makes a rotating movement on an imaginary pivot placed approximately half way between the elbow and the wrist (see figure 14).

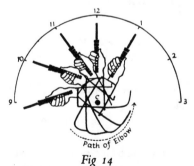

Fig 14

Sequence of movements in intensified Forward Cast
C – Centre of rotation between wrist and elbow

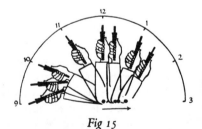

Fig 15

Elbow drift for distance casting
The shoulder also has similar drift, pivoting backwards. This gives a longer BA pull

Parachute and storm casts are two of the principal trumps in the caster's hand. I shall try and give you some idea of them, but to complete it a demonstration from an instructor is necessary.

In July 1937, on a river in Pennsylvania, that great American master, John Alden Knight, saw a fine trout lying under a big rock on the opposite bank. There was a slight current flowing round it and, in the middle of the river, there was a very rapid current.

Knight presented his fly, a Cahill, and the current in the centre immediately caught his line: premature drag. A refusal! He tried in vain to slow it down and, in spite of his great expertness, he could not get his fly accepted.

My long experience of the very rapid currents of the Ammer and the Traun had taught me how to get over this: the parachute cast. But it occurred to me that it might be tactless to give the great master a lesson!

I went up close and continued watching him without saying a word. A natural fly drifted by and the fish took it. Knight tried again: drag just at the moment when I saw the trout was preparing to take his fly. No matter, I'd take the risk.

'Why don't you try a parachute cast?'

'What do you mean by that?'

I explained it to him.

'Take my rod and show me.'

I dropped the fly with a parachute cast, but downstream of the fish so as not to alarm it, while watching my friend out of the corner of my eye. He seemed surprised but understood at once. I gave him back his Payne and he made a perfect cast followed by a long natural drift. The fly drifted down the current and reached the fish which took it without hesitation!

That night, at the inn, after two large cups of coffee, he said:

'Your parachute cast is a revelation to me, and to think I've never even thought of it.'

In Burgundy, I was once fishing on the Aube with Lambiotte and Tixier. The river was in spate and most of the trout were sheltering from the current in the smooth water along the banks. I was watching Tixier who, standing opposite two fine trout, which were rising regularly, could not succeed in making them rise to his fly. Disgusted, he sat down on a tree trunk and lit a pipe.

'There's nothing to be done, Charles! What a current!'

'My dear Tio, the parachute cast would allow of your slowing down your premature drag. Take your rod and I'll hold your right hand; but relax and let me guide it; try merely to follow my movement without taking part in it.'

A few minutes later, Tixier had succeeded in taking both trout!

The following year we met on the Andelle and, with his perpetual enthusiasm, he said:

'Oh, Charles, your parachute cast's marvellous! Thanks to it, I've raised my average.'

* *The parachute cast.* With the hand at approximately shoulder level, make false casts and drop the line while arresting the rod at twelve (the vertical position), lower the hand as much as possible while continuing to hold the rod vertical. The line will then fall on the water with the maximum of slack.

To retard the drag of the fly to the maximum, follow the line by lowering the point of the rod to nine.

Sometimes it is preferable to make sure of the distance with a trial cast behind the fish, precise judgment of the distance being difficult because the fly is pulled backwards by the weight of the line as it becomes taut.

THE PARACHUTE CAST

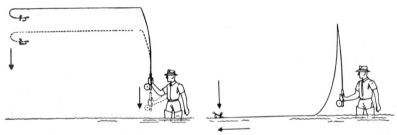

Fig 16 Rapid dropping of hand. Rod vertical   *Fig 17 The fly falls on a slack line*

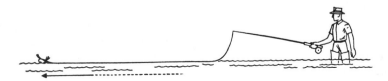

Fig 18 Free drift of fly for more than length of rod

I shall never forget my match in 1941 with Lambiotte on the Bourbe, one of the tributaries of the Risle, when staying with Edouard Vernes.

The weather was detestable, the terrible Normandy wind blew incessantly. We were on the reach where the big fish lie, and the river forms an S bend. Under the opposite bank were lying several trout, which we estimated as two pounders, taking all the ephemerids passing within their reach. Lambiotte was not as much at ease as usual, the wind seemed to be paralysing him.

My many years of fishing in Normandy during the Mayfly had taught me that if you cannot fish into the wind, the greater part of these wonderful days is nothing but disillusionment, irritation and discomfort, blisters and cramp, with far more moderate results than should be indicated by the numerous rises. In the process of experimenting, without knowing precisely what I was up to, but in trying to find some way of overcoming the wind without forcing my rod beyond its maximum, I noticed that the lower I cast and the more extended the line near the surface of the water, the more accuracy I achieved and the less I had to force. Finally, my average went up, and, on days of high wind I was, most of the time, more successful than the others, thanks to a cast which I afterwards called the Storm Cast.

It was an excellent opportunity of proposing a match with Auguste who generally beats me! He has a competitive spirit both as regards fish and fishermen, though he gives but little inkling of it.

The wind was becoming stormy. It was the right moment.

'A match, Auguste?'

'With pleasure! We'll stay on this reach, with a limit of one hundred yards up and downstream, both fishing where we choose.'

The exact fly and the precise tactics had only a relative value; it was necessary to beat the wind and place the fly with all speed, but with sufficient precision, so that the very limited drift possible should pass the fish without drag.

It was one of my very rare days of triumph over the Giant of Flanders! I took a dozen fine fish, of which four were over two pounds, whereas my terrifying adversary was almost empty-handed, and had a sprained wrist into the bargain! Auguste, who was most sporting throughout the match, kept on congratulating me. He always congratulates his friends when they bring off a good thing, for no one appreciates the difficulties of our favourite sport more justly than he does.

Even today, whenever I have succeeded ill, a victim to my habitual weaknesses (bad striking, lack of concentration, continually dashing up and down the bank trying to find more rises), and my friends, above all Edouard and François Vernes, see how depressed I am, they always remind me of that memorable day!

* *The storm cast.* (Figure 19.) It is above all the placing of the thumb on top of the handle which gives one hundred per cent success.

The wind offers least resistance on a level with the surface of the water, the finish must therefore be exaggerated.

Instead of finishing at nine o'clock and continuing to lower the point in an arc of a circle to stop it almost at water level, you must lower the arm, the hand, and the rod to the maximum, while keeping the last horizontal. To make this movement easier, you can lean forward a little

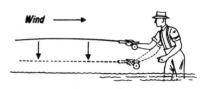

Fig 19 The Storm Cast

and even bend your knees. The line will then extend at the maximum speed almost on the surface of the water. The double haul consists of pulling on the line with the left hand during both FO and BA extensions, in order to accelerate their speed (used only for extra long casts, especially against the wind).

When the line begins to pull against the left hand, the latter must move close to the reel to obtain a maximum FO or BA extension and then move away from it again so as to pull on the line and accelerate it, returning to the best position for the following haul.

I often use simple haul, that is to say: haul with the left hand only at the last false cast BA, FO at the moment of dropping the line.

You must watch a competition caster for a demonstration.

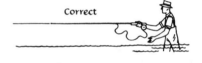

* *Shooting line.* Do not let go of the line until the rod is horizontally FO and you feel it wants to flow out (fig 20).

* *The roll cast.* One of the chief difficulties in fly casting on small streams or rivers that are overgrown with trees is that the ordinary cast must unroll in the air behind the angler, before it can go forward. As every fisherman knows, you cannot find trout in trees except in flood water but close examination of the nearest willow will reveal shredded leaders galore. Begin-

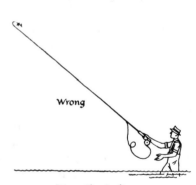

Fig 20 Shooting line

ners, especially, cannot stay out of them. The 'switch' or roll cast solves this problem. In a roll cast, the line does not travel more than a foot or two behind the angler, if at all. Bear in mind that you are not to lift the back cast into the air. First, work out about twenty feet of line by using a horizontal cast, parallel to the shore if necessary; then pull

In up cast, as here, low left hand and use of left-hand pull will allow rod to be brought back beyond vertical without rear line drop.

On the Risle, Charles Ritz demonstrates the finish of HS/HL 'forward power push', which will be smooth and comparatively effortless if up cast has been properly made.

A good HS/HL cast. Contrary to general advice, Jon Tarantino here twists his wrist to right, enabling lower part of rod to rest against forearm, producing more power leverage with a big rod and heavy line. He does this for long tournament casts only.

Tarantino demonstrating bad cast, the line moving slowly and, at the end of back cast, inevitably dropping low. HS/HL keeps line moving quickly in air, ensuring that it never reaches low position behind caster.

more line through the rings by hand. Allow it to drop on the water in front of you. The rod should be pointed forward and nearly horizontal to begin the cast. Strip a few additional yards from the reel and raise the rod slowly until it is just a little past vertical, that is, pointed back slightly over your shoulder. When the line has reached this position, with the belly of the curve slightly behind the right elbow, the forward cast is made immediately by driving the rod sharply downwards. The impulse given the line immediately beyond the rod tip causes it to travel forward before the leader and fly have entirely left the water on their backward movement, with the result that they are pulled after it in a big loop and unrolled on the water. You can get more distance by working out slack, and repeating the rod movements described here. Just remember that, as more line is worked out, it is necessary to put additional power into the forward stroke and to make sure that the line is moving towards you on the water when the forward stroke is begun. A good roll caster can handle fifty or sixty feet of line without too much difficulty.

* *Roll pick-up*. In fishing a quiet stretch of water, the dry fly fisherman can use the roll cast to considerable advantage in retrieving, without making a disturbance on the water. However, instead of making a complete roll, snap the rod forward only half way, pick the fly out of the air with a back cast, and then make a regular forward cast. These motions blend smoothly, and when fishing short line there is little chance of scaring nearby fish.

* *Switch cast*. The switch cast is a variation of the roll cast executed on either side of the body, the rod tip generally remaining below the head. This cast bears the same relationship to the roll cast that the side or horizontal cast does to the overhead cast. If the leader does not straighten out on the final delivery, a short pull of the left hand just before the fly hits the water will do the trick. This is handy when the wind is against you. It is frequently used by tournament casters on targets.

If an obstacle just behind you prevents your letting out sufficient line to start the cast, or if your fly catches in the bank or grass at your feet, strip several yard of line from the reel, then, holding the fly between your fingers, begin to switch cast. Keep the fly in your hand and release more line at each roll by stripping it from the reel until the required length is reached for final delivery. To prevent the line from tangling, while holding the fly and lengthening the cast, you must move the rod in a horizontal circular position. After some practice, you will get the right feel of how to move the rod to avoid tangling. It is not an easy cast, but excellent for use in tight quarters. For dry fly roll casting, use a full-hackled, bivisible fly, well oiled, to ensure good floating. This will take many fish that otherwise seem impossible to catch.

* *Line wave*. Line wave is invariably caused by poor casting, specifically when the angler's movements are not co-ordinated. Instead of the smooth blending between

back and forward strokes he breaks his rhythm and thereby loses line speed, which causes the taper to wave in the air. Line wave is sometimes caused by using a rod that is too soft for the weight of the line. The tip is thrown into the cast without recovering or shrugging off the load of the line. Being the most active section of the rod and of light construction, the tip bends freely under the line's weight, and unless there is some harmony between it and the mid-section and butt, there is no chance of precision or distance. If the rod tip is too fine in relation to the supporting rod taper, it will vibrate excessively, breaking up the rod curve and the transmission of speed. By the same token, with the tip-heavy rod you cannot make the fly travel slowly from rear to front, for the heavy tip gives too much speed to the line with a jerky motion. You have to make short, fast strokes, thus eliminating all hope of effortless casting.

Fig 21 Line wave

* *Distance casting.* With the modern rod, you can cast a line its full length provided your left hand is educated. There is no need to resort to heavier rods or mono-filament shooting lines in actual fishing. Either device is a crutch, and an obstacle in the path of good casting. If you are working on distance, bear in mind that the longer you keep your line in the air, the less chance you have of getting maximum line speed. The ideal is to get the rod at full load in about five motions – pick-up, lay-back, speed forward, speed back and shoot. If the rod is not at full load on the fourth motion, drop it on the water and start over again. I often see severe cases of 'caster's elbow' because people who have not held a rod for some time are trying to conquer distance by

pure muscle. Although fly tackle weighs less than sixteen ounces, the muscles you use in casting do not get much exercise in the course of the year. It takes about one hundred hours to build them up to normal efficiency, and another two hours to get them to peak.

Another tiring habit beginners get into is pulling the line violently when making a double haul. Line pull must be smooth, not fast. I saw one fellow actually rip the back of his shirt while making a forward pull, and ironically his cast did not go ten feet further than the distance he had reached previously with an ordinary cast. Line speed must be applied with smooth progressiveness and without jerking or vibrating the rod. I pull line on the pick-up on the forward cast and each time the rod is flexed in false casting. Apart from speeding up the line, it speeds the rod turnover. Quite a few pupils ask why I release line on my back cast. I only do this when the weight portion of the line is not at the proper distance from the rod tip at the start of the pick-up. It saves making an extra false cast. Unless you do it absolutely right, however, a back release will throw your line out of position and the rod will not come to full bend on the forward cast. Also, if the line is out of position, it will not turn over properly.

* *How to cast a closed and open loop.* For a closed loop the hand works back and forth in an almost horizontal lane.

For an open loop the hand works back and forth in a circular lane.

Fig 22 The closed and open loop

* *The curve cast.* The curve cast to the left is very easy. Use a side cast, semi-horizontal. For the last forward cast, stop the point of the rod about half way along its normal

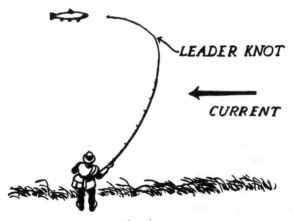

Fig 23 The right curve cast

course or trajectory. This will swing the leader round in a curve and drop the fly ahead of it. This is the most important and useful fishing cast, and should be used whenever possible. It will always work if, as you face the river, the current direction is to your left. The right curve cast is very difficult and cannot be satisfactorily explained in writing. * *Very important.* Beginners should start to fish using only the wet fly casts until they are able to land many fish with ease by this method, preferably using a full hackled fly on rising fish or, possibly, fishing only wet fly for one season. They should frequently check their back cast by looking at it. They will then learn and never forget how to hold a high line backwards and will not drop it during the false casts of dry fly fishing.

In 1957, I conducted a three-day course of casting in Yugoslavia for thirty selected anglers of the fly fishing club of that country. Only two could cast fairly well. None understood the principle of progressive line speed and high rear line.

At the end of the course all except two were safe for ever from casting a low rear line as they had mastered the wet fly cast with the high rear line. In my twenty years of teaching I never had such satisfactory results in such a short time, but we worked six hours each day. * *Conclusion.* The end-product is the catching of fish. To be a master of casting is the summit of the sport of fly fishing and gives the maximum amount of satisfaction.

Jacques Chaume, who started on the Risle, devoted his first fishing season to the exercise of casting and only began fishing the following year. He has become a caster of the first rank and his style is impeccable. Beginners, follow his example. It is the best way of achieving mastery and the rewards which await you will amply compensate for your patience and determination.

34

The bottle method

The results are guaranteed and incredible. It forms the muscles of the novice, maintains those of old hands and develops the grip of the fingers on the handle.

Devote ten minutes to it three times a week, or every day if you can. Take a bottle, the shape of a hock bottle for preference.

A. Rotate the whole casting arm in both directions.

B & C. Raise and lower the forearm vertically with the elbow against the body, then with the elbow free of the body.

D. Rotate the forearm in both directions.

E. Rotate the wrist in both directions. Vertical.

Left foot forward, make the movement of drawing the rod back without bending the wrist for the BA trajectory, then force the wrist down (as if you were leaning on the point of the rod) at the end of the FO trajectory.

Hold the bottle by the centre, rotate the wrist and the forearm in both directions. Horizontal.

Take a tennis ball and push the thumb into it.

Repeat each exercise twenty or thirty times.

During the first days use an empty bottle, and then gradually fill it with sand.

I insist that you try it!

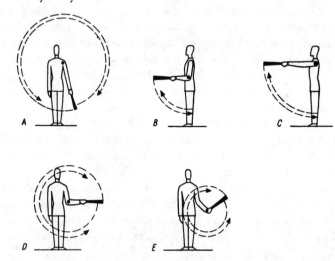

Fig 24 The Bottle Method

An important summary of advice to beginners

The main purpose of this book is to solve the mechanical problems of fly-fishing and make casting easy and relaxing. The sport involves the average newcomer in a most complex range of errors and faults, some of which may never be eradicated unless he has expert guidance from one source or another. These pages may help you to appreciate the value of mechanics at an early stage rather than relying on the years of experience needed to 'learn the hard way'. Those who apply the principles I have outlined are well on the way to becoming both casting-conscious and fully-relaxed fishermen.*

Learn how to cast before you start to fish. Above all, forget distance casting until later. Fish a short line. Long casts are for those with greater experience, because long casting makes it so much more difficult to present the fly accurately and delicately.

Study each situation carefully and select the best casting position before presenting the fly. Try not to scare fish by making them aware of your line as it moves forward or of line-shadow when false casting. This alone can add considerably to your catches over the years.

Learn how to spot fish moving below the surface and keep your eyes on the water all the time when fishing.

Decide from the very beginning of your fly-fishing career whether you consider it more important to match the natural drift of flies on the water or to match the hatch. The first is based mainly on mechanics – casting skills, streamcraft, the correct balance of rod, line and leader. It enables you to perfect your presentation of the fly and offers every chance of success. Attempts to match the hatch of natural insects should be considered only as a last resort. The theory is, in any case, based largely on imagination.

Remember that a splashy presentation, no matter how slight, is the worst of crimes! Oddly enough, few anglers guilty of this fault are aware of the fact. Result: when fish refuse to take they are convinced that, despite all their efforts, they have been unable to match the hatch.

Midge or mini-rods are very dangerous at times. Being much shorter than standard fly rods – 6 ft. or less – the fly travels perilously close to the fisherman's face when false casting. My dear friend Prinz Paul von Quadt fished with such a rod on the

* One of the most important points in *A Fly Fisher's Life*. When I first met Charles Ritz he studied my rod action and told me, 'I would like you to become a more relaxed caster than you are at present.' Thanks to his instruction and advice my enjoyment of the sport has increased a hundredfold. Many experienced fishermen will be amply rewarded if, for some months, they concentrate on casting in as relaxed a manner as possible. Only then does one realise how much unnecessary tension has been involved over the years. – J.P.

Andelle during the Mayfly season and hooked the fly into his right eyelid. If you must use one of these toothpicks be sure to wear glasses until you have acquired perfect control of rod and line.

Many anglers have told me, 'I like this rod, it strikes well' or 'I can never hook a fish with that rod'. This is nonsense. The ability to strike successfully depends on your skill, on *how* you strike, not on the rod. The trouble arises because you are too excited; too tense or nervous. You are strike-conscious. You may well face the same problem when you net and land a fish. Try raising the rod point instead of bending the wrist and moving the rod backwards.

The smaller the fly, the finer the leader point. Use a No.18, preferably with a double hook, on chalk streams and grayling waters, especially when fishing spent flies or black gnats.

Leaders must always be well stretched before you start to fish.

Avoid knotless leaders. They lack the stiffness necessary to gain a smooth turn-over of the fly on to the water. Use only leaders of the same type as those described on page 78 – the No.2 P.P.P. Rafale formula or eventually the No.1. Formula No.3 is for use when fishing with hook sizes 16 to 18.

I do not like automatic reels as they almost double the weight of tackle in the hand. They function well enough, but having used them for several years I could find no worthwhile advantage. Pierre Creusevaut shares my opinion. Today, people are fighting to gain extra quarter ounces. Why add ounces of hardwear?

Wherever possible, a beginner should face the river with the current flowing from the right. This ensures an ideal right-handed casting position, for the leader will curve more easily to the left and allow the fly to drift downstream ahead of the nylon.

Learn how to take a rod apart without twisting the two sections and always grip the rod with your hands close together before separating the ferrules. To avoid corrosion clean the ferrules after each fishing trip.

Before starting to fish, check that your line has been threaded correctly through all guides or rod rings.

Never fail to check the bend of your hook after a fish has been caught. Polish the point carefully with an Arkansas surgical stone. Needle-sharp points are essential and will avoid the loss of anything up to 10 per cent of the fish which take your fly. Many hooks are fashioned from poorly tempered steel – sole reason for vast numbers of fish lost.

I prefer boots and waders with felt soles. Iron studs are noisier and inclined to create vibrations likely to scare fish away.

PART II * HIGH SPEED/HIGH LINE

I am writing the following chapter because I believe that the HS/HL casting technique deserves a full explanation. In an earlier edition of this book, I explained the mechanics of fly-casting, and it was not until 1964 that I completed my observations and study of High Speed/High Line. The reader may find some repetition or differences in this new material, but I think both my old suggestions and my new ones are important for the angler interested in fly-casting: the first refer to classical technique, the second, and newer, to 'super' fly-casting.

Before *A Fly Fisher's Life* was published, I started giving fly-casting lessons in Great Britain, especially at the Annual Game Fair. I had as pupils beginners, old hands, boys, girls and adults with whom I obtained satisfactory results in quite a short time.

One year I offered £100 to the first pupil who could not, within fifteen minutes, cast a good wet fly line about fifteen yards.

A reporter from one of the leading newspapers tried it, believing it was easy money: any man who made such an offer was either crazy or had money to lose.

After thirteen minutes he was able to cast reasonably well and, as many other pupils were waiting, I told him: 'My friend, I think you should be satisfied now.'

He said he was well satisfied, even though he did not get the £100.

I often found it extremely difficult to communicate to the pupils the exact timing of a cast. I held their hands to give them the exact feel of the line speed but the moment I released them and asked them to cast alone, they still performed satisfactorily but the line speed was reduced. Even though the line was not too low behind, their casting was sloppy.

Friends who watched me cast said that my line had great speed and one could hear it whistle; and it never dropped behind.

This great speed was obtained by a good HS/HL rod movement, plus a very effective and continuous left-hand line pull.

A friend, Pierre Creusevaut, told me: 'Charles, that was fine, but your casting was rather jerky. I would prefer a smoother cast.'

I tried to change my style, but without satisfactory results. I lost line speed and after thinking it over found that my false casting, and particularly my back line, was very fast *because* of my jerky temperament. This was probably the reason why I could not pass it on to my pupils.

38

I then started to analyse exactly what I was doing and asked Pierre to watch once again. He said: 'I still see your very fast line but cannot discover how you obtain it.'

I tried again, and realised two things. *First*, I used a condensed jerk-jerk (which I named zic-zic) movement or impulse which enabled me to deliver great power and speed *instantaneously*, without losing the benefit of the rod-bend power. *Second*, I squeezed the handle of the rod before I started to cast, and I realised how my muscles worked, from the grand dorsal to the pinch of the index finger and thumb.

At the International Fly-Casting Championship in Zurich, 1960, I watched Jon Tarantino, all-round World Champion for many years, and probably still the best fly-caster in the world. I discovered that although he was casting for distance, which is different from casting on a stream for fish with a fly, his line travelled exactly the same way as mine, his power zone was similar and his casting was in fact HS/HL technique.

I had some slow-motion pictures taken of Jon's casting and mine. Then we viewed the movies and found that, as I had thought, whether you cast for fishing or for distance, to obtain line speed the method is similar.

I asked Jon Tarantino to come and fish with me on the Risle, a river in Normandy which I have fished for over twenty-five years. I wanted to see him present his flies on the many spots where I had cast and I knew exactly what one could achieve there.

I asked him to use the same kind of rod, line and fly as myself – an 8 ft. 5 in. P.P.P. Fario Club split cane rod, a D2 weight-forward line (see graphic) and a 9ft. 2in. P.P.P. leader with a point of ·007. To my great satisfaction Jon performed magnificently, better than anyone else could have.

This was the final proof that HS/HL technique was an ideal casting method.

I told Pierre Creusevaut that it was time for us to put it in writing and make some drawings.

We spent many mornings at the Paris Tir aux Pigeons Pond and soon discovered the movements were not exactly those we thought we were doing.

The dissimilarities were very slight, but sufficient to make just that difference between right and wrong. I concluded that we did not actually know what we were doing mechanically, and only slow-motion filming showed us exactly how we cast.

It took me another nine months to get it into shape. After many errors and changes, we finally produced the instructions and the drawings.

During the winter of 1963, the first article on HS/HL was published in the *Flyfishers' Journal* of the Fly Fishers' Club in London, and in *Trout and Salmon*. It was also published in French magazines, such as *Au Bord de l'Eau*, the *T.O.S.* and *Les Plaisirs de la Pêche*.

Then Tom McNally, of the *Fisherman's Digest*, an annual American publication, asked me for an article and I sent him HS/HL. It was also published in *Fischwaid* in Germany and in *Fischerei* in Switzerland.

Of course, there have been some comments, criticisms and so on, which is normal, but I am happy that, in general, it has been well accepted.

I have had practically no failures with the people to whom I taught this method – and I am still willing to put up the £100.

Whether you use a fly rod, golf club, tennis racquet, or throw a discus or javelin, the mastery of these tools can only be obtained by a full and complete knowledge of muscle power and the use of the hands, arms, legs and other parts of the body. All these must be perfectly blended and synchronised by training and building muscle strength.

Complete knowledge of the human machine and its motive power is necessary. This enables you to analyse yourself with absolute accuracy, to find the faults and gradually eradicate them.

Most fly fishers are hypnotised by the process of trying to catch fish and from the start become *unconscious* casters. They should first be *conscious* casters and concentrate on taking fish afterwards.

Full knowledge of casting will give the mastery, the confidence and the relaxation which permits the maximum enjoyment, even under difficult conditions, of your favourite sport.

As a start, consider *Isometric Muscle Training*: exerting a force against an immovable object. To improve HS/HL muscle control, we can add muscle development. Ben Fontaine asked me if I was familiar with isometric muscle training. He explained to me that it was a method being used in America to train athletes and increase their muscle efficiency and muscle memory.

He claims that muscles trained by the isometric method have a tendency to perform automatically at the right moment. To obtain 100 per cent efficiency, the muscles must be contracted to the maximum, which forces them to work and perform beyond what they are used to doing. The International Casting Federation has applied it to casting with excellent results.

The method for casting is extremely simple: take a stick, tie a piece of string to the end of it and fasten the string to a hook in the wall at approximately the height of the eye.

Six times every day for six seconds practise the back cast and also the forward cast, facing the wall and then facing away from it. For six seconds hold the stick as tight as possible, contracting the muscles to the maximum and pull or push as hard as possible. The height of the hook to which the string is tied can be varied.

A tennis ball can be squeezed, pushing the thumb into the ball as deep as possible and holding it there for six seconds to develop the thumb and index finger **grip**.

Here is an extract from *Trout and Salmon*, November 1964: 'May I extend to *Trout and Salmon* our congratulations and thanks for the outstanding articles on High Speed/High Line casting which appeared early this year.

'These have proved of immense value to the seasoned caster and a great assistance to the tyro. A vast improvement on the banks of the Towy in the casting ability became evident and the topic often was not the type of fly but HS/HL.

'It is interesting to note, too, that local tackle shops report a ten-fold increase in fly-fishing tackle sales.'

THE HIGH SPEED/HIGH LINE (HS/HL) CASTING TECHNIQUE

The natural position and movement of anyone who uses a fly-rod for the first time is to whip the rod back and forth, using a lot of wrist and forearm, the elbow remaining stationary at the height which seems to be, for them, the most comfortable.

This gives to the rod point a movement which overlaps the correct mechanical power zone on both ends and applies a curved pull to the line.

It makes it impossible to obtain a fast line speed and also stops all possibility of obtaining a good line lift.

It is the start and the continuation of defective casting.

Most fly fishermen are 'back-casters'; to master HS/HL casting it is necessary to become an 'up-caster'. The faster and higher the line, the longer it stays high.

Only a high back-cast (which should be renamed an up-cast) will deliver with ease a perfect forward cast with a light and delicate fly presentation, even at great speed. A perfect up-cast means a perfect forward cast (see figure 25).

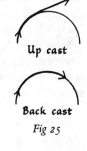

Up cast

Back cast

Fig 25

When a fish is rising, the faster the fly reaches its target with an accurate and correct presentation, the greater are the chances of it being accepted. The faster the line travels, the more efficient it becomes in piercing the wind. A high speed/high line keeps the fly drier.

I have found HS/HL casting particularly effective on lochs, lakes and reservoirs, and I have proved it many times on the Traun in Austria, when drift-fishing from a boat with very small dry flies.

HS/HL casting made it possible to reach any rise up to 60 feet away in from 4 to 6 seconds, using a good weight-forward line.

The 'back-caster', using the normal, slow, smooth line pull, may well achieve excellent fishing results. But I firmly believe that if the HS/HL technique is mastered, it will be found a tremendous advantage; the angler will remain relaxed even under difficult conditions (wind, obstacles, etc.), and will derive great satisfaction and pleasure from it.

HS/HL AND 'SQUEEZE-ZIC-BLOCK'

A high speed/high line can only be obtained by using a condensed, high-speed lift (see figure 26). The entire muscle power transmitted through the hand must be started, accelerated, blocked and stopped between rod positions 1 and 4.

I find the phrase 'Squeeze-Zic-Block' helpful in describing the three phases of the operation. I will explain this in detail a little later. It is sufficient to explain that 'Zic', the total power zone, must be condensed between the rod positions of approximately 2 and 4. This cannot be achieved unless the muscles from the hand to the shoulder are correctly used, and with split-second timing. Fly-fishermen are of three types: conscious casters, non-conscious casters and non-interested casters.

It is the conscious casters who try to analyse what they are doing and they usually continue to improve every year that they fish.

A fly fisher who can understand his casting – know exactly what he is actually doing – will always become a good caster and enjoy his fishing considerably more. He is unlikely to become upset when tired or when conditions are tough.

Some fly fishers in the expert class perform the 'Squeeze-Zic-Block' lift or pull subconsciously and cannot explain it with accuracy, because they are instinctive casters and have achieved mastership only after years of hard trial and practice. They succeeded because they were gifted and interested in their casting.

They were not hypnotised with the sole idea of catching a rising fish. Nearly every caster I asked to explain his wrist and forearm movement exactly was unable to do so.

Muscle power control has seldom been mentioned in casting chapters. Without its knowledge it is impossible to concentrate the muscle power into the part of the lift when the tip is continuing to go up, thus placing the line at the ideal rear height and angle for HS/HL. Power and speed lose all their efficiency the moment the rod movement stops rising.

This is what happens when casting without muscle control knowledge. From the correct starting position the rod tip is lifted up and back, following a circular trajectory from 1 to 4. As the lift is started so the grip on the handle is increased. Start of muscle control and arm movement are simultaneous. Automatically, the rod grip is progressive, instead of instantaneous.

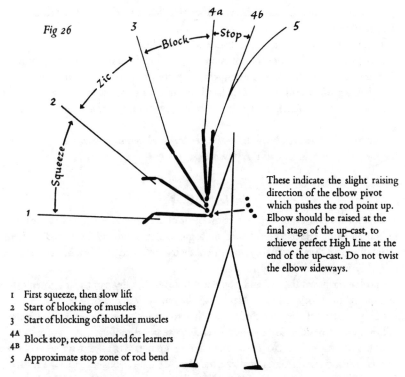

Fig 26

3

4a 4b 5

Block → Stop

Zic

2

Squeeze

1

These indicate the slight raising direction of the elbow pivot which pushes the rod point up. Elbow should be raised at the final stage of the up-cast, to achieve perfect High Line at the end of the up-cast. Do not twist the elbow sideways.

1 First squeeze, then slow lift
2 Start of blocking of muscles
3 Start of blocking of shoulder muscles
4A
4B Block stop, recommended for learners
5 Approximate stop zone of rod bend

The result is that the rod grip (or squeeze) becomes 100 per cent tight only after the start of the rod movement, and when the rod tip has reached almost 2.

This is too late, because from the very start of the movement the rod is not an absolutely integral part of the human casting machine (hand, arm and shoulder). Because all power transmission has to be delivered with split second timing, within a very short movement, only blocked muscles will prevent the 'power zone' from overlapping its exact limits.

Note to Figures: All rod positions, or descriptions of muscle movements, contractions, etc., are indicated in the sketches as accurately as possible. However, no two men, no two animals, are completely alike, nor do they operate in exactly the same way; therefore the sketches can only be approximate. The variation depends on what the individual finds best. This is why the old method of using the hours and hands of a clock has been discarded. Subconsciously learners always used to be hypnotised by the accuracy of a clock and tried to force themselves to perform 'clock-wise', even when they could not get good results.

For instance, I have indicated (in figure 26) the vertical position as the approximate stopping point for the rod at the end of the back-cast or up-cast. A really good caster, however, can often stop his rod further back and still keep his line high enough, provided he knows how to use left hand pull. Even so, beginners and those who are learning HS/HL are advised to stick to the vertical stop, until they have mastered both the back-cast and left hand pull. This will make sure that the rod point does not travel too far back.

For a fraction of a second there is rod wobble (like a machine with a loose bearing). The result is:

1. Loss of power and speed transmitted to the line.

2. A tendency for power transmission to extend beyond the correct stop limit of 4; then the rod drops too low, causing the very common low back line.

This does not mean a bad cast has been made or that a tempting fly was not presented. But the ideal, controlled casting with HS/HL performance has not been obtained.

The forearm has been brought to the vertical, or beyond position 4, to compensate for the delay in bringing in the power.

THE SQUEEZE

The *most important* thing is the exact moment of the squeeze (grip on the rod). When teaching casting either to old hands or beginners, and when I explained to them its exact timing, they invariably increased their line speed and height, and also considerably improved the final forward cast.

I no longer heard the old and popular phrase: 'Oh, why can't I straighten out my line on the final forward cast? Maybe it's the fault of the rod.'

Many anglers, if they are told of another rod which is supposed to eliminate this failure, do not hesitate to buy the rod and waste good money.

ALL YOU HAVE TO DO IS SQUEEZE THE ROD HANDLE TIGHT BEFORE YOU START TO MOVE THE ROD UPWARDS. Here are the various stages of the HS/HL lift:

* *Squeeze.* Tighten squeeze on the rod handle to a maximum; this will bring the arm muscles into play as well (see figure 26).

* *Zic.* Lift the rod slowly with the forearm (wrist down) until the line is straight and moving (approx. position 2). The power thrust of the rod comes when wrist and forearm go into action together to tear the line off the water. If done correctly the fly will zip off the water at high speed.

The elbow must move slightly up and down perpendicularly approximately two inches or so, according to the exact cast used. Its distance from the body can also vary. This elbow raise or lift is the only correct way to help the caster lift the forearm, hand, rod and line, and obtain a straight upward pull.

It makes it possible to pack in speed and power and concentrates them into the short power zone where the tip exerts a straight and upward pull on the line. The very slight elbow raise keeps the rod point waving upwards during the power zone trajectory. This is the most important point of HS/HL casting.

Block. Almost simultaneously with the power thrust *tense* all the muscles of the upper arm and shoulder. *This will block and stabilise the elbow pivot* and stop the rod dead, preventing it from prolonging the power zone. If the shoulder muscles are used correctly, a jerk will be felt on *the muscles of the back* extending from the shoulder down the right side. When the HS/HL wet fly lift has been learned, false casting will increase in speed and rear height.

Only in this way can so much power and speed be packed into a split second, and obtain so suddenly a perfect and total stop of the rod. The rod will then form its natural bend when the line starts to pull it back. This perfect stop produces the ideal narrow loop. By using the proper muscle control the elbow is blocked into a fixed position to give it more stability while false casting. This is also one of the most important points of this casting method.

You may have read that the caster is recommended to hold a book underneath the arm and hold it tight with his arm and elbow. This is only for the simple reason that it keeps the elbow pivot in a fixed position. This being the main axle part of the casting machine it is important that the elbow stays roughly in place, although it can and should move two inches or so.

FORWARD CAST

As soon as the pull of the line on the tip is felt, the forward power push is put in. If the back power pull has been made correctly, the forward line extension will be well above horizontal and will require only about half the effort involved in the up-cast pull. This forward power stroke will also be smooth (see figure 27).

The movement of the rod tip must not describe an arc. It starts with an arc, then from the vertical the tip is pushed slightly forward (horizontally) by lifting the elbow a little. This elbow lift is almost invisible when casting (it lengthens the forward drive and delays the lowering of the rod point). The rod should aim high, its tip pointing at an imaginary target slightly higher than your head. *Shoot the line the moment it is fully extended on the forward cast, or better still, the moment you feel its forward pull.*

Finally, the rod is brought down by wrist and forearm power (not only wrist), using Arm Action grip (see below), hand and forearm moving slightly forward. At this moment the grip of the thumb and index finger is tightened, and the grip of the other fingers is relaxed. This relaxation will help to prevent muscle cramp.

It is the best way to drive through the wind.

Almost always shoot the line for the final cast so as to avoid the fly hitting or splashing the water.

Fig 27 HS/HL *forward cast with push*

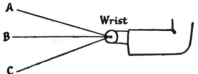

A Raised wrist B Straight C Depressed wrist
    (Wrong)   (Correct)
Fig 28   *Wrist bend ⅓ up, ⅔ down*

THE IMPORTANCE OF CORRECT WRIST ACTION
FOR HS/HL

Bend the wrist; never twist it because this creates rod twist and breaks up the HS/HL casting machine (see figures 28 to 31).

The bend of the wrist is very important; twisting the wrist to the right facilitates the movement but turns the reel and rod-rings sideways; this is *very bad*.

The wrist should be fully bent down vertically so as to drop the rod. When the rod goes up the wrist should move vertically back to straight before the rod reaches the blocked position.

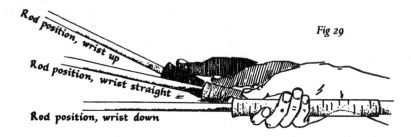

Fig 29

Rod position, wrist up

Rod position, wrist straight

Rod position, wrist down

The total *possible* wrist movement and bend is ⅔ down and ⅓ up. Failure to bend the wrist down means that total power is brought in too late. Practically no caster could answer when I asked what wrist bend he used.

The straightening of the wrist from a depressed position gives extra speed and helps to obtain more rod flex, providing the grip is at all times absolutely tight. It also prevents too much use of the forearm.

It is most important to check the wrist bend, and find out exactly what is being done. Twist of wrist forces the rod to deviate sideways.

46

Charles Ritz demonstrating the semi-sidecast using a 6ft 6in rod and High Speed High Line technique. Note the high-line forward finish.

The side cast, double hauling with the same 6ft 6in rod on the Tir aux Pigeons Pond, Paris. Note the wave-free line.

Muffet Hemingway, grand-daughter of Ernest, casting correctly after only three hours tuition. Right: A pupil demonstrates incorrect casting technique. Note position of the left hand in each case.

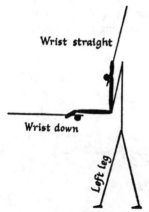
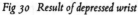
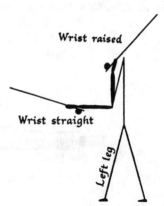

Fig 30 Result of depressed wrist   Fig 31 Result of raised wrist

GRIP OF THE ROD

There are three possible grips (see figures 32 to 34):

* 1. *Arm Action Grip.* Thumb on top is the only grip to use for HS/HL because minimum wrist twist is used. It allows the hand to give two different grips - together or separately. First the 'last three fingers' grip which fastens the rod to the arm; and second the 'thumb on top and index grip' which controls the rod. These two grips together give the best control.

Keep your thumb on top of the butt, wrist working at all times so that the flat of the reel moves always in the same plane as the rod (this is a proof that the casting machine is working correctly).

Arm Action Grip allows each of the five fingers to exert its full pressure on the grip. This grip requires a flexible wrist and no side twist. As this grip is difficult, the wrist can be *very slightly* twisted to the right.

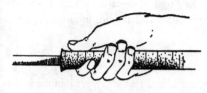
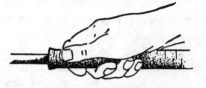

Fig 32 Arm action grip   Fig 33 Wrist action grip

* 2. *Wrist Action Grip.* Thumb slightly to the side. Using more wrist twist, thumb slightly on the left, reduces the efficiency of the squeezing power and induces more wrist and less forearm use. Exaggerated wrist casting is more tiring; it also permits the rod to travel too far back.

Fig 34   Index action grip

* 3. *Index Action Grip – Index on top.* Whoever started using this grip did far more harm than good to the casting world. It has only one advantage: when using the vertical cast on targets for tournament accuracy events, it reduces the chances of rod side-sway, but only for short distances. For fishing it has little value.

Index casters will never obtain HS/HL and become complete casters. This position gives the weakest rod grip and requires three times longer to develop.

None of the tournament accuracy casters who are in the 100 per cent class use the Index Action Grip.

At the I.C.F. World Championship in 1963 and 1964 some casters, for fly accuracy events, used the Index grip. But only Arm Action Grip casters took all the first places.

Some of my friends were surprised and could not understand why I attacked so bitterly the teachers who believe in index casting. This, unfortunately, is common in Switzerland, in the Paris area, and in Austria.

When teaching, professors who are not familiar with, or refuse to use, the casting which I recommend in the first sketch shown here are incapable of obtaining satisfactory results within a reasonable time, except by using the index.

This index casting reduces the power of the grip or hand squeeze on the rod, and makes it impossible to obtain line speed. The pupil who starts to learn fly-casting this way will always remain only a medium caster and should, in any case, never use a rod longer than 6½ ft.

This rod-hold also prevents him from using the many variations in fly-casting which are necessary to obtain mastership.

Pierre Creusevaut, Jon Tarantino, Ben Fontaine and Frank Sawyer join me in disapproval of it and never use it.

(See figures 35 and 36)

The normal caster has the right hand holding the rod, starting at about waist level; the left hand is about the same level and close to the right hand.

The right hand goes up and away from the left, and then back to its starting point. Therefore the distance between both hands, while casting, *varies all the time* and creates repeated line slack.

If the left hand is kept, with the arm slightly bent, beside the left leg below the waistline, the *variation* of distance between the two hands will be greatly reduced. Thus most of the line slack will be eliminated.

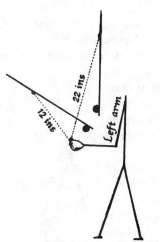

Fig 35 *Normal position of left hand holding line when false casting*

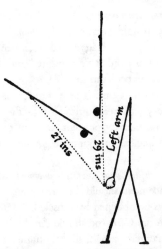

Fig 36 HS/HL *position of left hand holding line, when false casting*

This low left hand maintains an even and continuous tension on the line and prevents loss of line speed.

When holding the line in the left hand, if the thumb is stretched out and the line allowed to rest against it (thumb held open) the caster will become much more sensitive to the tension of the line.

By slightly adding line-pull with the left arm, extra line speed is obtained which will also reduce the line drop behind. This left hand line hold and pull is important to HS/HL technique. However, it is not the double haul used by tournament casters.

49

(See figure 37)

Instead of using the normal arm position, up-cast with full sky cast movement, raising the arm as high as the head and with an almost stiff wrist and forearm, using HS/HL muscle control. Keep the left hand in the pocket and hold the line in the right hand.

When a start has been made in mastering this upraised arm movement properly, when you obtain a high up-cast and a reach of over fifteen yards or so with ease, confidence and regularity, *and* when you have also the correct feel of the rod and line, then start in various stages to shorten the arm movement until back to the normal position.

General Conclusions

If you hold your rod *with thumb on top and palm of the hand perpendicular (as in figure 32)*, your exaggerated wrist bend problem does not exist, because this natural maximum bend is very limited and then you only have the exaggerated forearm movement problem to solve.

If you start casting as in figure 37, you cannot exaggerate your forearm movement – then both problems are solved almost 100 per cent – and you can obtain the famous HS/HL line feel in your casting hand. I would advise, therefore:

Watch first your forearm movement, which movement or displacement should be *very short*. This shortness can always be obtained by muscle blocking control.

Forward Cast: rod should aim high, pointing rod tip at an imaginary target, slightly higher than your head and shoot the line the moment you feel its forward pull.

I would say that ten half-hours of practice nearly always suffice, each time holding the arm a little lower, and trying a few false casts at each position.

The next step is to cast a wet fly straight up and down on the water – with the left hand holding the line. Let the fly come to rest on the water each time. (This is an essential step before trying to false cast as it will develop correct timing and rhythm.) Finally, try false casting with the left hand holding the line.

First practice

Last practice

Left leg

Fig 37

How to start the easy way

I also suggest concentrating on *low left hand line hold* to get used to keeping the left hand low, and prevent it from going up instinctively.

Several fly-casters who, after reading my article, tried to practise HS/HL technique ran into the following trouble: although the muscle contraction and the movement of the rod from the horizontal to the vertical were correct, the line refused to go high enough and also to obtain the necessary speed.

This was because they did not raise the rod sufficiently on the back-cast, which, as I explained, can only be obtained by slowly raising the elbow naturally at the same time as the hand goes up.

When starting to learn HS/HL casting it is extremely important that the method with the stretched arm indicated in fig. 37 should be used. Then the problem of raising the elbow does not occur, and by continuing to practise this system until the elbow is brought down slowly to normal it will be realised that automatically, when casting in the normal position, the elbow and forearm will go up slightly in the vertical line.

But if the cast is practised having the elbow pivot absolutely blocked as far as its height is concerned, it will be found that it will not succeed properly.

WHEN PRACTISING, ALWAYS KEEP YOUR EYES ON THE UP-CAST LINE HEIGHT AND SPEED. DON'T LOOK IN FRONT, ONLY LOOK BEHIND.

If you start to learn HS/HL as per figure 37, you will gradually master the perfect rod movement subconsciously, and discover the feel of the HS/HL cast in the easiest way, without having to force your mind to think about too many different movements at the same time.

It is then not necessary to master all the intricate, small and difficult movements (forearm, wrist, hand) which are so hard for beginners to learn.

I have had a few cases of casters who complained that they had sore muscles after trying to cast HS/HL. This was due to the fact that they kept their muscles taut during the entire casting time.

It is extremely important to relax the hand-squeeze on the handle of the rod between forward and backward casts. This reduction in squeeze is very, very slight, but is sufficient to relax the muscle tension.

You may also have another trouble when, after having mastered HS/HL, you use it for fishing and find that the fish often refuse to accept the fly.

This is due to the fact that when HS/HL is used, the line is travelling very fast forward and the fly will have a tendency to slap or hit the water. With the normal cast and slow line the fly can land easily.

It is absolutely necessary, in my opinion, to finish the final forward cast *with slight shoot* so that the fly arrives on the water the way a duck slides down on to a pond. The fly must glide down, not drop and hit the water.

I had an example of this when I was fishing in Bavaria. A young friend of mine who had been taught by his father, a first-class caster, fished with me on the famous Lech river. One day I said: 'Come along, I'll have a look at your casting and see if I can help you or not.' He was casting a superb line, very fast, and after a few minutes I told him: 'There is nothing I can teach you, your casting is perfect.'

Well, although his casting was perfect, for four days he could not net a single good fish, whereas myself and my other friends were having rather good luck.

He said to me on the third day: 'I don't know what is wrong.'

So I looked once more and this time I concentrated on the presentation of the fly and found that, every time, it tended to slap the water.

I told him: 'For Heaven's sake, use the shoot. You know how to shoot the line, *shoot* your line.' An hour later he came back with two lovely fish and said: 'Charles, you really helped me, I am so happy.'

I have discussed HS/HL technique many times with Pierre Creusevaut, Professional World Champion, Jon Tarantino, Amateur World Champion and probably today's greatest and most complete caster, and Ben Fontaine, the President of the International Casting Federation.

We all came to the same conclusion: HS/HL is the ideal of perfection in fly-casting.

I leave it to you to decide whether the opinion of World Champions on the HS/HL technique is worth considering. I hope that I have been able to help my friends of the fly fishing world.

My greatest reward will be to find out how many of you have decided to become HS/HL casters.

* *The latest method of teaching single-handed casting.* In 1970 Pierre Creusevaut and I taught the salesmen at the Mitchell factory in Cluses, France, to cast with a trout rod. None of them had tried before and as it was snowing we were obliged to use a hall with a low ceiling. This presented problems, for with a normal casting technique the flies hit the ceiling every time.

'Pierre,' I said, 'let's try this using only the rod tip.'

Our efforts on that occasion, and those of the Mitchell personnel, proved so successful that the experience is worth recounting for the benefit of anyone new to the sport.

When you first begin single-handed casting it is worth while using only the top section of the rod until you are able to cast 30-40 feet. Then, and only then, start practising with the complete rod.

This method has the advantage of preventing a beginner from using the rod as a whip. It is almost impossible to whip the line when casting with a rod top. The reason? Simply that the casting arm reaches upwards to compensate for the missing butt section. When you use the complete rod for the first time you naturally adopt the same action. The feel of the rod is appreciated immediately and a high back line can be cast correctly.

On most golf courses you are not allowed to play until you can handle a club reasonably well. Don't start fishing until you have the feel of your rod and can use it competently.

* *Casting with the entire rod.* I strongly advise those who start learning with a full-length single-handed trout rod to use a strap – a leather shoe lace, a ribbon or tape will do, but a rubber strap cut from an inner tube is ideal – to hold rod and wrist in the correct position. Strap or tie the rod handle to your forearm immediately

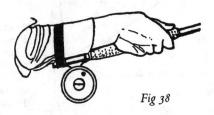

Fig 38

below the reel, ensuring correct placing of the thumb at the highest point of the rod handle. This will prove of considerable advantage to the average beginner, enabling him to acquire the correct action far more quickly and with fewer faults than those who rely on a free action from the start of their training.

HS/HL CASTING WITH THE DOUBLE-HANDED SALMON ROD

The movement on the back-cast is the same as that with a single-handed rod, but both hands are used. The most important part of the action shown in fig. 39 occurs in the 'Block' segment (3) when the rod point is pushed to the sky, raising both elbows.

The right hand controls the rod at all times, the left hand merely supporting the rod, countering its weight and length.

Both hands move together, up and down, at the same speed and along the same trajectory. Note that there is a tendency for the left hand to act as a piston, *moving back and forth* and so reducing casting efficiency and line speed. It is essential that this fault be avoided.

* *Casting with double-handed salmon rods – the shortest route to correct use of a trout rod.* I always teach double-handed casting first, even when my friends or pupils are only

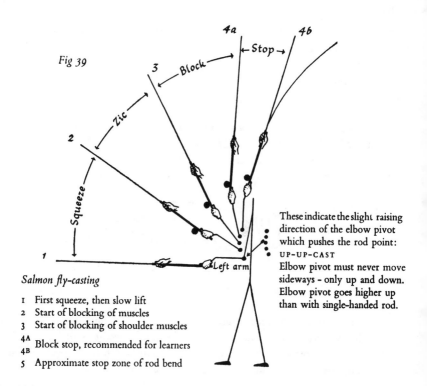

Fig 39

4a 4b

← Stop →

3 — Block

Zic

Stop

2

Squeeze

1

Left arm

These indicate the slight raising direction of the elbow pivot which pushes the rod point: UP-UP-CAST
Elbow pivot must never move sideways - only up and down. Elbow pivot goes higher up than with single-handed rod.

Salmon fly-casting

1 First squeeze, then slow lift
2 Start of blocking of muscles
3 Start of blocking of shoulder muscles
4A
4B Block stop, recommended for learners
5 Approximate stop zone of rod bend

interested in single-handed techniques. After reading what follows you will understand why.

You can learn double-handed casting within three hours and with practice will continue to improve without further assistance. By comparison, single-handed casting requires at least six hours instruction before you dare cast alone. Even then, it will be some time before you are able to improve without experienced help. Lacking this, your technique will almost certainly deteriorate and your chances of becoming a proficient caster may be no more than 50-50.

Why?

The fact is that all beginners instinctively use the rod as a whip. They horsewhip the stream. But fly-casting and horsewhipping have nothing in common; the movements involved in these two activities are quite different.

Since the double-handed rod is so much longer, all mistakes are amplified. You feel them. You see them. From the first lesson you are casting-conscious. Your left

54

shoulder acts as a brake, helping to steady your left hand. This, in turn, prevents your right hand from developing excessive wrist action and so whipping the rod.

To prove my point I picked two beginners – Suzie Babington Smith, whose father first introduced me to tubefly fishing for salmon, and Muffet Hemingway, daughter of Jack, son of Ernest. Results: most satisfactory. Their style was perfect and their casting mechanics bettered those of many experienced salmon fishers.

The immediate sense of casting control stopped them from dropping the line on the back-cast and forgetting what they had learned of the correct method. In a short time they were able to improve without further assistance.

The back-cast must be aimed high as the line is lifted from the water. Only in this way can one ensure that the line is fully extended *before* it starts to drop below the horizontal. Do this and you have an ideal position from which to obtain fast up-and-forward propulsion as your line moves into the forward cast.

Power for the forward cast is obtained by pressing with the right thumb against the upper part of the handle and aiming high, literally to the tree tops. In this way you achieve maximum line extension and the line will not fall to the water until the last moment. If you raise the rod-tip slightly at this point, fly and leader will drop before the belly of the line and your fly will dive immediately.

When it becomes necessary to change from casting over the right shoulder to casting over the left shoulder, reverse the position of your two hands – left hand up, right hand down. It is simple enough, 15 minutes' practice is all you need.

Having reached this stage, I then gave my pupils a single-handed rod and told them, 'Go ahead. Forget that you are no longer casting with both hands.' Their very first back-casts were high and the extension of line behind them was all that any instructor could wish for.

American steelhead fishermen – whose rivers are large, the wading deep and exceptionally long casting is often necessary – avoid touching the water behind them by holding their single-handed rods above their heads and using single-haul or double-haul techniques to gain casting speed and distance. As the rod hand controls all casting movements this illustrates yet again that the use of single- or double-handed rods follows the same principle.

* *Double-handed saltwater fly-fishing for beginners.* Salmon fishing in Norway and other Atlantic waters may soon be a thing of the past unless the Danish commercial fishermen temper their activities with some degree of good sense and concern for the future. Even then, only a limited number of anglers will be able to enjoy this sport. Salmon fishing today is very expensive – up to $2,000 a week for one rod, guides, lodgings, food and transport to and from Norway.

Taking big fish on a fly rod is every angler's ambition. Saltwater fly-fishing, a sport which is becoming more and more popular, is so much cheaper than salmon but no less exciting. Many species of fish in tropical waters, fish weighing 100 lbs or more, will take flies of the bucktail or streamer type.

The tackle used in this branch of the sport consists at present of powerful rods specially designed for single-handed double-haul casting with shooting head lines and monofilament backing. Only experienced casters can use these rods with maximum efficiency, for the fisherman must often present his fly rapidly and with great accuracy to the leading fish in a fast-moving school.

I would not advise any beginner to start with a single-handed rod of this calibre. They are very tiring and the average person must soon rest or quit the sport because of aching arm muscles or blistered hands. One solution: a combination single- or double-handed rod – the single rod measuring about 9 ft., plus an extension butt 2 ft. long, with a second reel seating to allow double-handed casting. Such a rod calls for relatively little effort and with the minimum of practice one can cast up to 100 ft., lifting all the line most of the time, with all the accuracy and speed so essential to success in saltwater fly-fishing.

Lefty Kreh is probably the greatest saltwater fly-fisher and guide in Florida. I saw him demonstrating double and single haul casting at the Federation of Fly Fishers meeting at Poconos, Pennsylvania. When I told him of my point concerning double-handed rods and their potential in this branch of the sport, he agreed that the idea was sound and of particular value to the novice caster.

CONCLUSION

I said that HS/HL is simple and that one can master it rapidly. Now that you have reached the end of this chapter, you may think that I exaggerated and that it is not all simple.

TO OBTAIN A SATISFACTORY HS/HL, ALL THAT IS ABSOLUTELY NECESSARY is to learn muscle control and correct up-cast movement and to *eliminate as much as possible the side twist of the wrist*, and watch the timing.

At Scarborough in 1963, Pierre Creusevaut used HS/HL for the first time for the salmon fly distance cast. He broke the Professional World Record with sixty-five yards.

PART III * RESEARCH AND TECHNIQUE

The split cane fly rod

Fly rods are like women: they won't play if they're maltreated! All rods can catch fish: their success depends on the hand that uses them. But there are rods and rods! Good ones are rare. To know how to select a rod without faults among the innumerable models placed on the market by the manufacturers of two continents is extremely difficult, even for an expert. The fisherman is therefore limited to searching for one he believes will suit him and seems the best to him. Lack of technical knowledge condemns him to uncertainty and often to useless expenditure.

The moments of hatch and activity on the part of the fish during a day's fishing are relatively short. Therefore, all loss of time should be avoided and all useless movements reduced to a minimum. The rod must do the maximum amount of fishing. The fisherman must have equal confidence in the rod and in himself. He must not thwart it, but endeavour to be in harmony with it and let its flexibility do the work. He must always be master of his smallest reflexes, be continuously capable of observing the most minute details and be able to relax as often as possible.

A faultless rod is one of the best trump-cards a fisherman has for attaining his goal. But how are you to know how to select one, particularly if you are only a moderate caster? I hope that my animadversions on rods (my hobby and my passion) will enable you to acquire the knowledge and understanding that every lover of the fly rod should possess. Moreover, I hope that the reader will find here something new.

* *How to select a cane rod without allowing yourself to be unduly influenced.* Before describing my methods of examining rods, here are a few considerations I believe to be of importance.

Let us first rid ourselves of a widespread idea, which I have often had occasion to point out as false or, at least, much exaggerated: the reel does not balance the rod; though in the past when rods were ten feet or more, very long and very heavy, a reel as a counterweight did produce the illusion of balancing the rod in the hand; but it is the line which plays the principal role owing to its weight and the shape of its taper. It is, indeed, on the line that the rod depends above all for giving its maximum, and yet retaining its balance. The ideal would be to be able to fish with the reel in your pocket.

Examining a rod in the shop enables you to determine its quality, its approximate power and its type of action; but actual casting on the water will alone show you whether it suits your particular physical and nervous make-up; in a word, whether it will tire you or not. For, indeed, after a long day's fishing, you do not want to feel, at the evening rise, that you are fishing with a broom handle. If you still have full control of it, if your wrists can manipulate it as easily as at the beginning of the day, you have a rod that suits you physically and temperamentally. This is the first and most important point. I must here excuse myself for talking of Parabolic rods most of the time. I must make it clear that I am not doing so for the purpose of advertising these rods, but merely as a convenient reference and in order to determine exactly the type of action. There are many first-class rods by other makers which will give you full satisfaction.

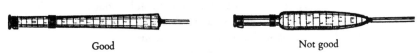

Good   Not good

Fig 40 The Shape of the Handle

The best advice I can give a beginner is to choose a cane rod of one of the following types: Parabolic 8½ ft. normal, Ritz Parabolic 8 ft. 2 in., or Ritz Super-Parabolic P.P.P., Master 8 ft. 3 in., or Powerplus P.P.P. according to the amount of money you have to spend. I only give these rods as examples; any other make providing a similar action will be just as suitable.

Still talking generalities, I must point out that, in a fly rod, even the shape of the handle is sometimes enough to tire the fisherman and give him cramp. Long, cylindrical handles with the minimum of curve and of comparatively small diameter reduce fatigue, the risk of cramp and the likelihood of acquiring blisters to the minimum, unless you have a large hand when the cork handle should be thicker.

I prefer extra light reel fittings (flange and ring), weight being the enemy of precision.

I consider that a rod should have eleven to thirteen rings according to its length. The ring at the point should be very light, as should the bottom one. They should be in hard chromium-plated metal. The agate ring belongs to ancient history. The intermediate rings I prefer are those in snake form, of fine tempered steel, either bronzed or chromiumed.

The ferrules, in rods of quality, need particular attention. Only nickel-silver, bronzed or chromiumed outside, can be considered. The portion of bamboo which enters the ferrules must not fit too tightly as this may result in the breaking of the rod tip at the joint. The male ferrule should be very slightly conical, in order to take up the wear and tear which is inevitable in the long run. The first condition a good rod must fulfil is that the bamboo should be guaranteed by its place of origin. The best is called Tonkin cane, such as Palakona, from Hardy, or Pingona. Tonkin cane contains about 20 per cent water. Seasoning, essential before manufacture, and tempering, should reduce the water content to 5 or 7 per cent. It is, of course, almost impossible to eliminate the water altogether without danger of carbonisation.

Correct tempering lies between the minimum condition in which the bamboo is under-tempered and the maximum entailing carbonisation of the fibres. There is, therefore, a golden mean that produces a cane at once lithe, light and infrangible. The achieving of this precise condition is a great secret that, naturally, I have no right to reveal!

While talking of wood, I must point out that some bamboos are camouflaged with brown dye, the object being to give them an appearance of having been tempered. It is not always very easy to detect this abuse. Nevertheless, bamboo often displays a difference in colour though subjected to the same tempering process. That is to say, it may turn more or less dark though retaining similar qualities. If, therefore, you find slight differences in colour on the various sections of bamboo on the different facets of the same rod, you should not necessarily conclude that this is a defect. Indeed, I would go so far as to say that it may well be the opposite, for it is obvious that camouflage will be applied to every facet equally to obtain a more generally attractive appearance.

The nodes should be at different levels in each section of the rod, that is to say that they should not be opposite each other. The most that is acceptable is that three strips out of the conventional six strips have their nodes at the same level, but only on condition that the strips are on opposite sides of the rod.

The essential part of the rod, as I have already said, is the top joint. If there are two, they must be identical, so that they are interchangeable without altering the rod's action.

When should you choose a rod? During the fishing season and after several days of fishing only, because the arm and wrist must be in proper training before sound judgment is possible. At the beginning of the season, I often have a feeling that my rod is defective, that it vibrates, etc. As I watch my cast, I see waves in my line, particularly with supple rods of 8 feet to 9 feet. This is nearly always due to too violent a movement of the wrist making the rod tip vibrate, owing to a lack of practice during the closed season. I correct this by slowing down the cast and reducing the force used, thus restoring the balance and preventing wavy line.

* *My method of examining a cane rod.* The first thing to do is to examine the six facets of the butt, that is to say the thick sections, by putting the rod to your shoulder and aiming with it as if it were a gun. You can see at once if the six facets are perfectly smooth or whether they have undulations in them.

Then examine each of the six facets, particularly in the neighbourhood of the handle and at the other end near the point of the tip. They must be precisely equal in width and show no glue line. The jointing of the six strips must be perfect and invisible.

Examine the joints of the six strips. They must show no signs of glue.

If the rod can pass this severe and meticulous examination, you may be certain of having found one manufactured by the most up-to-date methods and endowed with the maximum strength.

Now let us consider the question of the action, that is to say, the rod's efficiency.

* *How to determine the quality of a cane rod's action.* As far as I am concerned, I much prefer a supple rod, which does not, of course, mean a weak rod. It can be a powerful one, provided that its bending, under the tension of a series of tractions representing the successive curves it must take from a short cast to the longest, remains uniformly progressive.

To determine this, tie a piece of string to the top ring and attach the other end to a fixed point. Take the rod in your hand, and bend it progressively, meanwhile examining carefully the successive lines of curve, from minimum to maximum pressure: these curves should show no break or hump, but maintain a regular and decreasing progression from tip to butt. Then, having detached the rod, hold it firmly in the hand and give it a quick flick using the forearm only and without bending the wrist, then watch the rod till it comes to rest: if the tip of the rod gives too many vibrations and fails to stop quickly, it means that it is weak, of inferior quality, badly tempered or not tempered at all.

If you have flicked the rod very hard, it will have a tendency to show a curve with a break at about a third of its length from the tip: this is perfectly normal and correct, so do not be anxious. If the break appears nearer the tip, it is because the rod has a tip action owing to weakness of the tip. If, on the contrary, the break occurs towards the middle or near the butt, it is because the rod is too supple as a whole or too weak in the centre.

Most fishermen are content to flick the rod with a regular movement of the wrist which can give no precise indications.

60

* *The uniformity of cane rod tips.* In order to test this, take the male ferrule in the left hand, the ring end in the right and bend the tip, turning it in your fingers: if one of the facets shows any serious weakness, you will feel it at once. Then flick the rod tip with a brisk movement of the wrist and you will be able to tell quite easily, by comparing them, which are the most rigid and which the most pliant in relation to their diameter.

If you have to choose between several similar, or almost similar, rods mount them and place the ends of the tips on the edge of a table, placing all the butts in line so that the alignment is perfect, then the weight of each rod will slightly curve the tip near the end, the degree of curve will show the precise comparative difference in the strength of the rod tips. Half an inch or so is sufficient to show a disparity in strength. Make this experiment on all six facets to determine the rod's homogeneity. In rods of first class quality the difference should not be more than about an inch.

You are now in a position to judge of a cane rod as well as the expert can; you may nevertheless well find that it has faults the first time you use it in practice.

* *Malformation, weakness.* Since bamboo is a plant, the best processes of manufacture cannot change its basic texture. Very careful selection can eliminate wood which has not the appearance of guaranteeing the good quality of fibre necessary for the manufacture of split bamboo. But this quality can only finally be confirmed when, the rod having been completed after being tested for curve, the fisherman tries it out on the water.

A length of split bamboo is comparable to the leaf of a steel spring as far as elasticity and the breaking limit are concerned. To be constantly demanding from a rod the maximum it can give quickly brings on fatigue which is transformed into permanent and more or less serious malformations. The same thing happens to a rod after long service. In spite of all the care lavished on it, it will show signs of weakness in curvature. There is a decadence in the stamina of the wood, precisely as there is in that of the steel of a spring.

The malformation of a rod tip is but rarely due to a failure of the glue. The glues used today have the effect of soldering the six strips together. In general, a failure of this kind is due to a slipping of the fibres which partially detach themselves from the material sealing them together. A super-quality rod will become malformed if it is kept continuously bent for several hours, even if the curve is not more than half its maximum flexion. After several hours in a normal position, it will ultimately straighten out again and will not revert to its malformation while fishing. The fibres will have returned to their normal position.

In certain hands, rods will live longer than their owner, while other people will spoil them quickly whatever the quality of the rod may be. This is due to a twist of the wrist while casting or to defective holding of the rod when endeavouring to bring fish into the net. Too many rod tips are killed in this way.

Any failure of the glue is generally owing to shock and torsion either due to the style of casting (the thumb along the side of the handle instead of on top of it), or by taking the rod apart by twisting (this applies to rods not taken apart at night). I always disjoint my rods after every day's fishing. A slight rod deformation towards the butt of the rod is normal because the maximum casting power is applied in the last forward cast.

* *How I began working with split bamboo.* I began working with split bamboo at the Ritz-Carlton in New York in 1917. I was on duty every night in the Manager's department and spent most of my time in a little office in the entresol. I visited daily the great sports shop of Abercrombie and Fitch, some fifty yards from the hotel. The salesmen always seemed to be busy when I appeared, but nothing could discourage me and, in a very short while, I knew better than they did what the departments contained.

My salary of a hundred dollars a month prevented my being an important client of theirs and obliged me to slum by frequenting the pawnshops on Fourth Avenue where, for two dollars, ten at most, I was able to gratify my passion for fishing rods! For a few cents, I could proudly buy from Abercrombie and Fitch rod varnish, silk for whippings and cement for ferrules. Then, in my little office, which I had transformed into a workshop to the considerable disapprobation of the manager of the hotel, who only put up with my impudence because I was my father's son, I devoted myself to renovating my finds. I scraped them, I took the ferrules to pieces, I shortened the weak joints and strengthened my 'new' rods throughout with extra fine white silk that became invisible when varnished. I then showed my masterpieces to the salesmen in the big shop, who were astonished but interested! My rods had taken on a new life.

One evening, the manager invited me to fish with him on the following Sunday. The result was that one of my rods was approved and accepted by him! From that day, I became supplier of rods of all kinds to the hotel clients! Finally, my stock at Abercrombie's rose for I was no longer satisfied with bargains from the pawnshops. The salesmen got me in the end and sold me unfinished sections as well as all the fittings. The lathe in the locksmith's shop, in the basement of the Ritz-Carlton, supplied my cork handles. Finally, I acquired a stock of dollars which permitted me to realise my great ambition: my first fishing journey to Canada. Unhappily, this virus was the cause of my abandoning a career which should have been solely concentrated on the hotel business, for I had to maintain the independence that is so indispensable to a self-respecting fisherman!

*Lefty Kreh of Florida holding a tarpon taken on fly rod and line
using a leader with 12lb point.*

Pierre Creusevant and Charles Ritz

In 1927, after living for ten years in America, I returned to Europe, where I continued to work with split bamboo. Roger Pujo, of the *Bord de l'Eau* magazine, suggested that I should go and see Pezon and Michel in Amboise, near Tours, and visit their split bamboo workshops. A month later, I became their Technical Adviser.

* *The perfecting of prototypes: essential conditions and methods of work.* Perhaps I may be forgiven if I mention my own rods but, to be in a position to perfect fly rods as I conceive them, one must know the whole basis of manufacture, the mechanism of casting and be an experienced fisherman into the bargain. One must spend all one's time between fishing and the factory and in two continents. One must avoid at all costs becoming too individual: devote a great part of one's time to studying fishermen in action, so as to grasp the general basis of their technique of casting and also examine their principal faults. One must always keep up to date with every novelty, every new trend, and be on intimate terms with the very rare specialists. And, finally, one must have at one's disposal a practical experimental ground of the first order: a river highly populated with trout. I acquired this last advantage thanks to the generosity of Edouard Vernes, President of the Casting Club of France, on his fishing on the Risle, and during my numerous stays on the Traun, in Austria. Finally, I was able to find partners who were as passionately concerned with the question as I was: Edouard Plantet, works manager at the factory at Amboise, and my friend, the casting champion of the world, Pierre Creusevaut. It is entirely due to our perfect mutual understanding that we have achieved results. I think Creusevaut is one of the greatest judges of fly rods in the world. In an average year, he casts for six hundred hours.

In the same way that Weatherby, the great American armourer, has proved that for sporting rifles the methods of the artisan can no longer stand up to modern mechanisation, so it is with the manufacture of split bamboo. It is an identical problem and I am positive on the point. The tempering, the cutting of the sections and the glueing are mechanical operations; but it was necessary to await the birth of perfected machines invented by professional engineers. The great artisans of the past were no more than ingenious handicraftsmen, without any real mechanical knowledge. They improvised their machines as best they could, and succeeded in making them work thanks to their cleverness and dexterity. For instance, one of the artists in split bamboo cuts his triangular sections with two minute circular saws which move along a sliding carriage to which is fixed the length of split bamboo. They are pulled forward by the hand of the operator with the aid of bands. It is the machine for cutting sections which has finally superseded the artisan's methods: it turns up to 1,200 revolutions a minute.

The precision and uniformity of result reaches almost the exactness of working in metal. There is, however, one part of the process that depends entirely on the experience and acumen of a specialist: the choice of the raw wood and the selection of the sections once they are glued.

* *My methods of trial and perfecting.* Basic diagrams for the first prototypes. Study of the prototypes on the diagram of curves (normal minimum and maximum curve). The definitive establishment of the proportions by a simple and rapid process which I have called the longitudinal displacement of the cones (this is a little secret). Then the making of a new prototype and then two more with slight variations increasing or diminishing either the tips or the butts as the case may be.

Selective trials, eyes blindfolded, of these prototypes in the hand, without a line, to get the feel of the flexion.

Casting trials with a line, by Creusevaut, while Plantet and I observe the curves and vibrations. Every rod must permit a cast of twenty-seven yards.

Trials for slow and rapid cadence.

Trials for wave in the line.

Trials against the wind.

Trials for precision in placing the fly, fifty casts at targets at fishing distances to see that the rod tip does not deviate to right or left.

Trials for speed at targets. Fifty chronometric casts.

Each prototype has its own trial report, and the study of these reports gives us very precise indications for the final perfecting.

Trials of prototypes on the river in conditions with which we are familiar.

Each prototype is ready prepared with line, leader, fly and sixteen yards of line deployed on the water; then Creusevaut and I try three rods one immediately after the other so as not to lose the feel in the hand of the preceding one. This is very important. Use this method to select your rod, also to compare lines. You will be amazed to find how instructive and accurate it is.

After a definite choice has been made, the approved prototype must then be used fishing for a whole season. It will be tried out by a great number of anglers, good, bad and indifferent. When the people we have lent it to want to go on fishing with it instead of handing it back to us after a few minutes, we feel reasonably sure that we have come to the end of our researches.

There are not dozens of types of action, but one only, whose rigidity varies according to the length of the rod, and it must work progressively from the point to the handle without the slightest weakness, however used. The action may be more or less powerful, but the successive curves must be identical. This is the action which I have called 'Parabolic', though the term is only a figure of speech, and the curve of the rod

64

has absolutely nothing whatever to do with a parabola. This name used commercially dates from 1937. Since then, we have been researching into methods of increasing the suppleness still further without diminishing the strength. After many failures we finally succeeded, in 1949, in achieving a series of six different models, called Super-Parabolic P.P.P. (Progressive Pendulate Power).

I have said that the rigidity or suppleness must vary according to the length. Thus, the speed of a rod is in inverse proportion to its length (short: rapid; long: slow).

Short rod: the line moves backwards and forwards nearer the ground. It needs to travel backwards and forwards more quickly to avoid loss of speed which makes it touch the ground behind or become hooked up.

Long rod: the line travels backwards and forwards on a higher level. Therefore loss of speed is less dangerous. The cast can be slower, though this does not prevent its being fast if the caster's wrist demands it.

A supple rod without weakness will respond better to the wrist than a rigid rod which requires the whole arm to put it into action.

WHAT I DEMAND OF A GOOD FLY ROD

1. Feather light in the hand;
2. Instantaneous response from the action and extreme sensitivity to the least movement of the wrist;
3. Possibility of slow or rapid casting at all distances at will. The length of the rod will naturally modify this condition;
4. Progressive strength in a constant relation to the accentuation of the curve;
5. Complete absence of vibration in the upper part of the rod tip;
6. Great strength, but balance and suppleness;
7. Great effectiveness against the wind (50 per cent of fishing days are windy);
8. Great precision in placing the fly;
9. Reduction to the minimum of the caster's effort and general adaptability to the majority of fishing conditions.

The handle must be designed to ensure:

The maximum of comfort;

The minimum of fatigue;

The choice at will of three positions:

 The thumb on top;

 The thumb slightly to one side;

 The forefinger on top

The placing and the number of guides require special study to:

(a) Preserve the optimum curve of the rod during casting;

(b) Produce the least drag on the line;

(c) Allow the fisherman to grasp the line at any moment with ease.

* *Rods made to measure.* To make a rod to measure is, in my opinion, and speaking in all sincerity, out of the question. To balance a rod and achieve the optimum action, it is necessary:

1. To have numerous prototypes;

2. To make exhaustive trials in the act of fishing.

The net price of a unique model would therefore be impossible.

* *Comments on the ideal action P.P.P.* Here is an interesting example:

The three rods P.P.P.: Wading, 7 ft. 1 in., Baby Zephyr, 7 ft. 9 in., and Zephyr, 8 ft. 4 in., have two identical first joints. The 7 ft. 1 in. has its handle on the second joint. The 7 ft. 9 in. has also a detachable handle of 9·45 in. The 8 ft. 4 in. has a butt handle of 13·78 in. (cork and reel seat 10·63 in.). Thus, their power is identical, but the 7 ft. 1 in. is ultra-rapid, the 7 ft. 9 in. rapid, and the 8 ft. 4 in. semi-rapid.

Each of these rods has a rigidity appropriate to its length. Furthermore, the rod tips have a maximum length. The slightest extra weight on the rod tip (ferrules and guides) has a considerable influence on the action. The nearer the ferrule is to the point of the rod, the greater the weight. The first sixteen yards of a heavy line only weigh between ·035 and ·088 ounces more than those of a medium line. A ferrule weighs between ·176 and ·246 ounces. The lower you place the upper ferrule, the less weight there is on the rod tip and the better the quality of the action. Therefore, to achieve an ideal action, rod tips should be extra long with only one set of ferrules. On the other hand, the length of the rod tip is limited by the requirements of transport. But I was also in search of the ideal action, or as near as it is possible to achieve it, by effecting a perfect compromise between suppleness and rapidity with the maximum of strength.

Instead of trying to incorporate this action within a determined length, I preferred in the first place to discover the optimum length. In order to achieve this, I was forced to abandon the standard lengths of 8½ and 9 feet. The trials made for curvature and in the act of fishing have proved that 8 ft. 5 in. is the desirable length. I therefore arrived at the following:

Rod tip:	54 in.
Butt:	46¾ in.
Total length:	8 ft. 5 in.

and I finally obtained the Fario–Club, a rod which corresponded to all my needs for fishing trout and grayling at that time.

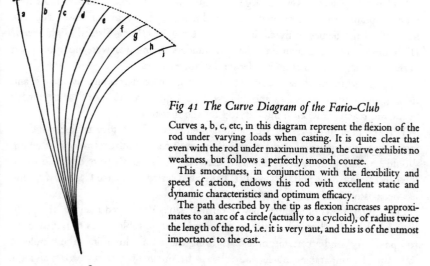

Fig 41 The Curve Diagram of the Fario-Club

Curves a, b, c, etc, in this diagram represent the flexion of the rod under varying loads when casting. It is quite clear that even with the rod under maximum strain, the curve exhibits no weakness, but follows a perfectly smooth course.

This smoothness, in conjunction with the flexibility and speed of action, endows this rod with excellent static and dynamic characteristics and optimum efficacy.

The path described by the tip as flexion increases approximates to an arc of a circle (actually to a cycloid), of radius twice the length of the rod, i.e. it is very taut, and this is of the utmost importance to the cast.

Fifty years of research and rod designing

Object: The LF/LL (Long Flex/Long Lift) flyrod, able to achieve perfect HS/HL (High Speed/High Line) casting.

Method: Maximum bend coupled with maximum-flex straightening power.

I first became interested in fly-fishing, casting and rod action when I was in New York from 1916 to 1927. I felt that the fly rods available at that time did not perform with 100% efficiency. Far from making correct casting the simple, gentle action it should be, many rods of that era were so badly designed as to ruin their owners' technique.

From those early days I searched for a material and for design theories which would ensure perfect action. That search ended in December 1968.

The main defects with split cane rods were weakness in the rod tip and a relative lack of flexibility in the butt. Some rods produced in the first quarter of this century were too soft in the centre section. With such equipment no fly-fisher could possibly develop the skills of which he or she may have been capable.

The rodmakers of those days, more especially the designers, were responsible for this sad state of affairs. It was they who failed to appreciate that the total length and bend of a rod must help the caster at all times to transmit power to the line, leader and fly, and that this applies when making short or long casts, slow or fast.

Rod building was governed largely by guesswork in those days and most new models sprang from liaison between a rodmaker and one of his customers. The science and mechanics of fly casting, such as Long Flex/Long lift and High Speed/ High Line, were unknown and the rod builders themselves were no more than average casters. Specialists in rod design did not exist.

Such specialists must have advanced knowledge of rod making, fly casting and fishing, and as instructors they should have considerable experience of the beginner's needs and reactions when using a flyrod for the first time.

The key men in car racing are the design engineer, the factory engineer and the test driver. It is my opinion that rod building calls for a similar team, one of whom should be among the world's finest fly casters. All the rods I have designed, from the prototype to the finished product, have been tested by Pierre Creusevaut, who has been associated with me since the early 1930's.

Until 1967, we concentrated mainly on split cane. We solved many of the problems involved, but the lack of flex in cane made it impossible for us to improve the rod power beyond a certain point or to bring the action down into the handle. A cane tip of comparable power must always be much heavier than glass and the longer the rod the greater the feeling of excessive weight. Since a cane butt is also less responsive, less capable of transmitting full power to the line, such rods are at a disadvantage, no matter how well they are designed. However, prior to the mid-'sixties fibreglass also lacked the qualities we sought, to such a degree that the finest cane rods proved superior to those fashioned entirely from glass.

We had always heard that by comparison with cane, glass rods had a soft, floppy action, and until recently this was so. But though glass is more flexible it does have tremendous flex-return power and a longer flex-range. Modern materials permit perfect control of power from rod tip to butt and are much lighter than cane. As we have now proved, light rods can be extremely powerful.

In the mid-'fifties, when the black Harnel glass rods produced by Pacific Laminated were on the market in Europe, I bought a nine-footer with the intention of matching a long, fibreglass top with the butt section of an 8 ft. 2 in. Parabolic cane rod. I painted the butt black, the same colour as the glass top. The result was a very good rod indeed: it could even cast a light spoon.

That tip could handle three different line weights – something a cane tip could never do – and though we recognised that the cane butt was too stiff and therefore lacked maximum power, fibreglass had not reached the stage at which we could rely entirely on this man-made material.

All glass fly rods were then tip-actioned and this, in my opinion, is far from ideal for fly-fishing. Even so, I painted a white skull and crossbones on the butt of our combination rod and presented it to my rodmakers, symbolising the coming demise of split cane.

We then made a rod with a glass butt and a heavy cane tip: the Variopower. The result was amazing. This was followed by an 8 ft. 6 in. cane/glass combination with enormous line-lifting power. To this day it is considered by many Pacific steelhead fishermen to be the best rod ever produced. It enables the caster to use a relatively short rod which eliminates much of the need for double haul casting – a technique which so often makes for poor presentation of the fly and lack of penetration when the fly reaches the water.

The cane tip used on that model was taken from the 130 gr. all-cane dry fly distance rod with which the great Albert Goddard reached 150 ft. using a semi-side cast. Despite its power, it was normal enough in the hand.

As fibreglass improved so Pierre and I accepted the possibility of designing an all-glass rod, lighter and still more powerful than the cane/glass combination, but we were determined to insist on using our own tip formula and to incorporate this with tapers giving through-the-rod action.

I had always hoped that before my working days ended I would find a rod manufacturer with progressive ideas; ideas extending beyond current market influences. The Trade spoke of tip action: always, tip action. I needed someone aware of the fact that in Europe we understood the finer points of rod design.

In 1967, Cornelius Ryan, author of *The Longest Day* and a member of the famous X Kilo Club in New York, stayed at the Ritz. We met, and talked fishing. I took him to the *Tir aux Pigeons* pond where we test all our rods and invited him to try them.

I explained LFLL/HSHL and the importance of casting mechanics. His interest was immediately apparent and he told me afterwards that his action improved from the very first cast.

We discussed the matter further over two Chivas Regal scotch at the Ritz Bar later in the day. Suddenly he said:

'Charles, you are wasting your time in Europe.'

He paused, marshalling his thoughts.

'Your theories are so advanced and have such potential that you *must* go to the United States. I have the very man for you – my friend Thomas Lenk of the Garcia Corporation. Let me talk to him.'

I told Cornelius that I had long since presented my theories in his country, only to be defeated by sales organisations convinced that nothing but tip action rods would be acceptable in their market.

There the matter rested. But the next year, fishing on the Nausta river in Norway, I interrupted my stay and crossed the mountains to meet Tom on the Laerdal, at Modelbo. I asked him to try my rods and that first meeting closed with an invitation to visit the Conolon factory in Santa Ana, California.

I arrived at Conolon in December, 1968, to be met by a disconsolate Pierre Creusevaut who had gone there ahead of me. He told me that everyone had been most kind, but that it would be no easy matter to persuade them that LFLL/HSHL rods could outcast their tip action models.

'Charles,' said Tom Lenk, 'you know that I accept your theories, but Pierre is right. It's up to you to perform a miracle and convince these fellows.'

Technically there was no problem. The co-operation we needed depended on our ability to overcome the psychological barriers linked with the well-established tip action rods. In the event, we were able to do this without hurting anyone's feelings.

In two days we made six prototypes, resulting in two superb fly rods of 7 ft. 1 in. and 7 ft. 10 in. Tom Lenk tried them both and immediately increased his casting range by more than 10 ft. Most important, he did this without forcing the rods or using extra strength.

I must express my gratitude to Tom Lenk for his open-mindedness, his great intelligence and understanding. His co-operation enabled me to achieve a satisfactory conclusion to some fifty years of research into the mechanics of fly rod construction and to produce a rod which is indeed a perfect casting machine.

Finally, I must thank my dear friends Pierre Creusevaut and Dick Barnes, without whom I must surely have failed.

* *Ritz-Garcia LFLL/HSHL rods*. Only very precise knowledge of casting and its mechanics, of rod construction and rod action, plus practical experience of dry fly, wet fly and nymph fishing can produce a rod which will do most of the work for you. Even then, the right material must be available and for much of my life that material did not exist. I found it, and the key to long years of research, when I visited Conolon for the first time.

The long-flex built into the glass blanks used at the Conolon factory ensures long line lift. It builds up flex-release power which keeps the rod tip in contact with the line as it extends behind and ahead of the caster. Its smooth power transmission means that rod vibration is a thing of the past.

Modern glass has a much longer flex than split bamboo; the more it bends the more it stores power. From the day the pole vault rules were changed, authorising

* Long Flex/Long Lift: High Speed/High Line.

the use of fibreglass in place of bamboo poles, the world record was broken many times. That super-power is now available in fly rod form. No fly-fisher seeking the ideal rod action should ignore the increased flexibility, power and lack of vibration apparent in these new rods.

Today – March 1st, 1971 – after building and testing many prototypes we have the perfect range of LFLL/HSHL all-glass fly rods, from 6 ft. 6 in. to 8 ft. 10 in. with an extension butt.

All these rods have been tested on the Nausta and Jolstra rivers in Norway, on the chalk streams of Normandy and the rivers Argen and Lech, in Germany. Not one of them has disappointed me. Thanks to their great power-flex as line is extended, casting distance is increased. Their terrific speed keeps the line high and reduces

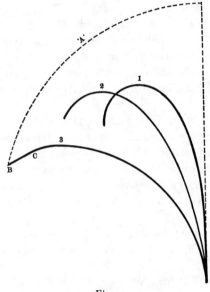

Fig 42

A: Power transmission zone
1: Flex of typical tip-action glass rod
2: Flex of Ritz PARABOLIC split cane rod
3: Flex of Ritz-Garcia LFLL/HSHL fibreglass rod

Note: (a) From B to C the tip of this rod has almost no flex, a characteristic vital to achieving long lift
(b) The scale is approximate

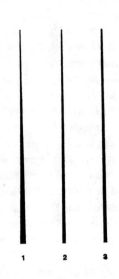

Fig 43
Cross Section of Rod Tapers

1. Typical tip-action glass rod
2. Ritz PARABOLIC split cane rod
3. Ritz-Garcia LFLL/HSHL glass rod

line-drop when false casting. Without exception, they feel pleasant in the hand and fish perfectly at all distances.

As a direct result of their long lift, power-flex and high speed, false casting is reduced by as much as thirty per cent. and the fly is on the water longer than it could possibly be when using an inferior rod. What matters most to the novice caster, with such a rod it is so much easier to learn.

The longer the line lift, the longer a rod's power-transmission zone. This long zone makes it easier to correct timing errors, provided the basic design is right. The action of the new Ritz-Garcia rods guarantees more positive assistance than could be obtained from tip-action rods or those made of short-flex material. For example, the 8 ft. 2 in. Ritz-Garcia fly rod will lift 54 ft. of line. One of the best U.S.A. rods has a maximum line lift of 44 ft. Our 8 ft. 5 in. model lifts 63 ft. One of the best American rods of standard design has an absolute limit of 57 ft.

We have found that split cane rods have a tendency to deviate sideways, due no doubt to the fact that bamboo fibres are less flexible and less homogeneous than glass fibres. Rods in the Ritz-Garcia LFLL range show no trace of this fault. Even in the hands of an average fly-caster they invariably cast a narrow loop and this, I maintain, is vital to accurate casting when fishing. In brief, no other type of fly rod 'casts for the angler' as these do.

Given blanks of this quality and tapers of the correct design, glass is not only ideal, it is the only material from which fly rods should now be made. This does not mean that other materials, still lighter and with still more flex-power, will not be used eventually for fly, bait or spincasting rods. I am already experimenting with such a material and have reason to hope that I shall be one of the first to perfect a fly rod of this type. But that is looking to the future: for the present there can be no question that glass reigns supreme.

Having reached that conclusion after years of painstaking research and experiment, I tested the Ritz-Garcia rods with several European fishermen whose opinions I value.

In England, I went to see my dear friend Dermot Wilson at Nether Wallop, in Hampshire. We tried the entire range from the casting platform behind the Mill House – a delightful setting, typical of England's finest chalk stream country. Dermot voiced not a word of criticism: the action, he said, was all I claimed it to be. And this was no case of being polite to an old friend from overseas. Never before have I seen this great enthusiast place the fly with such precision and delicacy.

Frank Sawyer also tested them. 'I like your new rods,' he wrote later, 'and foresee a great future for them. The main feature, as I see it, is that these are the first glass rods I have tried which can be used with a light line and yet, at the same time, command a long casting range without undue exertion. I found the line very easy to control as I could feel it perfectly. The rod works smoothly from tip to butt and the delivery of line and leader was as good as I could wish. This should be a good rod both for dry fly and nymph fishing. If desired, it can be loaded with a heavier line which could, of course, make casting a little easier for those whose timing is not up to standard. I am not yet ready to put on the black armband for the split cane, but it does seem likely, much as I dislike having to admit it.'

The final test. By now, my rods had been approved by many of the finest fishermen and casters in Europe and the U.S.A., but I was anxious to challenge some of the famous fly-fishers of Austria and Bavaria. This, I had no doubt, would prove the most difficult test of all.

I visited Hans Gebetsroither on the Traun, a famous river which is today more difficult to fish than ever before. Besides, the casting technique adopted by Hans and his friends is entirely different to my own. They favour the index finger grip and the use of very short rods. To my sorrow, this style of fishing has also been adopted by the majority of Swiss casters. Even so, I was up against a tough, know-ledgeable crowd.

When I met them on the river with my fibreglass rods they could scarcely con-ceal their dubious expressions. Some grinned openly, and little wonder; the Traun is the Mecca of split cane rods. Few of its anglers have ever considered any other material.

Most of them are dry fly enthusiasts, able to present a fly accurately under all fishing conditions. I handed my rod over and asked them to try it. One by one, they voiced surprise at its quality and action, but – they said – this did not mean that it was better than split cane.

I noticed that after presenting the fly and prior to casting again, each one of them brought his left hand into action, pulling in line three or four times before lifting into the back cast, and then false casting until sufficient line was in the air once more.

I told them not to shorten the line on the water, but to lift the full length and re-present immediately. False casting was unnecessary and the advantages of that fact were obvious. That advice was received with astonishment bordering on disbelief but confirmed when the rod behaved perfectly.

One fisherman asked another, 'Why does this rod lift so much more line than our own?' And at that point I knew they were licked. Their rods were made by a great rod builder named Brunner – a split cane artist who inherited a stock of the finest bamboo. It only remained for me to explain the mechanics of Long Flex

Long Lift and the vital importance of a super-power tip. For the first time, they acknowledged that glass rods of this quality are indeed superior to built cane.

But for me the finest test fishing was on the wonderful waters of the Lech, in Bavaria. There, one bright morning, my friend Kustermann, Jr, and I took six grayling averaging more than 2 lb each in a hectic half hour's fishing with Tup's Indispensable and barbless hooks. Some of those fish were struck at distances up to 80 feet using the 7 ft. 10 in. rod. We also tried the 8 ft. 2 in. rod to make sure once again that for river fishing the 7 ft. 10 in. model would lift all the line we could cast and was, indeed, the best for LFLL techniques.

Forgive me if I have devoted too much space to this subject. You probably realize that my rods represent a large part of my life's work, certainly one of its greatest passions. That being so, label me a raving enthusiast by all means, but one who is sincere and whose theories have withstood the most severe tests of time, trout and the considered judgements of the world's finest fly fishers.

* *The Line Test.* This is the fairest way for the average fly-fisher to compare his present rod with those I have designed. Do this first with your own rod, extending line on to the water until you reach the maximum length which can be lifted correctly into the back-cast. Then measure the line by laying it along the bank and pacing out the distance cast.

Next, using a similar line, repeat this procedure with a Ritz-Garcia rod. Both rods should, of course, be of the same length and the reels of comparable weight. I have no doubt that the measurements noted will convince you of the soundness of my theories and the benefits to be gained from Long Flex Long Lift.

Lines

The proper use of a rod's action depends on the line and the fisherman's hand.

Is your line properly balanced?

Does it suit your rod?

Without special knowledge, you can only trust to the sensitivity of your own hand and you can only reach approximate conclusions.

The dealers and manufacturers only give secondary indications: maximum diameter in the centre in hundredths of mms or as letters A, B, C, D, etc. The total weight of the line varies according to the material used (silk, nylon or dacron), the dressing and the length, which may be 25 or 30 metres, or 30 to 40 yards.

The more usual indication of weight, as distinct from the diameter of the line, is that given by AFTM Nos which classify each fly line according to the weight of the first 30 feet, excluding the level tip. (This length was chosen as the average amount of line aerialised.) The initials AFTM stand for 'Association of Fishing Tackle Manufacturers' and their scale numbers from 1 to 12, No. 1 being the lightest and No. 12 the heaviest line.

There are two types of lines:

* *Normal:* double taper, divided into three sections:

Front taper; Belly; Back taper.

The two tapers and the decreases in diameter are similar.

* *Weight-forward:* otherwise termed Forward-taper or Torpedo, divided into five sections:

Front taper; Belly; Back Taper; Holding line; Shooting line.

I only use lines with fine taper. They are obviously more fragile, but they are the only ones which can give one the assurance, whatever the conditions, of placing and presenting the fly as I conceive it should be done.

Fig 44

Double Tapered Floating Line
(seldom regular)

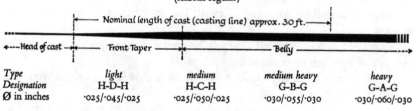

Type Designation Ø in inches	light H-D-H ·025/·045/·025	medium H-C-H ·025/·050/·025	medium heavy G-B-G ·030/·055/·030	heavy G-A-G ·030/·060/·030

Weight-forward Floating Line

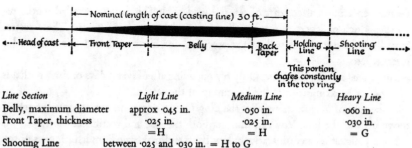

Line Section	Light Line	Medium Line	Heavy Line
Belly, maximum diameter	approx ·045 in.	·050 in.	·060 in.
Front Taper, thickness	·025 in. =H	·025 in. = H	·030 in. = G
Shooting Line	between ·025 and ·030 in. = H to G		

75

Size Equivalents

Trade designation	in 1/1000 inch	in 1/10 mm	in 1/100 mm round figures
A =	·060	15·24	150
B =	·055	13·91	140
C =	·050	12·70	127
D =	·045	11·43	115
E =	·040	10·16	100
F =	·035	8·89	89
G =	·030	7·62	76
H =	·025	6·35	64
I =	·022	5·59	56

The length of line determining the maximum weight that a rod can take before being overloaded is called the 'lift', the maximum free line. It is the greatest length that should be held in the air for false casts.

* *Double tapered line.* Maximum free line equals the forward taper plus a variable length of the belly section.

* *Weight-forward line.* Maximum free line equals forward taper, belly, back taper, and all or part of holding line.

A comparative trial between a double tapered line and a weight-forward line of the same belly diameter will prove that the maximum free line of the former will be longer than that of the weight-forward line and the action of the rod more delayed.

Weight-forward lines permit the fly to be presented more quickly to a fish seen rising, and are much more effective against wind.

Recorded times taken in presenting have nearly always shown a small average in favour of weight-forward lines.

It is the formula of the distribution of diameter-plus-weight on the free section, to attain the ·423 ounces (or more, or less: light, medium, heavy), which balances the line. This balance is a science that only the great competitive specialists are in a position to acquire after years of research and trial. This is very detailed work, requiring much patience, numerous diagrams and hundreds of splices. These casters have lines for distance as well as for precision, for front, back and side wind, calm weather, etc.

* *The method of trying out a line.* Only try out a line after several days of fishing, that is to say after breaking it in at the beginning of the season.

Make sure of having an assistant standing to one side, who can observe the whole movement of the line. You can thus get both the side and rectilinear view.

Place yourself on a comparatively low bank and make medium length casts of ten to fifteen yards, parallel to the bank, so that your assistant can get an accurate view of the line's extension and the placing on the water of the forward taper and leader (the same method should be used for trying out a leader), waves in the line (big or small), unevenness, loss of speed, and touch-downs behind and before.

If waves are apparent in the forward extension:

1. Make sure they are not due to a lack of delicacy of the hand and try to correct this: nine times out of ten some improvement will be obtained. A forward extension without some minor undulation is extremely difficult to achieve; it is the best proof of a hundred per cent delicacy and of perfect mastery of technique, which is very rare;

2. Extend the line on the ground behind you, cast and place it on the ground in front of you. If the end of the line is serpentine, the forward taper is too long, but this is not very serious in actual fishing. If the leader has a tendency to turn backwards, the forward taper is too short;

3. Make a few trial casts of sixteen to eighteen yards with shoot, and again watch in front and behind. If the shooting line is too fine there is a risk of getting entangled and a tendency to lose equilibrium in flight. Finish with a few short, slow false casts, while endeavouring to keep the fly almost on the level of the surface during the forward extensions. This is very important, for it is then that the defects of a too-thick forward taper can be discerned.

How to determine if the weight of the free section suits the rod and its action. Begin by extending the line without false casts, placing it each time on the water until, without forcing it, the rod just begins to be overloaded – you begin to touch down behind, have a sensation of weakness, too pronounced a dropping of the forward taper. The forward part of the holding line should pass through the top ring before you have a sense of overloading. Normally, the maximum length of the free section should approximate to thirteen yards.

It should be only the weight of the line that bends the rod, and the action of the rod alone which extends the line. If this is not the case, measure the maximum diameter of the belly with a micrometer and weigh the free section of the line. This information should allow you to determine whether the line is suitable or not and what dimension of line is necessary to match your rod.

A good caster, master of his left hand, can use a lighter line than the average; which will enable him to place the fly more delicately on the water.

When wading in rivers with rapid currents, when a horizontal cast is necessary and a curve cast essential, I often prefer a somewhat heavier line and a rather abrupt forward taper. Whatever the circumstances, the only lines I use today are the plastic lines of the type supplied by Garcia, Scientific Anglers and Cortland.

The gathering in a figure of eight of the line in the left hand keeps the line dry for most of the time owing to the hand's heat.

It is approximately the first three feet of the holding line, continually running backwards and forwards through the top ring under the pull of the left hand, that undergo the maximum friction. This is where the first signs of wear, fraying, etc., appear.

To sum up, make sure of knowing your line; you will often be surprised to find that its apparent faults are due to your casting. Moreover, you will eventually discover precisely what type of line perfectly matches your rod. The general tendency is to select too heavy a line which over-weights and prematurely weakens the rod.

The leader

To be sure of achieving the maximum chances of acceptance, it is essential to obtain accuracy in placing the fly and the forward taper of the leader at the first cast. Moreover, you must be in a position to achieve this result, in so far as it is possible, whatever the weather. This is the role of the leader. It is as important as the rod and the line and must be minutely balanced to complete uniform continuity, obtain a homogeneous whole and transmit the precision of the caster's hand faithfully to the fly. The leader must therefore be accurate and effective against the wind. It must also extend rapidly and allow a perfect presentation in calm weather on smooth water.

Before nylon was invented, I only attached secondary importance to the leader. I contented myself with a good leader of first quality gut, tapered to 1X or 4X at most, but I found that these leaders lacked strength and reduced the precision of my casting. By strengthening them, I obtained only slightly better results. In the act of fishing, they quickly became dry and rigid.

As soon as Rhodiaceta submitted to me the first samples of nylon, in 1939, I began my experiments again. Six months later, I abandoned gut for ever. Thanks to the leader in nylon of unequal length and diameter, which I called the Rafale storm leader type, I achieved a considerable improvement in accuracy and thus caught more fish.

* *Gut*. May be stronger when new.

The forward part of the taper can be readily sunk.

* *Nylon*. Maintains uniform strength after use.

Allows great variation in type of leader.

More supple when dry.

Eliminates the need for soaking.

The only possible leader for use in the heat of summer and when hatches are rare and spaced out.

Saves time in case of repairs or alterations while fishing.

I leave to the faithful all the advantages of presentation with the submerged forward part of the taper in gut. The many observations I have made of fishermen practising this doctrine have convinced me that the game is not worth the candle, except on very rare occasions and then only in the hands of certain masters. I prefer to ally myself with the majority of old hands in the search for positive and simple methods which may achieve good averages with the minimum of complication and manipulation.

All fish are aware of the leader. In 1949, in the Bay of Douarnenez, a big tunny weighing several hundreds of pounds followed my boat for forty-five minutes. It took all the sardines, sardine heads and pieces of mackerel we threw it, but persisted in refusing three whole sardines and a live mackerel on the hook! The leader was of very thick twisted nylon.

The butt of the leader should have a diameter equivalent to approximately 60 per cent of that end of the taper of the line.*

The ends of tapered lines vary generally between ·002 in. and ·030 in.; therefore the butt of the leader must be between about ·014 and ·018 in.

The ideal is to have as long a forward taper as possible but which still remains controllable. It is desirable, moreover, to reduce to the minimum the loss of transmission of power, and in consequence to preserve the maximum of strength and rigidity over the greater part of the length of the leader. To achieve this, an ultra-rapid decrease near the point is necessary, and the total length must be divided approximately into:

60 per cent of strength	·018 in.	·016 in.	·014 in.
20 per cent of decrease	·012 in.	·010 in.	·009 in.
20 per cent of point	·008 in.		

The diameter of the point must always be appropriate to the size and weight of the fly.

Hooks No.10	nylon point	·012 in. to ·010 in.
No.12	,,	,,	·010 in. to ·008 in.
No.14	,,	,,	·008 in.
No.16-18	,,	,,	·007 in. to ·0063 in.
No.20	,,	,,	·0063 in. to ·0047 in.

The Rafale storm leader formula for the leader is susceptible to slight modifications according to atmospheric conditions, types of line and dimensions of flies. In special cases, I content myself sometimes with shortening certain sections and,

* The dimensions of nylon thread are accurate to ·004 in. more or less.

with experience, you can quickly get to know what must be done to achieve perfection.

I must, however, add here that many of my friends, expert fishermen, content themselves with almost any leader and frequently catch as many fish as I do! But why not hold as many trumps as possible and thereby give yourself the maximum of confidence, the means of savouring the success of your presentations and, above all, make your task easier when the wind is bothering you?

The Rafale formula has been adopted by the majority of my friends both in Europe and in America. Sometimes fish will rise to the knots of the leader, mistaking them for midges!

You may think that a Rafale (Windstorm) leader is more visible to the fish than the old standard type. But a perfect cast presentation of the fly consists of placing the leader so that only the fly and eventually the point of the leader are visible. The storm leader increases the possibility of this by 50 per cent and gives you the feel of the fly in your casting hand because it blends perfectly with the line taper and point.

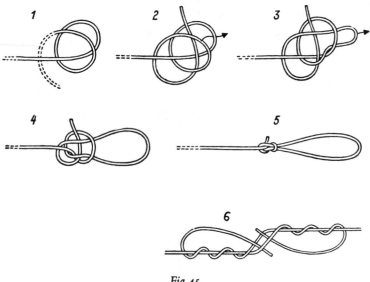

Fig 45

1 to 5 The best Leader Loop, the Perfection Loop. It is the only loop which runs true in line with the leader and does not deviate sideways. Length: ¾ in. minimum. 6. The best connecting knot for leaders; called the Blood Knot, because its inventor was named Blood; it has no connection with 'blood'.

* *Trying out a leader on the water. Trials by hand.* Before using a nylon leader, especially if you have made it yourself, fasten the loop to a hook or nail and give it a thorough stretch. This will slightly lengthen it, keep it straight and at the same time test it.

Take the loop of the leader between thumb and forefinger, stretch it backwards and then forwards with the whole arm. You will see that a Rafale, even of three yards, will extend perfectly.

* *Conclusion.* The leader is one of the means of transmitting the power of the cast to the fly. The speed and precision with which the fly is placed depends on the formula of its taper and its balance.

The form of the taper of the line and the leader have equal importance. The point of the latter is the principal agent in awakening the fish's suspicions. A bad leader can greatly reduce the qualities of hand, rod and line.

The knots reinforce the rigidity of the leader which assures greater precision in presenting the fly; suppleness is only necessary in the point, where a length of 20 in. is, in my opinion, the ideal compromise. Greasing the leader up to the point is advisable. It improves the efficiency and sensitiveness of your strike. I like a soft nylon. It makes better knots and the point lasts longer.

Formula: Normal P.P.P.

No.1 Trout Leader, 9'2" long, tapered from .018" to .010"
.018" — .016" — .014" .012" — .010"
3'7" — 2'11" — 6" 6" — 1'8"

No.2 Trout Leader, 9'2" long, tapered from .018" to .008"
.018" — .016" — .014" .012" .010" — .008"
3'7" — 2'5" — 6" 6" 6" — 1'8"

No.3 Grayling Leader, 9'2" long, tapered from .018" to .007"
.018" — .016" — .014" .012" .010" .008" — .007"
2'11" — 2'7" — 6" 6" 6" 6" — 1'8"

Formula: Super-Precision P.P.P.

No.1 Trout Leader, 9'2" long, tapered from .018" to .010"
.018" — .016" .014" .012" .011" — .010"
5'6" — 6" 6" 6" 6" — 1'8"

No.2 Trout Leader, 9'2" long, tapered from .018" to .008"
.018" — .016" .014" .012" .010" — .008"
5'6" — 6" 6" 6" 6" — 1'8"

No.3 Grayling Leader, 9'2" long, tapered from .018" to .007"
.018" — .016" .014" .012" .010" .008" — .007"
5'0" — 6" 6" 6" 6" 6" — 1'8"

Formula: Short P.P.P., coloured brown, green or grey

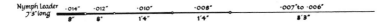

No.1 Trout Leader, 6'7" long, tapered from ·018" to ·010"						
·018"		·016"		·014"	·012"	·010"
2'3"		1'8"		6"	6"	1'8"

No.2 Trout Leader, 6'7" long, tapered from ·018" to ·008"						
·018"		·016"	·014"	·012"	·010"	·008"
2'0"		1'5"	6"	6"	6"	1'8"

No.3 Grayling Leader, 6'7" long, tapered from ·018" to ·007"							
·018"		·016"	·014"	·012"	·010"	·008"	·007"
1'10"		1'5"	6"	6"	6"	6"	1'4"

(instead of the ·018 in. thick section, the ·016 in. section may be extended)

Formula: Nymph

Nymph Leader 7'3" long	·014"	·012"	·010"	·008"	·007" to ·006"
	8"	8"	1'4"	1'4"	3'3"

Typical tapers shown exaggerated

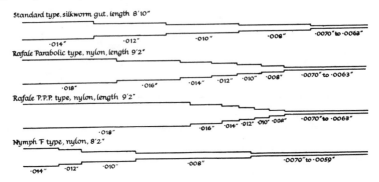

Standard type, silkworm gut, length 8'10"

Rafale Parabolic type, nylon, length 9'2"

Rafale P.P.P. type, nylon, length 9'2"

Nymph F type, nylon, 8'2"

The nymph type possesses an especially long and supple front taper in order to facilitate the submergence and unhindered drift of the nymph.

Fig 46

Double tapered leaders may, when there is no wind, produce a lighter and finer fly landing. I prefer, however, the P.P.P. type, which pushes the fly better, has more penetrating power through wind, and ninety per cent of the time will prove to be the most efficient and satisfactory.

* *Perfect non–splash presentation of the fly*. Add a 2 ft. length of nylon (approximately 0·18 diameter or 20 lb breaking strain) to the point of the fly line, using a nail knot

for this purpose. Tie a loop at the free end of the nylon and fasten a 9 ft. P.P.P Rafale cast or leader to this loop.

* *General conclusion on tackle.* The combination of a Ritz-Garcia 7 ft. 10 in. or an 8 ft. 2 in. two-piece rod with a No. 6 weight-forward line and a P.P.P. Rafale leader is a striking example of well-balanced fly tackle. It ensures that at all times and in all conditions the fisherman retains the feel of fly, line and rod. This, in turn, gives precise control of the fly's movement whether it is cast at slow or high speed. Thus, while progressively lengthening one's casts until the target distance is reached, there is no risk – even at much-reduced casting speeds – of the fly hitting the water or dropping behind. Speed can be varied, once the target length has been obtained, to ensure the best possible presentation of the leader: straight, curved or serpentine.

Artificial flies

Perfection in imitation will not compensate for defective or imperfect presentation.

But perfect presentation will compensate for imperfect imitation.

Importance should only be attached to the fly when you have sufficient technique to ensure good presentation.

Technique represents 85 per cent of success.

Precise imitation 15 per cent only.

The fish reacts above all to presentation and only in a minor degree to the fly.

The fisherman succumbs much more easily to the theory of the exact fly than does the fish.

Perfection in casting and presentation is the great qualification.

The exact fly is only a refinement of the expert; but if you believe in it, stick to it! Each to his own opinion.

* *The drawbacks of the artificial fly and their remedies.* Natural insects are taken:
   1. Because they are real;
   2. Because they are more numerous;
   3. Because they are alive and moving;
   4. Because their drift is always normal;
   5. Because they have no point of attachment;
   6. Because their movements and behaviour are in conformity with the different stages of their life and the evolution of their hatch.

The outline of the artificial fly, an imperfect imitation, is always deformed by the floating hackles and the hook. The more floating hackles the better it floats, the fewer there are the better its outline.

An artificial fly can be presented in only three ways: floating, wet or in imitation of a nymph. In all these three cases, you can offer only a puppet suspended from a cord, with the movements of an automaton, and activated by a combination of the current and the drag of the leader which, most of the time, presents it flat, sideways on, etc.

The only means of reducing these drawbacks are:

(a) *In the tying of the fly*

  1. To utilise to the maximum the mechanical qualities of the artificial fly;

  2. To present an outline which has the greatest possible verisimilitude.

(b) *Tactics and casting*

  3. To present it in the most favourable conditions.

(c) *Casting*

  4. To conceal as far as possible its lack of freedom.

(d) *Tactics and dressing of the fly*

  5. To animate it as much as possible.

Here are my ideas on the ideal fly. I insist above all on:

  Balance in floating.

  Optimum outline.

  Visibility for the fisherman.

  Bright hackles of the first quality.

  A waterproof body for preference.

  Solidity.

Hooks: the best quality obtainable. Light, short points. Shape, round. Eyes, for me, of no importance, up-turned or down. Sharpness of point, vital.

∗ *Equilibrium in placing and floating.* The most important condition according to the old hands and those who are most successful is that the fly should alight on the water perfectly straight, its hackles or wings cocked up. To achieve this the tying must be perfect. The hackles should be natural, *undyed*, and of the first quality and the body as waterproof as possible. The patterns on hooks Nos. 16 to 20 cannot always be strictly floating. They are often semi-submerged.

Dressing. The hackles and tail of the artificial fly should not be arranged merely for the purpose of reproducing a given outline, but also to give balance when floating and raise the fly above the surface. For instance, a very large bushy bivisible, in spite of a poor outline, is often very attractive, while no part of the body or hook sinks below the surface.

Instead of three or four traditional whisks in the tail, a little tuft like a tiny flat brush should be tied and curved downwards. I have always insisted on this tying for my flies and I believe that it gives far from negligible advantages. In any case, it inspires me with confidence and that is already a great deal.

This tying of down-turned whisks was suggested for the first time some thirty years ago by an excellent fisherman on the Ain, M. A. J. Gros de Marigny, who described it in a remarkable series of articles in *Pêche Illustrée* in 1923. All the fishermen on the Ain, Simonet, Née and Charpaux have, since then, adopted this tying which is alone able to give the fly balance and assure it a correct position on top of the water. L. de Boisset considers it an essential part of the flies of the Gallica series.

Preskaviec, whose knowledge and experience is incontestable, has assured me that after much experimentation he has finally succeeded in achieving a tying of floating hackles which, so to speak, do not penetrate below the surface. He selects semi-supple floating hackles which, as soon as they come into contact with the water, bend at their extremities and thereby increase their floating surface; whereas, if the hackles are too rigid, they have a tendency to pierce the surface of the water. He has also created a pattern of sedges with horizontal wings covering the hook, which has given me excellent results.

* *Visibility for the fisherman*. Wings of visible colours. Mandarin, Summer Duck, the bivisible combination. Avoid brown; pale colours for preference.

* *Optimum outline*. Minimum deformation of the outline by the floating hackles.

* *Visible hackles*. Undyed hackles, blue dun for preference or ginger, the only ones which reflect the light. Avoid dyed hackles as far as possible. Fine natural hackles being very rare and expensive, most manufacturers of flies use dyed hackles which are too supple. Dyed hackles are only permissible on Nos.16 to 20, because of their lack of rigidity.

* *Solidity*. A secure tying to prevent the fly turning round the hook, the windings at the head sealed with varnish.

* *Colours*. L. de Boisset, in his book *Les Mouches du Pêcheur de Truites*, believes that the essential is to give the body of the fly the dimensions and, particularly, the colour which conform to that of the natural insect. Lambiotte and I have frequently noted the truth of this and, in 1952, repeated observations of trout on the Loue, the Doubs, the Risle and the Andelle, proved to us the soundness of this theory. What the fish see above all is the body of the fly. The colour of the hackles is probably secondary provided they are luminous and rigid. The blue dun, undyed hackle holds first place, but is almost impossible to obtain today. Then comes the ginger hackle, easier to obtain but less visible on the water, and finally the Bivisible Hackle, 70 per cent ginger and 30 per cent white, which is very visible and easy to obtain in a good quality.

85

* *Hooks*. Hooks must be of fine wire, with a first-rate point, not too long and a rather open gape. If you use the knot I prefer, the up-eye is best.

If the hook is over-tempered, there is a great danger of it breaking. If the hook is not sufficiently tempered, it is often inclined to bend open at the strike or when subjected to pressure.

Since you can almost no longer get English hooks such as those of Partridges of before the 1939-1945 War, which were almost unbendable and unbreakable, you must be content with a compromise; but the hook has a tendency to open a little when the tyer makes the finishing-off knot round the eye, on a No.16 for example.

The necessary pull to obtain a secure tying and a good knot often deforms the gape of the hook. The same thing generally occurs in taking a fish, not enough to risk losing it, but with a second one it will often be fatal.

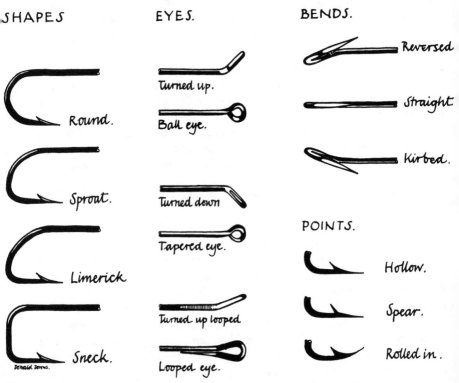

Fig 47 (*This and facing diagram by Donald Downs*)

Gape/Length Combinations for a Typical Hook.
(№ 8)

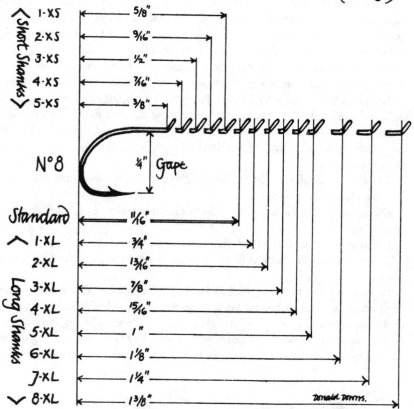

⟨Short Shanks⟩

1·XS	5/8"
2·XS	9/16"
3·XS	1/2"
4·XS	7/16"
5·XS	3/8"

№ 8   1/4" Gape

⟨Long Shanks⟩

Standard	11/16"
1·XL	3/4"
2·XL	13/16"
3·XL	7/8"
4·XL	15/16"
5·XL	1"
6·XL	1 1/8"
7·XL	1 1/4"
8·XL	1 3/8"

Donald Downs.

NOTE. Measurements do not include the hook eye.

Further variations (not shown) include differences
in the gauge of wire, to suit hook purposes,
ie., for dry, wet & salmon flies.

Fig 48

87

Very fine wire hooks often allow of hooking fish, particularly grayling, when they seem to be untakable.

For many years I have used barbless hooks for trout and grayling fishing, breaking the barb with a pair of pliers. Rarely have I lost fish for this reason. It is a technique I strongly recommend to all fly-fishers other than beginners. Prince Von Quadt shares my views on this aspect of sportfishing – barbed hooks are absolutely forbidden on his wonderful river Argen, in Germany.

The point does not, of course, apply to salmon, but with lesser members of the gamefish family there are many advantages. Trout and grayling can be released so easily and without damage by holding the fly with one's fingers or with pliers and shaking the fish free. There is seldom any need to handle a fish and this, to my mind, is conservation and sportsmanship at its best. Having practised this method for so long, I cannot do other than despise those who proffer barbed hooks knowing the damage they do.

* *Handling flies.* Simplifying the handling of flies can give the fisherman advantages that should not be neglected:

The reduction of loss of time during the rare moments when the fish are taking the artificial fly.

The fisherman's comfort by reducing causes of irritation.

The maintenance of a stock of flies in impeccable order and the facilitating of their selection.

To avoid wasting time, use small fly boxes, preferably of plastic, with very deep compartments, which shelter the flies from gusts of wind, and of dimensions adapted to the size and shape of your pockets. Their low cost allows of having several boxes of different kinds adapted to various requirements. They facilitate extracting the fly without spoiling the hackles. They should float if they fall into the water. For my own

a

Fly box with magnetic bodkin

b

This is how I fasten my fly to the leader:
Half-Blood (Clinch) Knot

Fig 49

88

personal use, I have invented a little box in light wood of five compartments with bottom and lid in plexiglass. Two magnetised bodkins, kept in the box, extract the flies. A series of from two to six boxes permit classification according to the fisherman's personal ideas, while four boxes can easily be carried in the pockets owing to their small size.

* *Knots*. There are many different opinions on this matter. In my own experience the simplest is the best. Pass the nylon through the eye, then make four turns round the nylon, pass the end between the eye and the first turn and back through the loop thus formed, then draw tight. It is a quick knot and it is very easy to remove the nylon from the eye when the fly is being taken off.

* *Greasing*. Many stained coats decided me to abandon the old oil bottle for greasing flies. I prefer the box of line grease, and particularly a new French product – 'Letarpon' (silicone vaseline) – which is remarkable. It is made up in a little tube like paint which makes it much easier to use, or in a small plastic box. I use a match or sliver of wood, cut flat at one end, and apply the oil to the body of the fly only. It is easy, quick, and does not rumple the hackles. It is no use greasing good hackles; it is enough to make the body waterproof and increase its powers of floating if you want it to sit on the water. Silicone, however, does not make the hackles stick together; it also makes them more brilliant.

If I mention my all-purpose tool-kit once again, it is because it has been for nearly twenty years my inseparable and serviceable companion.

A little screw-driver for the reel, etc. Fine-pointed extracting-pliers for seizing the hook by the gape and removing the fly with a quick jerk: this is easy and avoids disfiguring the hackles. A needle mounted in a wooden handle for undoing knots and cleaning eyes. A small hook disgorger for removing the hook in difficult circumstances can also be used as a picket for attaching a big trout and keeping it alive. A flat Arkansas stone, in the shape of a safety razor-blade, used to sharpen the points of hooks and knives, does not shorten the points (files and carborundum stones $= 0 + 0$). I insist on extra sharp points to the hooks: it undoubtedly gives you an advantage in hooking a fish.

Before putting flies away in the boxes, always check the points, put them to the stone, and check their gapes. Keep an empty box for used flies.

* *Maintenance of flies*. Crumpled, deformed hackles: steam them. Dry fly hackles that are too supple and too long (therefore, poor floaters): cut them slightly underneath, parallel with the extremities of the fibres.

* *Patterns of flies*. When I wrote my first book in collaboration with Tony Burnand, the Universa series was our all-purpose collection for trout. Today, my preference is

for a selection that includes modified American patterns which are ideal for placing upright on the water. They are extremely visible and have never let me down. And, of course, Lunn's Particular.

For grayling, I am less radical. The frequent periods of systematic refusal oblige you to have all-purpose patterns, security flies. The time passes more agreeably and your irritation is appreciably calmed thereby. It is indisputable that small flies, hooks 16 to 20, are in general those which interest trout, and particularly grayling, most. On much-fished rivers it is an advantage to fish fine and small.

My two collections have always been amply sufficient for the rivers of France, Austria, Germany, England and numerous rivers in North America. However, I consider that every fisherman must preserve his entire freedom of judgment concerning the choice of patterns. The choice and purchase of a fly in the shop, the selection for presentation, as well as the possession of a fine stock offering opportunities for agreeable discussion are, for most of us, among the great pleasures of fly fishing. The possibility of being able to select among a number of patterns which please and inspire confidence is, for many people, a matter of great importance.

Here is my personal approach to the subject which, though it has value for me, may have none for anyone else:

FLIES FOR GRAYLING IN CALM WATERS AND MEDIUM CURRENTS

Hooks Nos. 16 to 18 and eventually down to 20 – except for Sedges

* *Gloire de Neublans.* White hackles. Dark brown silk body. Good when fish are feeding freely. Specially conceived for bad light. White whisks. Particularly useful towards the end of the afternoon.

* *La Loue.* Pink hackles. Body pink quill. White whisks. A very visible fly. Optional.

* *La Favorite.* Mauve hackles. Body brick-red quill. White whisks. An all-purpose fly and easily visible. Optional.

* *The Brown Ant.* Coch-y-bondhu hackles. Body shaped two sections, ant-fashion, peacock herl and pheasant-tail herl with dark orange silk in the centre. Pale blue dun hackle, wing tied flat over back.

* *October Dun.* Blue dun hackles. Body of heron herl, blue dun and thick. Pale grey whisks.

* *Purple Iron Blue Dun.* Lilac and ginger hackles. Body red silk. Ibis red whisks.

* *Scarlet Quill.* Bright ginger hackles. Body bright red quill. Whisks similar. Optional.

* *Sulphur Dun.* Hackles dyed sulphur yellow. Body yellow quill. Yellow whisks. Can

be seen when other colours are invisible. Useful in a very bad light and in waters with reflections. Optional.

* *Choroterpes Picteti Imago.* Style Lunn's Particular. Type Spent. Wings in cock hackle fibre of medium dun. Hackles medium ginger cock. Body peacock quill. Whisks grey-white, series Gallica. My favourite.

* *Choroterpes Picteti Subimago.* Type Spent. Short hackles, ginger cock. Body dark brown silk, ribbed fine silver thread. Wings of pale dun hackle tips. Whisks golden honey dun. Optional.

* *Tups Indispensable.* Very visible in rapid currents.

* *Red Tag.* Ribbed in gold. Optional, except on the Traun, where it is indispensable.

* *Sedge.* No. 16 hook. White wings. Peacock herl body. Ribbed gold tinsel. Red hackle at shoulder. For afternoon and end of the day.

* *Sedge.* No.16. hook Brown wings. Red hackle at shoulder. Body pale grey silk. Afternoon and end of the day.

* *Tricolore.* Nos.16, 18. Ragot type. Spider with three hackles superimposed black, ginger, blue dun, gold tinsel tag. Ginger whisks. VERY VISIBLE. Floats very high.

* *Black Ant.* Nos.16 and 18 hooks. Often the only acceptable fly.

For rapid currents and particularly in rivers where there is little food, the exact pattern has but little importance. The most important thing is that the fly should be large, visible at a distance, and easy to follow for the fisherman: Cahill, Wickham, Tups, Bivisibles, Panama, President Billard and Pont Audemer, Nos.16 to 12 hooks, for the evening.

TROUT FLIES

The placing of the fly with the hackles upright and the rare opportunities of animating the artificial fly are mainly applicable to trout flies, owing to dressings which allow of the necessary dimensions.

The possibilities that exist of exploiting the elements of forgetfulness or surprise by changing the size, because of the greater number of natural insects that interest the fish, make it necessary to use hooks of 12 to 14 and even 16. For Mayfly 10 to 12.

* *Light Cahill.* American pattern. Light green body – ribbed with yellow. Modified pattern (Stenonema canadensis), Nos.10 to 11 for the Mayfly. Nos. 14 and 16 at other times.

* *Quill Gordon.* American pattern. (Iron Fraudator.) Nos.12 to 14 and 16. Mandarin or summer duck wing hackle, blue dun hackle, grey quill body.

* *Née Fly.* May be grey hackle with green body, grey whisks; bivisible hackles

(brown and white), yellow body; or red body or green with yellow ribbing with bivisible hackles. Or black body. Nos.14 or 16. All seasons.

* *Gold or Silver Sedge and Sedge with Preskaviec tying*. Wing of pheasant hackle, red hackle, brown silk body ribbed gold or silver. Nos.12 and 14.

* *Panama*. Green body ribbed yellow. Two hackles, red and summer duck, red whisks. All seasons. Nos.14 and 16 (modified pattern).

* *Tups Indispensable*. Nos.12, 14 and 16.

* *Large Bivisible*. Brown and white, hackles right down body. Brown whisks. Nos.12 and 10 Mayfly and evening. Big trout.

* *Plumeau*. Stiff hackles thickly tied. Standard pattern: summer duck hackle followed by red hackle, pheasant tail whisks. Stiff or collorette type: badger or pale coch-y-bondhu hackle, long and stiff, bronze peacock herl body. Special cases and big trout. Nos.10 and 12. Thick hook.

* *Tricolore*. Ragot type. Fly of the spider type without body, all hackle. Nos.14 and 12.

* *Blue Dun or Sherry-Spinner*. According to choice, Nos.14 or 16.

* *Pont Audemer*. Bunched summer duck hackle for wings, dressed forward, fat yellow silk body, ribbed peacock herl, red hackle; and *President Billard*: wings of hen pheasant tail, body green ribbed yellow, white hackle followed by another of red, red whisks. Nos.14 and 16. The most visible in a bad light.

* *Wickham's Fancy*. No.14.

At the end of the season or during hatches of small flies, I use grayling flies.

* *Preska Sedge*. Nos.12 and 14.

Fig 50

Preska Sedge

* *Sawyer's General Spinner*. Red tying silk. Whisks, three fibres of white cock hackle. Body, four fibres of cock pheasant tail. Hackle, game-cock or Rhode Island red – four turns of hackle only.

WET FLIES. GRAYLING AND TROUT

Above all, hackles must lie close to the body, be blue dun, gleaming, supple and sparse. Their movement must animate the fly during drift.

Lightness to preserve as normal a drift as possible, except when fishing holes or pockets with eddies behind large submerged rocks where, sometimes, heavier patterns are effective.

Slow currents, small sizes:

A. Pale green body ribbed yellow.

B. Red body, ribbed yellow.

C. Dark red body, ribbed black, with small wings of very narrow slips of the web of the feather.

D. Butcher.

Rapid currents: medium size No.12.

It frequently happens that an old fly, having lost a good part of its hackles, succeeds better than a new fly. Why? Many patterns have too much hackle, which prevents their sinking properly while the old fly will sink better and drift at the right depth.

NYMPHS

* *Sawyer's No.1 Type A.* Cock pheasant fibres for body and thorax. Weighted with extra fine copper wire under dressing, and with pheasant fibres spun on wire and the two lapped together. Whisks of body material. Nos.15 and 16.

* *Sawyer's No.2 Type B.* Fibres of brownish-yellow condor wound in with weighting copper wire as in previous pattern. Thorax, fibres of blue pigeon. The same weighting. Nos.15 and 16.

To conclude, if you wish to reduce your stock to the minimum, here is my simplified and select all-purpose collection made with undyed hackles obtainable today.

* *'Ritz' Cahill.* Bivisible hackle. Body green, ribbed yellow. Hooks: Mayfly No.11, standard Nos.14 to 16.

* *Modified President Billard.* Bivisible hackle. Body same as Cahill. Hooks Nos.14 to 16. The small, very upright brown feather wing ensures maximum visibility for the fisherman when light conditions become difficult, especially just before the evening rise.

* *Modified Panama.* Bivisible hackle. Hooks Nos.12 and 14.

* *Née type.* Bivisible hackle. Bodies yellow or red. For green, use dark grizzle hackle. Hooks Nos.14 to 16.

* *Choroterpes or Lunn's Particular.* Pattern optional. But only one of these two: Hook No.14: in this size, wings must be upright. Hooks No.16 to 18: wings spent.

* *Sedge. Type Hans Gebetsroither.* Hooks Nos. 14, 16 and 18. For Traun evening rise strong hook No.12; also No.10.

93

* *Tups Improved Model*. Bivisible hackle. Body thin. Hooks Nos.14, 16 and 18. Also small double hook No.16.

* *Wet Flies*. Belgian pattern; feather wing; dark red body, ribbed black. Ritz standard pattern: body green, ribbed yellow, and body red, ribbed yellow. Very thin and supple dyed grey hackles. Hooks Nos.12 and 14. Sawyer's nymphs.

All hackles should preferably be natural and not dyed.

Pattern for Hooks: Hamilton, tapered, up-eyed. (See Hardy Catalogue.)

The selection of a fly

The beginner is always attracted at first by pretty flies and their great variety. His lack of ability to observe, his lack of technique and experience in fishing, cause him to attribute most of his failures to his inability to find the right fly.

Fine hackles, good hooks and impeccable dressings are very expensive, particularly the hackles. Only a very limited number of experts, both in Europe and in America, are capable of tying what I would call the perfect fly and their charges are much higher than most fishermen are prepared to pay. I knew one dealer, a great tyer of flies and a great connoisseur, Colonel Ogareff, who had the creative passion and made new patterns every week. Each Saturday, he sold his customers a new fly: the week-end fly. In general, he was right. His flies were impeccable, of the highest quality and, moreover, gave his customers and friends such confidence that his flies did more fishing during the week-end than any others and took more fish.

But to return to the beginner. He arrives on the river bank and starts fishing. Rises are rare, there is not much hatching and the fish have plenty of time to examine the lure. Bad presentation will prevent his having any chance of success. He persists, constantly changing his fly, but his presentations continue to be defective. His box of flies gradually becomes full of crumpled flies, their eyes blocked up by the ends of the leaders. Finally, the principal hatch he has been waiting for begins. The fish are anxious to take the first insects and are less wary. And our beginner is suddenly overcome with joy: he has caught a fish. At last, he has found the right fly!

But then refusals begin again while the hatch reaches its climax. There are too many flies on the water. Our fisherman is dismayed; in despair, he starts swearing, casts furiously, ceaselessly flogging the water. His hand begins to blister. His rod is no good. Nothing is going right! All the pleasure he foresaw before he left for the river, all his enthusiasm while he discussed the day's fishing with his friend, while they were driving at seventy miles an hour to gain a few extra minutes for the evening rise, have now turned to despair. But then, suddenly, he catches another fish. (Daylight is

Fly fishing in salt water is popular sport in Florida. Here, an angler hooks a large snook

Dermot Wilson with Barrie Welham of Garcia Tackle, Great Britain. The trout, taken from the Mill Pool at Nether Wallop, was England's second-largest fly-caught rainbow: 9lb 12oz.

right: John Piper, angling writer and broadcaster.

The Mill House, Nether Wallop, Hampshire – England's most unusual tackle store.

fading, the leader is less visible.) Once again he is convinced that the dealer has advised him well and that he has found the right fly.

That evening, at dinner, our young fisherman will produce for the older hands the theory of the right fly. He is perfectly convinced, and has made up his mind to increase his stock of flies. His hasty and premature conviction will become his most serious obstacle and will considerably retard his progress, while at the same time leading him into useless expenditure. He will neglect to concentrate on improving his casting and presentations, as well as his faculty of observation. He runs the risk of remaining in the class of moderate fishermen, while refusing to follow the advice of the old hands. He ignores the fundamental rule that the fisherman counts for 85 per cent and the fly for only 15 per cent.

It is a fact that we all have our favourite flies. Before the war, on the Risle in Normandy, over several years, the President Billard was the favourite. Today, one rarely hears it spoken of (though the fishermen of Brionne, and my friend Beaudoin, perhaps the most effective fisherman in the Risle Valley, have remained faithful to it). Why? Have the hatches varied? Perhaps. It is more likely, however, that it is a question of the evolution in the making of flies and new methods of tying them. This particular fly had wings made of feather web. Wings of hackle points, which are much more successful, have rapidly replaced them. The fisherman, for all his weaknesses, always maintains his practical sense. During the false casts with a medium fly with traditional divided wings, you can hear their sharp buzzing sound and are apt to conclude that more strength is necessary. These Mayfly patterns are useless for long casts. However, the President Billard still holds its place. It always falls very straight, its small, brown, upright wings, shaped like sails, remain vertical on the surface. It is therefore very visible. There is nearly always wind during the Mayfly. It is the special tying of the wings that makes them visible, while the placing of the floating hackles allows the base of the hook to penetrate beneath the surface, making its outline different from that of the conventional flies. It is very easy to pick out on the water. I particularly recommend its use on all rivers when fly visibility gets bad.

One of the great rods of the period, my good friend Moreau, only fished with a big Plumeau which, according to the circumstances, he presented dry, half wet or wet. He loved casting and fishing but loathed manipulating tackle.

My inseparable fishing companions, V., S., L. and G., also have their preferences for very varied reasons.

V. has three: a mole fly with a green body, a Dun also with a green body and the Béhotière with a green body, his favourite. His fishing lodge is called La Béhotière and the pattern was created specially for him by Colonel Ogareff.

S.'s favourite fly is always the one on his leader. For years he has been using the stock he began with, hoping that one day he would no longer have the embarrassment of having to select. He only regrets not having more Panamas, a fly with a great reputation on the Risle and which bears no relation to natural insects.

L. always brings with him, in his fishing bag, a surgical instrument box containing at least twenty small flat plastic boxes of twelve compartments each, all well furnished and carefully marked, as well as two or three big American boxes and one or two ordinary ones. This is his stock for enjoying security and tranquillity. His favourite is Née's fly, particularly the grey with the yellow body of the spider type. Née is the only fly-maker who can supply him quickly, when he is in need, with flies with blue dun undyed hackles. He accepts his tying, which could be improved by the American type. For the Mayfly, he uses a Light Cahill only.

G. has a great angling friend who, every year, makes specially for him splendid big patterns for the Mayfly. If he exhausts his stock before the end of the Mayfly, he despairs and no longer takes the same pleasure in fishing, manifesting a distinct loss of enthusiasm.

On good days, they all have a very similar level of success. Their averages are regular. Bad days are equally poor for all four. The year I gave them superb Tups Indispensables, made by the celebrated Roger Wooley, they had considerable success.

In the United States, the Fan-Wing Royal Coachman, a real miniature glider with its big wings of white feathers, and the big bivisible are the favourites for the evening rise. They were invented to be visible to the fisherman in the dusk. During the day, the Cahill, Hendrikson and the Quill Gordon are very popular patterns. Their outlines are similar, and they were conceived especially to give pleasure to anglers. Their qualities of floating visibility and firm tying are impeccable.

Albert Godart, the Belgian professional champion, likes ginger-coloured flies with yellow bodies and believes in size and outline. He insists on bright hackles and first-class tying with bushy tails. Being a great caster, he has no difficulty in deceiving the fish.

Simonet, the best fisherman I know, uses two spiders, a grey with a yellow body and a ginger-brown with a red or yellow body. He ties his own flies. He fishes most often with the grey. His knowledge of all the good localities and the perfection of his presentation would make the trout rise to any good fly!

My good friend Pierre Dufay, one of the old hands on the Loue, prefers for grayling only small hooks garnished with a few fibres of almost invisible feathers, and a second fly with large hackles to serve him for a mark.

In Germany and Austria, where the dealers were last to make up their minds to offer fishermen modern tackle, the unfortunate angler had to content himself with old-fashioned stock and the selection was limited to standard models: Red Spinner, Wickham's Fancy, March Brown, etc. Today, these conditions have considerably improved.

In 1930, most of the fish in the Traun had never seen a dry fly. At that period, my friend Jacques Spier, a beginner who had never fished except with a dry fly, arrived at Bad Ischl, on the upper Traun. The first day, having acquired the services of a ghillie, he began fishing in the very centre of the town. He saw a fine fish, sheltering behind a big stone, not in the least disquieted by his presence. He pointed it out to the ghillie.

'That's Adolf, Sir, it's no good trying for him, he's been there for years and never takes!'

Jacques, as a beginner, blindly followed my advice in those days, when the Tups Indispensable enjoyed my entire confidence. He tried nevertheless! He presented a Tups. A few moments later, the ghillie was having some difficulty in getting the fish into his creel. It weighed 4½ pounds and had succumbed to the first dry fly, when all the fishermen had been trying it with a wet fly!

The President Billard, the Cahill, the Tups, the Brown Bivisible and the white, yellow and rose sulphur Dun of the Loue series are the most visible when the light is bad. I attach great importance to the colour of the hackles. At my age, you save your eyes. All brown gives me headaches. I can just about stand the grey, but I prefer the white collar of the bivisible type.

On the Doubs, during the last war, we were a company of friends who preferred the rose fly, which took most grayling. Its colour admirably suited the light of the vast gravel beds where the flies are always very difficult to follow. We thought it was the fly of the moment more often than any other. Unconsciously, we found ourselves using it most of the time owing to the difficulties of visibility. Had it been as visible, the mauve would have taken as many fish.

On the Traun, where the light is better, we prefer the mauve. Perhaps because the bottoms are darker. The rose gives us less confidence. The yellow always remains in the box. One hesitates to consider a fly of this colour qualities, but it has its uses and there is no reason why it should not take as many fish as the rose or mauve. One year I fished for trout with the rose flies on Nos. 12 and 14, without lowering my average.

I think we all agree about the matter. For us, the question of flies and women are similar! It is no good trying to understand why a certain fisherman has a preference for ginger-haired women or a Wickham's Fancy or for a brunette and a Black Gnat. Moreover we like change, which is the good fortune of the tackle-shops and the despair of our wives! The pause due to the selection of another pattern and the putting on of a fly after repeated failures is not only comforting to us, but indeed a most excellent means of deceiving the fish.

I hardly dare tell of my early efforts. No one could have been more stupid! When I reached the river bank, I was in such a state of excitement that I lost all sense of proportion, and all powers of observation and reasoning!

During my first days on the Beaverkill, in the United States, in 1920, I was utterly hypnotised by the idea that the exact reproduction of the insect the fish were taking was my best chance of success. As for my presentation, it consisted merely in ceaselessly flogging the water and running up and down the river in continuous search of some locality where a trout would take my fly, a locality I could never find! I bought myself every fly the dealers recommended. My stock increased so rapidly that one day my fly box consisted of a large case of four trays with innumerable compartments containing some two thousand flies!

In spite of constant change of fly, I never succeeded in finding the right one. My evenings were devoted to putting my splendid collection in order, and my creel was still waiting for its first fish! At last, the day came when I discovered that three friends of mine, at the same hour and on the same reach, had all had considerable success with different flies, while I remained empty-handed. 'Penny', the best fisherman of our little group, said to me at dinner that night:

'Here are six patterns: Cahill, Lady Beaverkill, Woodruff, Hendrickson, Quill Gordon and a Coachman for the evening. If you can't take trout with these, you'd better give up fishing! Promise me to fish with these six flies only during the rest of the season, to concentrate more on your casting and to think about what you're doing with your left hand. If you don't get better results after keeping your promise, I'll give up fishing myself!'

It was my salvation! I gave the children of Roscoe Village the greater part of my collection, only keeping the well-tied flies with good hackles.

In 1931, during my first stay on the Ammer, my friend Trinks, who died a few years later on this river, rod in hand, gave me a few Tups tied by Woolley. They were a revelation to me. My Tups always floated well erect and I could see it as soon as I placed it on the water. I caught more fish. The following year, I had an assortment of Tups on Nos.10, 12, 14 and 16 and decided to use these patterns only during my whole season on the Risle. I had excellent results. The following year, the Tups became very popular among my friends and, until 1941, when my stock became exhausted, I remained a convinced and obstinate devotee of the Tups.

During the war, it was impossible to communicate with Woolley. Mme de

Chamberet could make me flies, but good hooks were unprocurable. One day I went to see M. Gastine, who informed me that, when Mainwaring had gone into liquidation, he had bought up all the remaining stock of flies Colonel Ogareff had had tied by Woolley or Hardy. Within a few minutes, I had all Gastine-Renette's drawers out on the counter. Alas! Not a Tups! Questioning the salesman, I found my suspicions were correct: one of my dear friends, a great seeker of bargains (I hope that when the good Samaritan reads these lines he will feel a certain remorse) had made his selection the previous week! When I had met him the day before, he had taken care to say nothing about it! What could I do? I put on my spectacles and went into action. There was only one solution: to choose the best patterns with Partridge or Seeley hooks. I became the owner of about three gross of flies of the most varied patterns on Nos. 10 to 16, as well as an admirable collection of grayling flies. From that time until 1946 I used only these flies, selecting, according to the circumstances, those which had the hook and were of the size I thought suitable. I did not have to complain till my stock was exhausted once more.

At the end of 1946, on my first journey to America after the war, I took care to acquire a stock of American flies of the Cahill, Quill Gordon, etc. type.

Several of my friends have adopted for trout, more or less definitively, the Cahill on a No. 10 for the Mayfly, and the Cahill and Quill Gordon on Nos. 12 and 14 for other periods. At the moment, I am a devotee of the Cahill, President Billard (modified pattern) and Lunn's Particular for trout, but with the compromise of the grey with a yellow body and the Panama, as well as a small assortment of consolation patterns. The day I become tired of it, and if my sight grows worse, I shall perhaps end up by using the Fan-Wing Royal Coachman or Mayflies with wings only, as Colonel Vavon did.

For grayling, until 1952, my fly box, like those of my friends, Creusevaut, Straub, Cavallasca, Lambiotte, Gauthier and Co., was amply furnished with small flies of the Loue and Gallica series, which we believed to be indispensable. In 1951, André Ragot came to Gmunden with a pattern of a spider fly: the Tricolore. Black, brown and white hackles, in three sizes: 17, 15, 13, on which he takes all his grayling and obtains first class results.

Owing to laziness, during two months' grayling fishing in 1952, I used a Tricolore most of the time and, today, I am content with that fly on 18 and 16, the Gloire de Neublans, the two Choroterpes, the Red Tag, the two little Sedges, the Tups and the October Dun.

I believe that the success of the Tricolore is due to its excellent floating.

Here is André Ragot's description of the Spider Tricolore: 'It is all hackle and has no body; the Traun-Tricolore has a little turn of flat gold tinsel between the hackles and the tail, but this cannot be looked upon as a body. In my opinion, these flies resemble a natural fly in the state of subimago, having just hatched and got rid of its larval envelope, whose wings, legs and whisks are still entangled, forming an indefinite mass on the water. Like the spent, they are easy prey for grayling, for they lack the agility of an imago'.

* *American Hair Flies.* My friend Ben Fontaine, who has been President of the International Casting Federation for several years, is a typical fisherman of the American West. He uses standard American flies which look like anything but the natural insect; indeed, most of them are very odd-looking creatures. I own a box full of them, presented to me by Jon Tarantino, but until I fished with Ben I had never dared to cast one over a living fish.

The best patterns are deer hair yellow, deer hair natural and deer hair Grey Wulff. I have seen Ben fish these three patterns on the chalk streams of Normandy, and on British waters, and take more fish than either Pierre or me. Naturally, I had to investigate. Why should these apparent monstrosities prove so successful?

The fact is that the hair fly rides high. It is stiff; it floats well and you can see it on the water. It looks like a nice fat ham. Of course it must interest the trout.

I cannot accept that fish are at all fussy about exact imitation – which is, in any case, beyond the most highly skilled fly dresser and must remain so for as long as iron hooks run through the centre of artificial flies. Ben Fontaine has taken so many trout with these patterns that his experience alone proves that matching the hatch is a pastime best reserved for those who enjoy it. I give them welcome and wish them luck, but it is not, in my opinion, the important thing.

The all-important thing in fly-fishing is to match the drift of the water and to use a pattern which you can see clearly, which floats right, stays high and dry, and in so doing is capable of exciting the fish below.

The results obtained with American hair flies – on chalk streams where the fish are said to be the fussiest of all and to require exact imitation of the natural insect – destroys all the old theories. We come back to consideration of the mechanical problems, even when choosing a suitable pattern of fly. It is always a question of mechanics.

Conclusions

How to select your patterns:
Trout and grayling:
1. Calm waters: small flies not over-bushy. Rapid waters: larger and more bushy flies.

Trout and grayling:

2. Gauge the light and select a pattern easy to see and follow, especially in a wind.

Trout and grayling:

3. In case of refusal, change your pattern.

Trout:

4. In case of refusal after presenting several patterns, change the size.

Trout and grayling:

5. For deep water, big flies.

Trout:

6. In case of refusal, try a Panama (Spent), it always has surprises in reserve, particularly at the most unexpected moments.

Trout:

7. For fish feeding on the surface that will not take, always try a larva or a nymph.

Trout:

8. For evenings: dry fly. Bivisible, President Billard, Pont Audemer, then Sedge, which must always end with drag.

Trout and grayling:

9. Evening: mountain rivers: first very small flies, little Sedges, then big Sedges, President Billard.

10. Early in the season, when you take too many small fish, I recommend using barbless hooks; also when you want to keep big fish only.

PART IV * GRAYLING

Grayling and the fly

L. de Boisset, France's leading writer on fly fishing, has revealed this sport in all its splendour in his book *L'ombre, poisson de grand sport*. Only the real fisherman appreciates its true worth.

In England, some people put the trout at the head of the list, others consider the salmon outclasses it. In general, the grayling is only fished in order to eliminate it from the river.

Those who have gone after grayling among the gravel beds of the Doubs, fished the shelving bottom of the Loue, or the rivers of Austria, Bavaria, Switzerland, Yugoslavia or Czechoslovakia are compelled to recognise that *Thymallus thymallus*, taken on the dry fly, must be placed at the head of the Salmonids.

In my view, the sporting qualities of a fish are dependent neither on its size nor its weight, but on the effort of concentration, the skill and mastery it demands from the fisherman. The reasons which make me prefer grayling fishing to any other are as follows:

The necessity for the precise determination of the area of drift.

The narrowness of the channel of drift in which acceptance is probable.

The length of drift without drag.

The extreme precision with which the fly must be presented.

The necessity for concealing the point of the leader.

The grayling's habit of taking the fly downstream (in retreat) after a quick, swirling rise.

The fineness of the leader tippet.

The minute size of the flies used.

The sensitivity of a nylon leader tapered to ·007 in. to the slightest breeze.

The difficulty of the strike owing to the shape of the mouth and the manner of taking the fly.

Thousands of fish must be taken before averages can be obtained or observations of any positive value made. The Traun, that magnificent Austrian river, is ideal for experiment thanks to its exceptional wealth of grayling.

June is the most productive month owing to the very frequent hatches entailing the most extensive period of feeding activity. But in order to control my observations with the greatest possible precision during nearly twenty years spent fishing the best rivers in Europe, I have chosen the month of August, when the fish have become more difficult.

While in the actual process of fishing, you are too often liable to come to hasty conclusions and allow yourself to be influenced by facts which do not lend themselves to generalisation. You are too absorbed, and the opportunities for making observations of general validity are thereby limited.

To achieve results of any value, you must avoid being dogmatic, base your reflections and your deductions on the observations of experienced friends, as well as on your own, talk matters over every evening, and discard all conclusions which are not of a positive nature. As far as possible, all doubtful cases should be put to the test during the following days. Only hypotheses which seem to lead somewhere should be retained.

Hans Gebetsroither, an eminent fisherman, head-keeper of the Traun for more than twenty years, has always accompanied me. He has a slight tendency to allow himself to be influenced by his respect for the precisely imitative fly, but he maintains always a true sense of the value of perfect presentation. Hans is an incomparable encyclopedia of fishing, and I acknowledge with gratitude the invaluable assistance he has always given me.

The difference in behaviour of the grayling and the trout when faced with an artificial fly

I naturally leave the trout all its hierarchical prestige. Without it, the art of fly fishing would never have been evolved or become a world-wide sport.

I always enjoy myself on any trout stream.

In 1948, my friend P. Dufay, an experienced grayling fisherman, came to make the acquaintance of the Andelle trout for the first time. From the very first day, he showed himself to be an excellent trout fisherman. On the other hand, my old friend Pierre Creusevaut, for whom trout hold no secrets, took a good week to master the grayling on the Traun. I could quote many similar instances.

If I had to classify fly fishermen, I should place the grayling fisherman in the first rank, then the trout fisherman of the chalk streams and, finally, the trout fisherman of other rivers. I believe that all my friends, who angle for both grayling and trout, are of the same opinion.

The technique and tactics of grayling fishing, which are the least known, can be applied almost in their totality to trout. I therefore propose to deal with both species at the same time.

As far as trout are concerned, I shall limit myself to those facets of the subject which are exclusive to them, and to such observations as I have made in practice since *A la Mouche*, written in collaboration with Tony Burnand, appeared.

TROUT

Will take the fly in any direction from the position in which it is lying, whether *on the bottom*, immediately below the surface, or sometimes half way down.

Behaviour not uniform with regard to artificial and natural flies. Indifference, interest, curiosity, susceptibility to boredom, anger, etc.

Activity somewhat variable.

Temperamentally a Latin type. Impulsive.

Wary of signs revealing the presence of a human being, or of abnormal conditions to his *modus vivendi*.

Precautions in approach more difficult owing to limited time in which the fly must be presented.

Less conservative and difficult in choosing than grayling. Sometimes reacts positively to sudden changes in size and outline of artificial fly.

Large bony mouth. Powerful bite.

Tackle in general less light and above all less fine than for grayling, more efficient against wind. Possibility of placing a fly with wings erect.

THE CAST

Presentation zone circular and less regular in shape than for grayling, permitting casting with less slack and delayed drag. Greater choice of types of casting. Necessity for precision with first cast to obtain 70 to 90 per cent chance. Afterwards, the percentage grows rapidly less.

In bad weather and moderate winds, as far as I am concerned, my average decreases by 50 per cent.

GRAYLING

When lying in position is always *on the bottom*, and will only take the fly behind that position, and then only in a long, narrow rectilinear zone downstream.

Behaviour more uniform towards both natural and artificial flies. Almost constant curiosity.

Activity more regular, particularly between ten o'clock and four o'clock.

Temperamentally a Germanic type. Consistent.

Less wary of the signs revealing the presence of a human being.

Approach more easy and time less limited for presenting fly. Extremely wary of the leader, though activity will continue.

In slow and moderate currents will only accept small flies, numbers 16 to 18, and certain shapes and colours.

Small, cartilaginous mouth, situated somewhat beneath the head. Less powerful bite.

Light, fine, tackle, very sensitive to the wind, necessitating great delicacy of wrist. Impossibility of placing fly perfectly with erect wings owing to small size.

THE CAST

Absolute precision essential. The necessity to cast with a great deal of slack, to delay drag to the maximum, limits the choice of types of cast and increases their difficulty. Precision and correct presentation not indispensable at the first cast. The 70 to 90 per cent chance continues during several successive casts and correct presentations.

In bad weather and moderate winds, my average touches nought.

DIFFERENCES IN CATCHING ZONES, OBSERVATION, PLACING AND PRESENTATION OF FIRST AND SECOND CASTS

The proverb, 'If the mountain will not go to Mahomet, Mahomet must go to the mountain', can be applied only to trout, not grayling.

Grayling will not take the fly laterally, so to speak, but nearly always going downstream and in retreat.

Trout will take the fly for preference on the spot, but also upstream, downstream and laterally.

Fig 51 Grayling

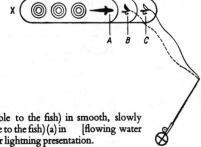

From A to X: Extent of the field of action
From B to X: Fish's field of observation
From C to X: Here the fly must float, but not drag
From C to A: Presentation here

⊕ Angler's position
→ Grayling
◎ Probable position of take
⚓ First presentation (which should be invisible to the fish) in smooth, slowly
⚓ Second presentation (which should be visible to the fish) (a) in   [flowing water
  fast-flowing water with surface waves; (b) for lightning presentation.

Principal elements to exploit: curiosity, constant activity during the period of feeding, approach during period of activity less careful than in the case of trout. Persistence often rewarded. Extensive length of drift. Rapid presentation not essential.

Fig 52 Trout

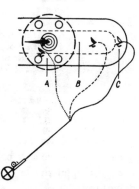

A: Extent of the field of action
B: Fish's field of observation
C: Here the fly must float, but not drag
From C to A: Presentation here

⊕ Angler's position
◎ Take probable
○ Take also possible
→ Trout
⚓ First presentation (which should be invisible to the fish)
⚓ Second opportunity of presentation (which should be visible
  to the fish), often more effective, even on calm water
⚓ Presentation can also be made here in the last resort

Principal elements to exploit: extensive feeding zones, excitability, drag at the end of the drift, unexpected reactions on the part of the fish. Presentation should be as rapid as possible during feeding periods.

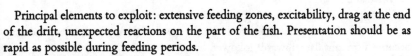

* Gravel beds, depths of three feet at most, slow currents. The course and direction of the rise, according to depth.

Why one should cast further upstream for moderate depths and slow currents.
Estimation of the points of rise.

In the diagram, the fish is lying at a depth of three feet behind a small stone. It may also lie nearer the surface. If the stone is larger, or the current weak, it may maintain its position without sheltering behind an obstacle. The end of the rise with a slow drift gives the fish an opportunity of examining the fly for a greater length of time.

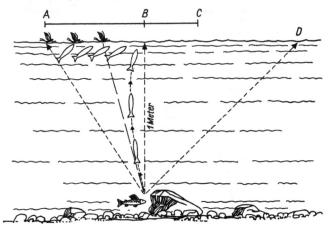

Fig 53

A: Limit of field of action, take
B: Lie of grayling
C: Presentation about here
D: The fish can start seeing the fly from about this point

Probable takes
Path of fish whilst rising
Grayling

* *Deep water, slow and rapid currents.* At depths of six feet or more, the fish rises more quickly. The acceptance or take zone moves downstream of the fish's observation post. The approximate position from which observation may begin also moves downstream.

The opportunity for examining the fly is more limited and lasts a shorter time.

The speed of the rise depends largely on the speed of the surface current and may become a straight dart upwards followed by a vertical dive.

The approximate position for placing the fly depends on the depth and the speed of the current.

A vertical rise may result in a break on normal striking.

The diagram shows the two extremes of rise, the normal and the dart upwards.

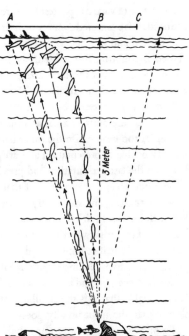

Fig 54

A: Limit of field of action, take
B: Lie of fish
C: Presentation about here
D: The fish can start seeing the fly from about this point

Probable takes
Path of fish whilst rising
Grayling

3 Meter

* *Conclusion*. The lateral displacement of the grayling's position when taking the fly may vary according to the depth of water. At moderate depths (up to approximately three feet), it is extremely small, much smaller than that of the trout. For depths of more than four and a half feet it may, in certain cases, be three feet or more.

At the evening rise, during the hatching of sedges on the Traun, for instance, the grayling adopts the habits of the trout and remains just below the surface during the feeding period.

The grayling's behaviour towards the fly

* 1. *Calm waters, slow and moderate currents*. The grayling examines every fly that drifts over it, whether natural or artificial. During a period of activity it is nearly always interested. It always gives an impression of careful selection. It might therefore be supposed that grayling fishing necessitates more frequent changes of fly than fishing for trout. Success tempts one to believe in the precise fly, but it is possible that the presentation of varied types results in creating a state of confusion. For example, the same artificial fly is examined every time it drifts past and is refused, while certain natural flies are rejected and but one among them selected. The fisherman's fly is examined and classed as doubtful. But suddenly he presents a new type, the fish has become curious again and commits the fatal error. The same result might equally well have been achieved with a different fly.

In most cases, the refusal of the fly at the first cast is due to defective presentation: drift outside the positive area, an imperceptible drag at the last moment, the point of the leader too visible. On the other hand, acceptance at the first cast after a change of fly may be due to presentation and drift being impeccable. Unaware of the difference between the last presentation and previous ones, one is more often than not inclined to attribute acceptance to the fact that one has found the right fly.

When the grayling sees the fly, it begins by observing it and does not rise vertically but with increasing drift, so as to take it downstream of its fixed position. It shows no haste but takes it slowly after a final examination. It seems always to hesitate almost imperceptibly before taking the fly, but this is not an absolute rule. When the fish is being very active, making a good meal and the whole menu is to its taste, the examination is less careful and is sometimes followed by its taking the fly without hesitation. It is probable that it is the smallness of its mouth which makes it take the fly more slowly than the trout usually does.

To outwit an apparently uncatchable fish, provided it is showing regular activity towards natural flies, it often suffices to place the fly on the water, while the fish is on the move and feeding, in such a way that it sees it only at the last moment as it returns to its fixed position. It may be necessary, when the exact distance has been found, to continue making false casts, very likely a hundred, before the fly can be placed on the water, owing to the rapidity with which the fish moves. But, in these circumstances, it will not have seen the fly fall – which is bound to arouse suspicion – since the natural flies only drift towards it. The fish is taken by surprise and takes the fly by instinct without the usual preliminary examination that would have revealed the difference between a natural fly and an artificial.

An active fish during a big hatch of a variety of insects will make a choice, experience having taught it that some are more juicy and tasty than others. The fish is therefore extremely busy. It suddenly sees an artificial fly presenting a very different appearance from the natural ones. The outline is larger and more complex owing to the hackles, and the fish will be perplexed and hesitant, though it is possible that its suspicions will be lessened by the fear of allowing a choice morsel to escape. If the angler has not put the fish on its guard, it may well succumb to the temptation. The shape of the feathered fly, floating higher than do the natural ones, is presumably less precise and more difficult to determine by the eye of the fish, of whose powers we know nothing.

That great master Skues, in his book *The Way of a Trout with a Fly*, puts forward the hypothesis that the trout has a sense of taste, which would go far to confirm the grayling's tendency to prefer certain insects to others. This is also true of trout during the Mayfly, when they select for preference the large females and disdain the males.

I remember that once on the Traun, after numerous failures, Hans was of the opinion that the reason for refusal was due to the body of my artificial flies and the instance of the Haeger Wiese has proved that he was right.

Fear, suspicion, wariness, the close examination of the artificial fly, can all be diminished or indeed suppressed, and forgetfulness induced, by ceasing temporarily to present it. This applies to fish that have refused consecutively to take on two or three occasions after an examination of the fly, but whose rhythm of rise to natural flies is uninterrupted. Should they cease rising altogether, you must wait till full activity is resumed. It is up to the fisherman to decide whether a change of fly is also necessary. He can tell only by experience.

Hatches normally succeed each other throughout the day with very different effects. Those towards the end of the afternoon are the most difficult and only the very smallest flies will produce results. Between hatches, the fish are practically untakeable. I shall never forget two places on the Traun where the current is fairly rapid, one below the dam at Marienbrucke and the other at Dantzer-Mühle; on days when the water was normal, and there were big hatches with continuous feeding lasting often for nearly two hours, I never succeeded in persuading a grayling to rise boldly. Most of the flies in my boxes were tried, presented by Hans and myself. Hans admits that he has never been able to discover the explanation for these repeated failures. It may be that, during these hatches, only live flies with moving wings were taken.

In spite of a great number of fish, two or three good fishermen, working conscientiously, will soon educate the grayling and run the risk, should they return the following day, of making fools of themselves. This has happened to me on more than one occasion. Forgetfulness on the part of grayling can only be exploited on condition of not abusing it.

It also sometimes happens that grayling appear to take the fly delicately with the ends of the lips and a minimum of suction and therefore do not get hooked. This has twice happened to me: once on the Salza, in Styria, and again on the Ammer, in Bavaria. Dr Toupet was fishing a bend of the Salza where several fish were rising continuously. He found it impossible to hook them. I joined him and, having failed too, attached a little Tups with a minute double extra fine hook to my leader, thanks to which I succeeded in hooking three grayling by the end of their lips and my friend, following my example, took two more.

I have observed the same phenomenon with Kustermann on the Ammer. Sometimes the grayling will take almost invisible insects of the ant type a few centimetres away from the artificial fly, which would give one to suppose that the strike has been defective. The grayling's small mouth is often the reason for failure, especially if it takes too quickly.

If one is prepared to admit that fish possess a certain degree of intelligence, the trout is in a higher class than the grayling. But the latter compensates for this inferiority by a more precise and detailed inspection before selecting a fly. It is a tireless worker and always subject to a rigorous self-discipline. It fights less intelligently, always plays itself out, has no tricks and is finally taken completely exhausted. It does not know, as does the trout, how to use the obstacles on the bottom, so dangerous to the leader. It does not react to the landing-net. Its nervous system must be of considerable delicacy. Once in hand, a light flip on the nose often renders it motionless and facilitates the difficult removal of the hook. If placed in a retaining pool made of large stones, it makes no attempt to jump out as does the trout.

The sight of the fisherman and his tackle often makes no difference to its continuing to rise; this is not the case with the trout which, more often than not, retreats at full speed at the merest false cast, even if it is behind it. On the other hand, it can be easily alarmed at the sight of other fish coming from downstream or by a fisherman in waders.

* *2. Rapid currents. Deep waters. Holes and pools. Rapids and waterfalls.* As far as deep waters and slow currents are concerned, there are no definite rules. A fish can be just as difficult and refuse to accept any of the small flies. However, everything depends on the depth at which it is lying. In general, the type of fly used will have less importance because the fish must take it more quickly and will have but a limited time in which to examine it, even though there is good visibility due to a calm or gently rippling surface.

In fast currents, pools with eddies, rapids, waterfalls, etc., the type of fly used has less importance still. The fish can only see confused outlines, while its field of vision is much reduced. Flies drift quickly and the fish has to fight against the current and rise very fast. It takes the fly *at speed*. Flies with hackles of good floating properties are necessary and they should not only be clearly visible to the fisherman, but of a size to allow the grayling to see them and follow them easily: hooks numbers 10, 12, 14. In general, the fish will then be suspicious only if the fly drags and will not take it except at the precise place at which it feeds.

The Salza near Gschöder

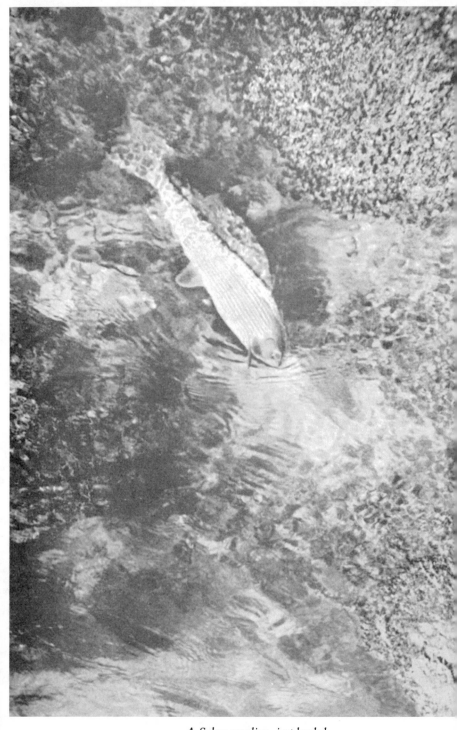

A Salza grayling, just landed

In rapid, shallow water, the grayling is generally easy to deceive, though still suspicious of the point of the leader. It has greater difficulty in determining the type of fly owing to the rough surface which affects the clarity of its vision. Moreover, the movement of the surface water, as well as that of the fly, creates a scintillating light from the reflections of both the water and the hackles, giving the fly an aspect of life.

When a grayling takes the fly quickly, one has a better chance.

As soon as the wind begins to ripple the surface of the water, the rises at once become slower.

I have rarely seen an active grayling become suddenly inactive. One can therefore prepare one's presentation with care and without being hurried, as for trout.

If we could only question the fish, we would better understand how to avoid our too numerous failures!

Fishing for grayling with a fly

I. THE DRY FLY

To begin with, it is essential to determine with great exactness the area of drift so as to achieve absolute precision in placing the fly. To this end, advantage must be taken of every available means: large stones on the bottom, differences in colour on the bottom, vantage points on the banks. Those who are expert in estimating distances accurately at a glance have a considerable advantage.

An excellent method for determining the distance is to place oneself first downstream of the rise, to make certain of placing the fly behind the fish. Then to move slightly upstream of where the grayling is lying and, if one cannot see the fish, make certain of presenting the fly up to six feet in front of the point of rise. If one can see the fish, place the fly about three feet in front.

On the wide shallows of rivers such as the Traun, the Doubs, and the Loue, it is very difficult to place the fly accurately at the first attempt. If the point of rise has not been accurately marked, it is better to wait for another.

The grayling refuses to move laterally to take a fly. It normally shows no fear of the line's shadow during the false casts or the placing of the fly, but a sight of the point of the leader immediately makes it wary, though this will not prevent its accepting the fly at the next cast, if the point is behind the fly. Nevertheless, it is better to avoid this. I have nearly always noticed that, when the fly hid the point of the leader at the first presentation, its being taken was almost certain.

Slow currents

(1) Avoid as far as possible presenting upstream.

(2) Use as much as possible the semi-horizontal cast to the side when you are on the left facing downstream. This cast, correctly executed, produces a curve cast to the left and is not difficult, particularly for medium distances. The curve cast to the right is extremely difficult to master.

(3) When the curve cast is not possible, substitute a cast down stream at 45°, raising the tip of the rod just before placing the fly, and follow this by lowering it to obtain the necessary slack to assure a long drift without drag.

(4) Take up a position slightly upstream of the fish.

Rapid currents. The same rules as for slow currents, plus (3) above, modified to casting 100% downstream instead of at 45°; and also the parachute cast.* The faster the current, the more effective a downstream cast will be.

Fishing from a boat. I have practised this particularly on the higher reaches of the Traun. Fascinating and probably more difficult, it requires an expert technique for casting at all distances. To determine where the fly should be placed the same method should be used as for wading, owing to the better vision of the bottom. Use this opportunity to the maximum. Every large stone is an indication. Owing to the fact that one is on a higher level and casting fairly far, the different variations of vertical or semi-vertical casts are the best with plenty of loose line in the hand to give slack and very long drifts. For the most part they will take the place of the curve cast.

Pay attention to the direction of the currents; in deep waters they often have eddies which alter the direction of the drift of the flies.

Fishing when the boat is in movement becomes a 'sprint', particularly if you are attacking fish upstream of the boat. Fish alarmed by the boat will quickly warn those feeding within range of your rod. Every second counts. The movement of the boat is constantly altering the length of your cast and necessitates a maximum of concentration in watching the target. You nearly always get drag too early. You must be ready to shoot line as you need it, and get it out very quickly indeed. The whole operation becomes a matter of dexterity, speed and the rapid judgment of distance.

Striking. If you are inclined to be nervous and strike too hard, tighten with the arm only; do not use the wrist which is inclined to react too quickly. I would advise trying to raise the tip of the rod slightly towards the sky, with wrist and forearm rigid. If you are fishing downstream, the movement must be still more delicate. Nevertheless, the strength and speed of the movement must depend on the length of the cast. For long

---

* For a description of the parachute cast see p. 28.

casts, particularly if there is much slack in the line, you sometimes need to strike fairly hard; sensitive hands may strike from the wrist but the risk of breaking is greater.

2. WET FLY FISHING

I do not despise wet fly fishing as do most of my friends, perhaps because I have much to learn about it. I concede it the following advantages:

On most rivers there are currents where, at certain hours, the wet fly will give the grayling fisherman better results than the dry fly. In high winds or when the grayling is sulking, it is sometimes altogether preferable.

When bored with fishing on the surface for recalcitrant fish, fighting against the wind and bad light, it is the best method of relaxation and can give you splendid moments.

When you begin to understand the technique of the wet fly, the search for places where fish are lying becomes fascinating. The more you practise it, the more you realise that it is far from being merely a question of promenading a train of flies under water. It is full of tricks and subtleties, and requires an eagle eye and quicker reflexes than does the dry fly.

In my view, the fact that it is not highly considered is mainly because most fishermen do not use adequate tackle or have never tried to study it seriously and without preconceived ideas.

For this form of fishing, the rod is no longer a shooting machine but a receiving post, with super-sensitive antennae, capable of registering immediately the slightest reaction of the fish to the fly.

* *Rule No.1.* Never take your eyes off the fly or, failing that, the leader or the extremity of the line and, above all, try to see the fish.

My own method is partly inspired by that practised and perfected by the French fishermen on the Ain, in particular by Beau and, after him, Roussiller, two celebrated fishermen of Pont-d'Ain. Their tackle consisted of a reed rod with a tip of white bamboo eighteen to twenty-one feet long, a reel with a level line and a horse-hair leader carrying up to ten small flies. Between the line and the leader there was often a length of rubber to deaden the strike. The rod was manipulated with both hands. It is the length of the rod, the fineness and lightness of the line, the leader and the flies which allow of dropping the leader only on the water, and at the same time giving it great sensitiveness.

For those whose timing in casting leaves something to be desired, casting a wet fly is the best means of attaining perfection.

113

Rule No.2. Always hold the rod high in the most vertical position possible.

Rule No.3. Fish with as short a line as possible to reduce resistance to a minimum and improve vision.

Always fish very slowly in a fan-shape, probing the river to the bottom.

When it is not possible to fish the whole of an interesting area with a short line, make three casts, one short, one medium and one long, before moving downstream three, six, eighteen, twenty-four, or thirty-six feet to cast again. If you are in the middle of the stream, work first to the right, then to the left.

Drift. Always cast well across the stream, sink the flies and let them drift downstream at the speed of the current while keeping the line as little tight as possible. In certain currents, you can sometimes drag either under the water or on the surface.

Striking. Since you cannot know the precise area in which the fish will take, you have to be constantly on the alert. The novice always strikes too late or, rather, he strikes when he feels the fish on the end of his line, at the precise moment when the fish, having felt the hook, is opening his mouth to eject the fly while escaping as rapidly as he can. Owing to the fish's speed, too strong a strike prevents the point of the hook from catching in the fish's mouth and penetrating.

You must strike early and it should be no more than a tension of the line, raising the point of the rod to the vertical with the forearm. Striking with the wrist is dangerous unless you are very expert.

It is very often at the end of the normal drift, when the tension of the line is reacting on the flies, that the fish is taken. The only plausible explanation is that, as the fish follows the fly unable to make up its mind to take it because the fly seems inert, it suddenly mistakes the beginning of this movement for the real thing and says to itself: The fly's alive and it's going to escape me.

Marking the line is sometimes very helpful. A paint mark nine feet from the point of the leader is an excellent alarm signal.

The leader must be very supple, therefore very fine, in order to assure more or less natural drift with the minimum of drag or deviation. On the other hand, it must be manageable and conform at the top to the end of the line, so as to allow a uniform join.

Two or three flies are sufficient and considerably reduce the risk of tangling the leader.

High speed fishing with the wet fly upstream. This method replaces the dry fly when fish are rising during a hatch, on rough, rocky water, for instance, where there is a certain quantity of weed. At certain times, fish show their fins and appear to be feeding particularly on hatching nymph. You should fish a short line, using mostly the roll cast on rising fish. It is advisable to vary the speed of the fly during the down-stream pull, even making it very fast. The roll cast enables you to fish the fly very close, before rolling it again. It is, I must add, a very good method of filling the creel rapidly, when conditions are right, but should not be abused. It is, however, full of interest and far from easy.

Captain T. B. Thomas is probably one of the leading experts in this type of fishing.

* *Tackle*. While for the larva, the nymph and the submerged, drifting fly, small hooks, Nos. 14 to 16, are to be recommended, I have always obtained the best results with the wet fly with Nos. 10 and 12, except for slow currents when Nos. 13 and 14 may be used but weighted under the body with ultra-fine copper wire (see Chapter on *Flies*).

Bright flies are excellent, also tinsel bodies, a little red on the tail.

I prefer a weight-forward line on condition that its maximum diameter is not more than ·040 in. The rod works better, casting is much easier, especially when there is a wind, and excellent sensitivity is preserved.

* *Conclusion*. Tackle should have the maximum of sensitivity for registering, and great suppleness to produce natural drift as nearly as possible.

3. FISHING WITH A SUBMERGED DRIFTING FLY IN VERY RAPID CURRENTS

* *Artificial larvae, nymphs or wet flies*. Sometimes the grayling will take both on the surface and under the surface, sometimes only under the surface, larvae or nymphs either rising from the bottom to hatch, or drifting and circling below the surface. It is then that the submerged, drifting fly becomes necessary, particularly for short distances, near the banks, in pockets, etc.

The technique is very much the same as for the dry fly. Let the fly drift without drag towards the fish but below the surface at a suitable depth, sometimes even only partially submerged. To achieve this, place the fly upstream or at 45° or even down-stream with slack, lightly forcing the fly on to the water to submerge it or, in the case of longer casts, move the tip of the rod horizontally downstream; this is essential with nylon. The great difficulty of this technique is the strike which, even when one can see the fish, must be carried out with extreme delicacy and speed.

* *Indications for striking*. The same as for fishing with a nymph (see Chapter on *Nymphs*).

* *Flies*. According to circumstances and availability, larvae, nymphs or wet flies may be used.

Choose types which sink easily, but they must not be too heavy for fear of their diving instead of drifting normally with the current. The hackles must be tied with 'kick' in order to allow the current to produce movement.

* *Ultra-rapid currents, eddies.* Fishing pockets with eddies behind big rocks is often rewarding, particularly when the fish seem inactive elsewhere. It is necessary to make the larva, nymph or wet fly sink rapidly as if it were caught in the eddy, which often interests a fish at the bottom of the pocket or under a rock.

It is often necessary to weight the flies and, in general, strike by eye.

4. HOW TO PLAY THE FISH

The grayling fights till totally exhausted. If you do not force the pace a little, it takes a long time to tire, with all the dangers of breaking or losing the fish by loosening the hook-hold. Here is the best technique for tiring the grayling quickly without taking useless risks:

It is to your advantage to bring the fish to the surface as quickly as possible. It will tire itself much more rapidly. When it jumps, you hold the line taut. To make it come to the surface, it must be got off balance. This is done by lowering the rod towards the horizontal. If, for instance, you incline the rod to the left and then suddenly swing it to the right, you turn the fish round and get it off its axis. It can thus no longer take advantage of the current to fight, and you gain line. You can do this several times if necessary. Moreover, in order to recover its equilibrium and regain the advantage of the current, the fish will tire itself all the more and come quickly to the surface where it must be held. Once tired, it rarely continues to fight (beware of the fish that goes between your legs!). You can then take it by hand to remove the hook as rapidly and delicately as possible in order to return the fish to the water. If you take too much time over this operation, there is a danger of killing it. It will struggle when in the hand and make its last effort. Sometimes a flip on the nose, which does it no harm, will keep it still and enable you to remove the more easily these very small hooks which are so difficult to grasp. I recommend long thin tweezers for this operation; you save time and the hackles are spared. This is very important if you want your flies to last the normal time.

When a fish fights hard, it is an indication that the hook is buried deep in the mouth. When the fly is attached to the end of the lips, the tongue or the corner of the mouth, it fights less vigorously. As in men, some fish, of course, are stronger than others as well as being more cunning and combative.

Observations relative to grayling fishing

To illustrate the preceding pages, it may be useful to give some examples derived from observations made in the actual process of fishing.

First example. On the upper Traun, where it flows out of the lake of Hallstatt, Maurice Straub, Freddy Cavallasca, Pierre Creusevaut and I were fishing one day from four to six-thirty.

Straub, Pierre and I had chosen to begin on a long, wide, shallow reach with a semi-rapid current and a depth of four and a half feet at the maximum in the centre and gravel under both banks. There were numerous and regular rises. Confident of rapid and relatively easy success, we all three went into action. Utter failure. It was impossible to get the fish to take. I gave up in disgust. Hans* drew my attention to several rises on the opposite bank where the current was stronger and there was a certain amount of depth:

'Follow me, Herr Ritz. These fish can be taken. You'll have to fish them upstream owing to the speed of the current. The fish have not been alarmed and you're sure to be successful.'

A few minutes later I was in position behind several fine and very active fish. It was evening. It was very difficult to see and follow my fly on the water and my first casts lacked precision. At last I got the distance right and took five grayling which I returned to the river. We were at the end of a hatch; visibility was also growing bad for the fish and they had not been frightened in spite of my first defective casts because they were in full activity during the evening rise.

Straub, a patient man who never admits defeat, had stayed where he was and was resolutely attacking a fine grayling which, in spite of its eagerness to take the majority of natural insects drifting over it, continually refused Straub's beautifully cast Neublans pattern. A Wickham's Fancy had the same fate till the thirty-first cast when it was finally taken. Persistence sometimes succeeds. But there may have been other reasons for the fish suddenly changing its mind:

(1) The final cast was made while the grayling was on the move to take natural flies. It only saw the Whickham's Fancy at the last moment, when it had returned to its position.

(2) Fish, like human beings, are not infallible and may make a mistake during prolonged activity.

---

* Hans Gebetsroither, head keeper on the Traun.

(3) The thirty-first cast took place at another stage in the hatch when, for unknown reasons, the fish's reactions towards the flies had altered. Fish vary in their determination to take.

Freddy was further upstream, at a junction of the main stream with a small tributary, where the current was rapid and broken, thereby diminishing the fish's ability to see. The grayling were but a little distance away, in feeding positions close to a concentrated drift of insects caused by the junction of the two currents. The fish were very active and it was possible to see them clearly and fish with precision. While we were constantly refused at the beginning of the hatch, Freddy, who had only been fishing grayling for two years, was taking them one after the other.

* *Second Example*. Another of Freddy's triumphs:

On a broad, calm reach with very little depth near the banks but about six feet in the middle, Straub, Pierre and I were conscientiously fishing a superb hatch with but moderate results. Freddy took the boat and anchored it in the middle of the stream. Result: sixteen for Freddy from the same position and twenty-five for us three. But he sportingly admitted that the fish were taking relatively easily where he was while ours, in more shallow water, were selecting carefully and accepting only perfect presentations. Obliged to rise from the bottom in deep water, his had to travel a longer and more tiring distance, while having less time for inspection.

* *Third example*. On the Hager Wiese, just below Hamstock Mühle, there is a long, shallow reach, some fifty yards wide and ideal for wading. The grayling were regularly distributed over approximately one hundred and fifty yards while there were continuous hatches and numerous rises throughout nearly the whole day. Hans said to me:

'Herr Ritz, this is where you'll find perfect conditions for trying out on these greedy feeders that large assortment of flies you usually refuse to take out of the boxes. You'll see, they'll beat you, but the presentation of nearly the whole of your *carte du jour* will be a most instructive experiment.'

After lunch, Hans advised me to get to work at once, so as to take advantage of the afternoon hatches which are the most interesting.

Until three o'clock, the rises were comparatively few and far between but fairly regular. There were not many varieties of insect and but few in number. Correct and accurate presentations were taken nearly every time. I took grayling on Tups, Favorite and Red Tag. Hans watched me and said nothing, spending his time pointing out rises and visible fish. I said to him:

'You see, your grayling are easy to take, the four I've just caught accepted three different flies.'

'Warten sie, es wird kommen, und sie werden bei allem was heilig ist schwören!' ('Wait, the moment will come and you'll swear by all your gods!')

Suddenly, activity increased, rises succeeded each other with the regularity of a metronome, but there was refusal after refusal. As they examined the natural and artificial flies as they passed, it was clear that the fish had become hard to please. Hans, who had been waiting for this moment, asked me to give him my boxes of flies and selected a Purple Iron Blue Dun, which was immediately refused, then a Choroterpes Picteti (Gallica), a Scarlet Quill, and finally an October Dun, all on No.18 hooks. Same result! Then we tried various types of Woolley whose names I have forgotten. Hans overwhelmed me with innumerable suggestions and I spent most of my time tying knots in the ·007 in. leader; it was no longer fishing but a matter of manual dexterity! Suddenly Hans exclaimed:

'I think I've found it! I believe it's the shape of the body that interests them. Look! They're examining your flies from nearer and nearer to, and doing the same thing with the insects. They're taking a certain number of white flies. Put on a Gloire de Neublans with a dark brown body.'

The first grayling I tried it on rose as if he were about to take it, but refused at the last moment. Hans pointed out that my drift was too much to the right and slightly outside the feeding area. I waited two minutes and cast again. The Neublans was taken! Three more out of six tries were taken. Then followed refusal after refusal! Hans began searching in the box and gave me a little Spentwing pattern with white wings and a garnet red body with a white band. The body was fairly thick. It was one of the masterpieces of Roger Woolley on a No.20. It took two more fish and, after several refusals, a third. To complete the experiment, I tried other patterns but they were systematically refused. These patterns had varied bodies and bore no resemblance to those of the Neublans and Woolley's Spent. I therefore went back to the Neublans and finished with two more grayling.

Straub, fifty yards downstream, had been casting continuously and with his usual persistence. After repeated refusals, he had tried out a variety of flies till he caught his first fish on a Neublans. With his usual enthusiasm he cried:

'Charles! Hurrah for the Gloire de Neublans! Hurrah for Gérard de Chamberet! It's the only fly they're taking today!'

It must be concluded from this experiment that the behaviour of the fish varied in accordance with the different phases of the hatch. Easy to begin with, they were becoming more difficult in the middle and easier again towards the end.

When the grayling becomes very difficult, it seems to attach great importance to the colour and shape of the fly. Our success was due to the fairly thick garnet red bodies of the Neublans and Woolley's Spent.

A few days later, the same experiment was made on the canal above Hamstock.

* *Fourth example.* At Theresienthal, towards eleven o'clock one morning, I was having continual failures, in spite of varied and correct presentations. I was fishing in sight of the fish. Hans was of the opinion that, in spite of several refusals, the fish could be taken: he shortened the hackles with scissors and advised me to weight the fly to make it submerge. The current was moderate with minor eddies. He advised me to pay particular attention and, if the fish moved during the passage of the fly, to strike the instant it stopped. He was right: we kept two splendid fish for luncheon. (This was an adaptation of fishing with a nymph.)

On certain reaches of the Traun I have often seen every fly refused at the height of the hatch. It may then happen that, once perhaps in every fifty casts, a fish, whose rhythm of rise has become almost automatic, will rise, I might almost say blind, and take the artificial fly. There is no doubt that, when these conditions arise, which they nearly always do in similar circumstances and at similar times, only continuous flogging of the water will achieve results. Changing flies is quite useless provided you have selected one near in appearance to those the fish are taking.

* *Fifth example.* At Radl Mühle a fine grayling was rising regularly. I tried it very carefully with a dry fly. My cast was impeccable and perfectly accurate. After three presentations followed by refusals, I stopped casting. From where I was standing I could see that it was taking flies approximately six feet downstream from its position. My casts had not in the least disquieted it. It was continuing to rise. I gathered all the line that was out in my left hand to maintain the exact distance. I waited a few moments. I began casting again without dropping the fly, keeping the line in the air. The moment I saw the fish move downstream to take a fly drifting over him, I placed my fly a yard above his normal position. The fish returned to its position and saw my fly a fraction of a second before it passed and took it.

At the previous presentations, it had been in a position to see the placing of the fly, the whole of its drift and perhaps the leader. These were all reasons for refusal. The different manner of presentation caught it unawares and did not give it time to recognise my fly though it had seen it from the start.

* *Sixth example.* On the Salza, in Styria, on a delightful reach of about one hundred yards with a rapid current and fairly shallow water, I took five fish, fishing upstream. I lit a pipe and went over the same water again, fishing downstream and casting very short. I took nine fish. The consistent presentation of the fly before the leader increased the acceptances. It is a very effective method and should always be tried wherever possible. This is the method generally used by Dr Duncan on the Traun. It should also be tried for very long drifts for fish lying in positions bordered by trees and, therefore, unfishable laterally.

* *Seventh example*. On the Traun I saw good rises opposite me, in a slow current, opposite Mitterau. I noticed grayling rising regularly. My first two casts were too much at right angles. I moved two yards upstream and, at the third cast, being better placed and having made my side cast less difficult, I succeeded in curving my leader to the left and was immediately accepted. I very rarely succeed in this unless I place myself upstream of the fish or even opposite him.

* *Eighth example*. Again on the Traun, Straub was wading in a shallow reach in brilliant sunshine. He took up his position ten yards from the bank where there were bushes and shade, very little depth, and no rises. He took six fine fish along the bank.

Pierre Creusevaut and I, fishing the sunny part of a gravel bed, where there were very active fish, were so persistently refused we had to find another spot. This is very frequently the case on the Traun. In fine weather, when the sun is immediately over the river, you have to fish the shallow, shady banks, but you must be extremely accurate, placing the fly delicately at the first cast and with the minimum of false casts.

* *Ninth example*. Again on the Traun, at Steyermühle, in 1951, Hans, Dr Schwarzaugl, a friend and I were fishing a gravel bed with a slow current. There were splendid hatches, continuous rises and many fish, but also many refusals and few fish caught. After about two hours, the doctor had put back nine grayling and was beating us hollow.

Schwarzaugl is a great enthusiast and a persevering caster. He fishes like a machine-gun and never stops as long as he sees rises in front of him! This is an effective method when you are being repeatedly refused during big hatches, for it allows you to take advantage of the grayling's all too rare errors, super-selective as they are at these times and taking only midges or small flying ants. In general, during May and June, grayling will take anything you present them, both large and small flies. That year, there had been no hatches of big flies up to that time.

In August, 1950, during our fishing holiday on the Traun, the Neublans and other patterns of the Loue series gave good results. In 1951, it was the Choroterpes Red Tag, little Sedge, and the Red Ant which were successful while the Neublans gave practically no results at all.

* *Tenth example: Fishing from a boat. Deep-lying fish. The Traun at Astecker*. Pierre Creusevaut and I were fishing below the Astecker Dam. The boat was anchored about twenty yards from a wall along which ran the tail-end of the current from a sluice. It was a semi-rapid current and there was a depth of six feet. It was five-thirty, and the

evening hatch was beginning. A group of grayling was rising regularly, but the positions of the rings were not consistent. We therefore concluded that we had to do with cruising fish which, given the depth, was unusual. But this seemed to be confirmed by the small number of acceptances.

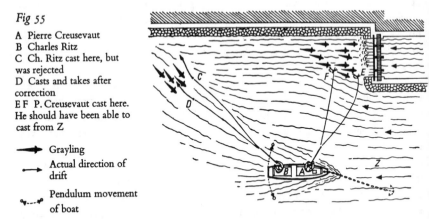

Fig 55

A Pierre Creusevaut
B Charles Ritz
C Ch. Ritz cast here, but was rejected
D Casts and takes after correction
E F P. Creusevaut cast here. He should have been able to cast from Z

→ Grayling
→ Actual direction of drift
⌐--→ Pendulum movement of boat

Pierre was in position A in the boat (see diagram) and was being successful only because of the frequency of the rises. Nevertheless, the rises were intermittent due to the gaps between the groups of insects in passage, or to that curious tendency of the salmonid family, during a period of activity, to take almost regular rest intervals between their rises. Most fishermen have noticed this fact.

I was in position B, and downstream of me there were three or four fish feeding in position and rising from the bottom. My fly was refused at every cast, though I should have been getting more acceptances than Pierre. As my fish were lying on the bottom, I had to take great care with my angle of cast in relation to Pierre's in order not to get entangled in his line. Wishing to let him cast to the maximum extent, I was obliged to keep my line high behind me, or to make my cast while Pierre was drifting.

I suddenly discovered the reason for the refusals. The depth of water in the two areas we were fishing was approximately the same, but my direction of drift was not parallel to the bank as was Pierre's. He was drifting at an angle to the wall, and moreover, was slightly zig-zagging. This may have been partly due to the movement of the boat, which was only anchored by the bow and was veering from side to side. After two attempts at placing my fly accurately, I discovered the correction necessary and succeeded in taking three fine grayling between one and a half and two pounds and another of just two and a quarter on a Favorite Mauve fly, the prototype of the

Loue series. Hans was putting all the fish back into the river and, if I caught one at the same time as Pierre, he made me keep it in the water until he had released Pierre's.

In the upper part of the Traun of Gmunden, the population of grayling in deep waters, owing to the war, was much diminished and Hans estimated that it would take three or four years to return to normal.

As my fish were rising from the bottom, I had the benefit of the rapid rise and the limited time for examination. As far as Pierre was concerned, there was no way of increasing his percentage of acceptances. His fish, owing to the size of the hatch and the great distance they had to go in rising from the bottom, often turned aside in mid-course to take the next insect: this is a very infrequent circumstance and might lead one to suppose that on occasion the grayling, like the trout, takes up its position half way to the bottom during a period of activity, but this is not the case. In a more rapid current, they would have remained on the bottom, for the grayling, unlike the trout, always avoids having to fight a strong current. These fish were therefore in a much better position to examine the flies. Moreover, Pierre's rises were slightly upstream and mine downstream.

* *Conclusion.* Grayling always rise from the bottom on which they invariably take up their position but, in the case of a massive hatch, they will occasionally, instead of returning to the bottom, and this is particularly the case at moderate depths and when the strength of the current requires an effort after taking a fly, turn back half way in their dive to capture the next insect and thereby kill two birds with one stone. Hans Gebetsroither is positive in stating that he has never seen a grayling take up its position half way to the surface, except during the evening rise.

* *Eleventh example.* Here is another case from the Salza, in Styria, of fish from the bottom moving near the surface.

On the opposite bank, which was bordered with rocks and splendid holes, I saw several fish rising with frequency and regularity in a hollow of approximately two yards in diameter. I waded into the water and got as close as possible, but not near enough to be able to observe the surface currents with exactness. For nearly an hour, I presented ceaselessly a medium Tups, the only possible fly for the place owing to the conditions of visibility. Moreover, on the Salza, the pattern is normally of but little importance in so far as its resemblance to the shape of the natural insect is concerned. Ultimately, I took two grayling during the last quarter of an hour. I thought I had succeeded in achieving the cast without drag and I was partly right.

The next day, I decided to go to the opposite bank and examine the hole. It was overhung by a six-foot rock. I lay flat on the rock and, to my intense surprise, saw a sort of natural aquarium some nine feet deep, with over a dozen splendid grayling swimming about in it, rising and diving, though not to the bottom, and feeding on the insects passing above them. I was surprised to note that the current consisted of circular eddies with, in the centre, a calm surface of less than a yard in diameter, the only possible place for a fly to float without immediate drag. From what I had been able to judge the evening before, it was certainly there that my two fish had taken the Tups, with a semi-parachute cast and slack.

Having selected a position on an overhanging rock from which I could cast without being seen, I took five grayling before they dispersed in general alarm. It appeared that the nature of the eddies in this aquarium allowed the fish to lie without fatigue and with ease of movement anywhere between the surface and a depth of three feet.

* *Twelfth example.* One afternoon on the Doubs, when fishing the gravel bed at Lilliaton, there were dark clouds obscuring the sky. It was impossible to keep the Favorite Rose in view after each cast. The wind was carrying it away and I was losing sight of it. The light was very bad, with steel grey reflections. The rises were numerous and regular, the fish easy to reach. At every rise of a selected fish, I struck, imagining an acceptance, but without result. In despair, I tried my luck with a Sulphur Dun with sulphur yellow hackles and found that I could see it. I came to the conclusion that I had never been over the rising fish. The rises at which I had struck had been made in every case for natural flies. I corrected my cast and caught several fish.

* *Thirteenth example.* On the Ammer. Before the last war, owing to the difficulty in following the drift of small flies on the Ammer, I used only patterns mounted on Nos. 12 and 13 hooks, which gave me excellent results.

After my experiences on the Traun, the Loue and the Doubs since 1939, where only Nos. 16 and 18 took grayling, I hoped to give Kustermann a lesson and improve my results on the Ammer with the little flies of the Loue series.

We arrived at about four o'clock on the reach by the power station which produces the electric current for the railway between Munich and Oberammergau. After several fruitless attempts, the speed of the current and the poor visibility obliged me to change my little flies for No.14s. I had the impression that the little flies did not incite the fish to rise. I caught but two little trout and the grayling continued to remain invisible. After about an hour's fishing, I met Kustermann. He had four fine grayling and two trout in his creel, all taken with a large Tups Indispensable on No.12. I then decided to try a Cahill which I used on the Normandy rivers during the Mayfly. It is an American pattern with light brown hackles, very stiff and bright, with a light tan fur body mounted on a No.9 hook. Three fine grayling accepted it within a few minutes.

The Ammer is much less rich in ephemeridae and in its variety of larvae than the Traun. Its current is more rapid and the bottom is composed of stones and sand with very little weed or mud. The fish have a very limited choice of food. Owing to the current, the fish generally lie deeper, often in holes, and they rise more quickly. The colour and reflections of the crystalline water are very tiring to the eyes.

On the Alm, another river a few kilometres from the Traun, you find the same conditions as on the Ammer and the fly problem is identical.

On this type of river, when you cannot follow your fly in the current with the eye, you must continue to watch the channel where you imagine it to have fallen. A rise will often mark the exact line of its drift, but it is generally too late to make an effective strike and it is better to cast again and strike only when you are certain.

There is no doubt that the grayling of the Ammer prefer large meals! A large Wickham's Fancy is excellent, but it does not float so well as flies with wool or fur bodies. If you have the luck to be fishing at the right moment, your catch will always be above average but, to achieve real success, the fisherman must avoid the least error and study and perfect his tactics before presenting the fly. The big grayling in these areas only rise when the atmospheric conditions and the state of the water are favourable. They are extremely wary. They will take only in definite areas. The fisherman must have absolute mastery and impeccable accuracy. It often happens that you can make only a few casts before a general alarm suddenly stops the fish rising. You must take great care not to disturb the water and get into position only with the greatest precautions. Kustermann, who is a great expert in this kind of fishing, is positive about these conditions and has proved it to me many times.

* *Fourteenth example.* My finest grayling.

I took it on the Ammer in 1937.

There are big holes several yards deep in the Ammer. Their surfaces have rapid currents, which in certain cases tend to centralise the insects floating on the surface during a hatch. The fish that live in these holes only very rarely rise and then only during a short period, preferring the food on the bottom, which is more abundant than that drifting down on the current.

The river lies three hundred feet below the farm belonging to Grundle, a farmer of Swiss origin, a great drinker of *most*, a Swiss cider made of pears and apples. The river is only fishable after a week or more of uninterrupted fine weather, for the current is otherwise too strong and the fish do not rise.

Kustermann had taken up his position on a rock which overhung the Hell's Hole and pointed out to me several big grayling rising. The fish are generally only active on the surface towards the middle of the day and sometimes in the evening, at which hour it is impossible to get to them, because of the three fords you have to wade through in daylight to reach the Hell's Hole. These fords are very narrow, in places only a yard wide, with a great depth of water on either side.

From where I was standing, it was very difficult to see the rises; they were barely perceptible owing to the blinding reflections. I was in continual danger of being washed away by the current and only my wading staff enabled me to keep my balance as I moved. At last, I found a place sheltered from the current behind a submerged rock. I was not very comfortable, nor very firm on my feet. Only the hope of taking one of these huge fish kept me there at all. Kustermann signalled two rises which were invisible to me. He did his best to mark them for me.

I tried a side cast with shoot, but my fly was tangled with the leader. After five agonising minutes, my eyes got used to the light and I saw two almost imperceptible rises; they were not true rings but minute, rapid splashes. I was waist deep in the accursed current, but in order to get a view I had to rise on my toes, for every inch counted. The parachute cast alone could give me a drift of three yards without drag. I felt like an electric battery, quivering all over! It was now or never! And now my big Tups Indispensable was at work, the drift was perfect. The fly came down the current at full speed, as if it were riding an avalanche. I took up the slack of the line as best I could. Kustermann cried:

'He's taken it, he's enormous!'

I struck. Nothing. I was properly broken, without having felt any pull at all. I was shattered and ashamed. I suddenly heard Kustermann's voice shouting:

'You're striking too hard, you should draw the line tight. Wait a minute and try again, you've still got a chance!'

I replaced my broken leader with a new one. A second attempt had the same result. I was on the point of giving up, but I thought of my good friend and teacher, Dr René Toupet, one of the greatest fishermen in France, and of the advice he had given me on how to keep calm when in difficulties. While waiting for the next rise, if God so willed there were to be one, I filled my pipe; it's the best medicine I know for calming the nerves!

Kustermann shouted again:

'Go to it!'

I cast quickly. Suddenly, the rod bent; it was going to break; I could barely keep the butt vertical. The reel sang; then nothing, just slack. My God! I was broken again! Suddenly, a monster leapt clear of the water several yards to my left and my rod, which had straightened out, bent to the point of breaking. Thank God! I trembled with excitement! I was in Heaven! But now the grayling was starting downstream at

above: Grayling reach on the Traun
below: Grayling reach on the Loue

above: On the gravel beds of the Doubs (Dr Massia fishing for grayling)
below: On the Risle (a typical chalk stream, and one of the best)

full speed, in spite of all my efforts to stop it. My reel would be empty in a few seconds if I could not stop this projectile. There was only one thing to do: go down the accursed current and try to follow it. In fear and trembling, I staked all on the gamble. Twice I thought my last day's fishing had come! Fisher, the ghillie, leapt down the bank and rushed into the water:

'Herr Ritz! Wait for me! Don't move forward, there's another hole. I'm coming to show you the only possible way.'

The fish was pulling harder and harder. My rod was quivering. Had I enough line in reserve? I have no reserves of backing on my grayling reels. If I pulled too hard, I ran the risk of tearing the hook out if the fly were not attached to the cartilaginous part of the mouth. While Fisher was joining me, the grayling, still going downstream in the full force of the current, made two superb jumps, trying to rid itself of the hook. I raised my rod on each occasion but was at once compelled to lower the point again in order not to be broken.

At last, there was Fisher! And, with one eye on the fish and the other on the bottom of the river, I succeeded in reaching the right bank of the river downstream. I was now in calm water, not too deep. I regained control of my legs. I could now try and get the fish off balance by moving the point of my rod backwards and forwards from right to left and gaining a few inches of line each time before the fish recovered its balance and could use the current to start fighting again. Finally, I succeeded in stopping it for the first time, but it was not long before it went off again; however, I felt that the end was near. I had got it all right! I looked round for Kustermann. He was just behind me and smiling broadly.

'Charles, he's at least three pounds! But hurry up, you must not lose a moment in getting him to the landing-net. Get as near as you can to your fish and bring him into calm waters.'

I succeeded in doing so and tried to lead it to the landing-net. But the fish was too heavy and was carried away by the slightest current. After three failures, I realised that there was no question of bringing it to me. Precious time was being lost and I was maddened once more by my powerlessness. There was only one resource left me: to place Fisher ten yards downstream, his landing-net in the water, and try to guide the fish down into it. At the fourth attempt, Fisher's net was round my finest grayling: 4lb 2½oz precisely, on the scales of the pork butcher from whom Kustermann always bought sausages on his way home from fishing.

Kustermann then explained to me the reason for my two breakages: these fish rise at full speed from a depth of several yards, leap on the fly and dive again at once. The strike almost always takes place at the moment when they are diving and the least movement of the wrist will bring about a break; a slight tightness of line will alone allow of contact with the fish being maintained.

* *Fifteenth example.* Concerning the value of animating an artificial fly.

Before the 1939-1945 War, I went to Tutbury, in England, to see Roger Woolley, the famous maker of flies, with the certainty of obtaining valuable information from him. It was during this visit that he confirmed the value of movement and partial animation in an artificial fly. Here is a striking example:

It is near Tutbury, on the Trent, that Woolley tries out and perfects his theories.

At the slack end of a current issuing from a dam, several grayling were rising every day and regularly refusing his finest creations. After several days of observation, he had come to the following conclusion: the cause of their refusal was due to the inertia of his flies. The grayling seemed to be particularly interested in insects that moved on the surface.

One evening, on returning to his workshop, he decided to try a new method, using only a few very long and rather stiff hackles. The following day, he presented his new pattern with delicacy and precision, then, with imperceptible movements of the point of his rod, succeeded in animating the fly. These slight movements made the long hackles bend and quiver. Several grayling succumbed to his ingenious idea.

Later, Woolley created several patterns in the Life Like series for grayling and trout which were much appreciated by his customers. Colonel Ogareff, before the war, sold them at Mainwaring's and on several occasions I was able to confirm the excellent results they gave with difficult fish.

PART V * TROUT

The trout and the fly

I do not propose to recapitulate here what has already been said, with more or less talent, in innumerable works of instruction on how to take trout with an artificial fly.

I propose to limit myself merely to an examination of certain peculiarities I have noted during a long experience of trout fishing, in particular on the Normandy chalk streams, and I shall give by way of illustration examples taken from the life of incidents in which I have been either actor or witness.

There are, indeed, certain precautions that must be taken when trout fishing, precautions which are peculiar to this fish and are of less importance when fishing for grayling. I can confirm, from my own experience, what every author who has written on the subject has emphasised, that the first condition of success is not to frighten the trout you are out to catch. And that sufficient precautions can never be taken to this end.

The fisherman and his tackle must remain invisible to the fish, even if you have to crawl on your stomach. The trout must not be allowed to see anything but the fly and that only from the moment it begins to float. Sight, sound and vibration are all fatal! The position of the sun may be either a great handicap or a trump card. Natural phenomena must be used to the greatest possible advantage in concealing your approach.

That great decorator and fisherman, Henri Ruhlman, invited me one day to his fishing on the Lieure, a tributary of the Andelle, a tiny stream full of big trout. To make a bad cast there is fatal! We walked down the bank keeping several yards from the edge. As soon as we saw a good rise, we went down on our hands and knees to reach a position from which to cast. Once in position, we waited for the next rise to present the fly as quickly as possible and with the minimum number of false casts. Fishing became a stalk, but was amply rewarded. Had we behaved like most fishermen do, we might have taken one fish in ten, instead of an average of one in three.

Stevenson, one of the most experienced rods on the Risle, and a great gentleman, always fled when he saw the local anglers striding casually along the bank. He preferred to take refuge on the little tributaries, armed with his leather kneeling pad, certain of finding there better opportunities of taking fish of a respectable size. A great and wise sportsman.

Nailed boots and the wading staff frighten trout, which is not the case with grayling.

To conceal yourself from view is indispensable but it is not enough. The correct presentation of the fly is no less necessary to success. *Precision at the first presentation is essential.* In general, the fly should fall slightly upstream of the fish, but this rule is not absolute. Placing the fly immediately above the fish, or to one side, or behind it may sometimes succeed after refusals on placing it upstream.

Once the fly is on the water, you must be ready for anything at any moment. In consequence, it is of advantage to let the fly drift downstream of the fish and then slowly tighten the line to make a very slight drag over at least a yard, still in the hope of a rise.

As for the strike, concerning which there has been so much discussion and such variety of opinion, it varies from the rapid to the extra slow. You must be prepared to strike immediately if the circumstances require it.

The food of trout in chalk streams

In chalk streams, rivers rising in chalk and with abundant weed, the stock of food is equivalent to the larder of an extremely luxurious restaurant. The fish has too great an abundance to choose from. The *menu* does not interest it. It likes to choose *à la carte* those dishes which appeal most to its appetite or its greed, unlike the trout of mountain streams which in general have a tendency to eat their way through the *menu*, whether it be good or bad.

At certain times of day, according to its state of activity, the fish will systematically refuse every dish except the one of its choice. It likes comfort, dislikes making an effort and prefers to eat sitting at a table rather than help itself from the sideboard. For instance, on the Risle or the Andelle, the trout will leave insects such as the Coleoptera which are too tough, in order to select the more tender Ephemeridae. They will take the female *Danica* rather than the male *Vulgata*, the veins of whose wings are coarser.

Molluscs and Crustacea (Gasteropods and Gammarids) are their main food. Trichopterans in the larval state are much appreciated, particularly during the evening rise, the main time of hatch. An imitation Coleoptera offered when the trout are feeding on Ephemeridae is like serving a dish of green peas you have omitted to shell!

The trout's preference for soft-skinned insects is perhaps due to the fact that, before swallowing them, it grinds or squashes them in the rear part of its mouth or, perhaps, merely because it finds them more tasty.

Here is a list of what the larder contains in the order of quantity consumed:

Crustacea. Fresh water shrimps.

Ephemeridae. In their successive states of larvae, then in winged form of Dun or Subimago, of Spinner or Imago, whether alive or floating dead with extended wings or, in the case of certain species (Baëtis), going to the bottom to lay their eggs.

Trichoptera. (Sedges.) In their larval state as they move about the bottom; and at the moment when they have abandoned the chrysallis and rise to the surface preparatory to hatching.

Perlidae. (Stone Flies) and willow flies, not very abundant on chalk streams.

Alder Flies. In their first state active in the mud, and also when they climb on to the bank to bury themselves as chrysallids, followed by hatching, in order to become land insects.

Coleoptera. Some live under water, others evolve above the surface. Generally gobbled up by trout.

Smuts. (Minute flies.)

Mosquitoes. In their aquatic states as larvae, nymphs and winged insects.

In chalk streams, as numerous examinations of trouts' stomachs have proved, larvae taken under the water or near the surface constitute two-thirds of their food during periods of activity, and winged insects only one-third.

The lavishness of this larder presents the fisherman with a double problem: in the first place he must discover what particular kinds of food are favoured at the moment, he must then select the best way of offering the trout an imitation which pleases it.

The dry fly purist tries above all to find the main dish of the day among his patterns. In case of failure, he is content to attribute the failure to his bad casting or tactics. If the trout persist in refusing, he will either try to persuade them to accept dishes that are totally different from those on the *carte du jour*, by offering them a wide variety of floating flies, or he will cut his losses and wait for a better opportunity.

I do not in the least wish to impose my own ideas on him. But why accept failure and condemn oneself often to mere idle contemplation? Why view the use of the same lure less wings and hackles with sovereign contempt? Why deprive oneself of the pleasures and satisfactions of a more difficult art in which observation, a sense of anticipation, quick sight and expertise are required to the maximum extent? Why, in short, when the trout are neglecting winged insects and floating flies to feed on larvae, should you not tempt them with a nymph?

It is a method that derives at once from the dry fly and the drifting submerged fly, which I mentioned in connection with grayling.

The angler can always find obliging and qualified instructors for dry or wet fly fishing. Those with a sound knowledge of fishing with a nymph are extremely rare.

And yet fly-fishing becomes doubly interesting the moment you begin to understand the causes for failure with a dry fly. There is great satisfaction in being able to say to yourself: 'I've found the right tactics!'

Fishing for trout and grayling with a nymph

Fishing with a nymph has been treated fully in many remarkable books, but I suspect that their weightiness, the extent and complexity of the subject, and the wide variety of observations reported are all reasons why most dry-fly fishermen know nothing of it, neglect to try it or despise it.

I resign to the innovators the prestige that is their due; to Skues, in the first place, who was a great master, and after him, to Mottram, to the Americans, Knight and Bergman, and, finally, to Sawyer.

Having read their books, I tried on several occasions to take trout on a nymph, but I succeeded only rarely, when the conditions were more than ideal. Most of the time the theoretical knowledge derived from my reading became mere chaos when on the water. This went on till the day I watched Sawyer fishing an English river.

The natural nymph is taken at two different stages: in the active state of the larva moving in the water, and again when, almost inert, it reaches the surface to burst out of its nymphal shuck to become a subimago.

HOW DOES THE FISH TAKE THE NYMPH?

In deep water, the fish takes the active larvae of which it is in search:

(1) In weed and mud;

(2) While they are on the move;

(3) When they are in process of sinking again, having unsuccessfully tried to pierce the surface of the water to hatch;

(4) Just beneath the surface, before breaking through it and hatching, while moving in the small circles which give negative results when fished with a dry fly.

In shallow waters

(1) While the fish is searching among the weed, its tail appearing on the surface (tailing);

(2) While seeking nymphs above the weed as they emerge from their hiding places. Its activity is shown by a humping of the surface of the water or by a ripple due to the half-turn the fish makes after taking the nymph (bulging);

(3) When you see the fish in position in a gap among the weeds, taking everything within reach.

The insect's position
  It may be completely submerged.
  A few inches below the surface.
  Floating on the surface for its metamorphosis into a winged insect.
Tactics to be adopted
  They vary according to circumstances:
  (1) The essential is to determine the position of the fish taking the nymphs.
(*a*) If you can see the fish, it is easy enough to determine its behaviour by observing its periods of stillness, its pauses, its reflection, its turning over, its movement, the opening and closing of its mouth.
(*b*) When you cannot see it, you may be guided by an eddy, an effervescence on the water and, if actually fishing, by a sudden acceleration in the sinking of the leader or by its coming to a stop.
  (2) Having discovered the fish's position, it is useful to know how it takes the nymph:
(*a*) When the trout is tailing, it is almost impossible to interest it.
(*b*) If it is bulging, it is fairly difficult because this is a fish that has just changed its position.
(*c*) The ideal conditions are united when the fish, either in a fixed position behind weed or in a current, is regularly taking larvae and neglecting surface insects.

THE CAST

Present with great precision. Cast either directly upstream or at forty-five degrees upstream, or laterally. Sometimes, slightly downstream. In placing the nymph always allow sufficient time and distance for the nymph to have submerged completely to a natural drift at a point immediately upstream of the fish.

  On the 10th July, 1952, I arrived at Netheravon, on the Avon, to watch Frank Sawyer fish. He is a big man with red hair and in his fifties, sympathetic, modest and realistic. He has been keeper of The Officers' Association Water since 1927.

  The water is several miles long and the river full of trout and grayling. It was two o'clock in the afternoon and we decided to go to the river at once.

* *Deep water. Fishing rings.* When we came to a reach of calm water with a depth of approximately four and a half feet, I noticed rises, small rings, regular and spaced out. I was under the impression that they were rises after midges. Sawyer began getting out his line and said that the rings indicated that the fish were taking nymphs beneath the surface. He cast upstream and placed his nymph about six feet from the selected ring. The nymph sank at once. Visibility was good and we could follow easily the floating part of the leader which grew shorter during the drift. Sawyer explained to me that you must watch the leader at the point of immersion for that is where the smallest reaction will become manifest when a fish touches the nymph. Suddenly he very slightly raised the point of his rod, a movement followed immediately by a delicate strike and he had taken it. I had not clearly understood what he was about, but, having landed a fine trout, he said:

'When I thought that my nymph had passed the fish without being taken I slightly tightened my line *to give animation to the lure*, which often incites a fish to take.'

We went on to the next. This time I was able to see clearly a sudden acceleration in the sinking of the leader followed by a strike, and a grayling of 1½ lb was taken. The third and the fourth fish were victims of the same tactics, but I must admit that once again I was able to see nothing. The last time, according to Sawyer, the sudden sinking of the leader was imperceptible, but there had been a slowing down in its drift.

Some of the fish he caught were taking nymphs almost on the surface (visible rings) as the nymphs were trying to break the surface to hatch, but others were in different stages of evolution. The rings reveal the presence and approximate position of the fish. In general, fish that are not near the surface lie at a depth corresponding to that of the water. It is therefore desirable that the artificial nymph should sink very deep to reach the fish. To attain precision, you must know the speed of the current and the rapidity with which the lure will sink so as to determine the point at which it should break the surface to ensure its passing close to the fish. The speed of the current is a fixed factor, that of the sinking of the nymph can be regulated (by a change of nymph), as can the place where the lure breaks the surface. The taking of a fish is indicated by a change in the movement or speed of the drift and the submergence of the leader.

After about an hour's fishing, my instructor had caught eight fish and missed two. This excellent average was due not only to his great mastery but to the fact that he knew the conditions by heart.

When my turn came, my eyes were already tired and the light was slightly less favourable, though still good. How should I make out? I am always inclined to strike nervously! In the result, I took two grayling out of five, thanks to the assistance of my instructor. By the end of the lesson I was astonished to find how much assurance I had already gained. I thought of the grayling in Austria and of Hans. What splendid times were in prospect!

* *Shallow waters. Fishing by sight.* 'Now we shall fish by sight', said Sawyer. 'I've kept it till the last for it is undoubtedly the most exciting method and requires the most rapid reflexes.'

134

We went downstream. It was not long before we saw a fine trout, lying in a pocket with a sandy bottom, in process of feeding on nymphs. Sawyer showed me how the fish fed with sudden, rapid movements towards an invisible prey, the appearing of the belly. At last, I began to be able to note it a little for myself: slight movements of the head and tail, the appearance of the inside of the mouth. The master took three fine trout and then made me try. I failed miserably with the first two. Too late each time! Finally, the third, moving to take my nymph before it arrived within reach, gave me the necessary warning. We could not see the cast and therefore our only mark was the movement of the fish. This, in my opinion, is what matters most, but . . . there is always a sixth sense!

Striking in this kind of fishing requires the most sensitive of reflexes. Casting must be very accurate; the same technique as for the dry fly but combined with calculations as to the speed of sinking so as to obtain the drift which will present the nymph correctly. The fish very quickly grows wary. Therefore the first presentation is very important.

Sawyer decided to try another locality:

'Let's go over to that big tree by the little artificial dam I built of concrete blocks, we'll find a colony of grayling and trout there. It's an ideal observation post. The light there makes it possible to see the fish's slightest movement.'

When we got to the spot, having walked well away from the bank to avoid any possibility of alarming the fish, we hid behind the trunk of the tree, from where I was in a position to observe a unique sight: some twenty fish, among them several fine trout, were grouped together and ceaselessly taking nymphs. There were three grayling near the bank and Frank took them one after the other without a failure. But how quick his reactions were! I was able to see only the last take his nymph. Then he took two trout, one of which weighed two pounds. And he did all this without alarming the fish, thanks to his first presentations being as accurate as if he were fishing with a dry fly. He immediately took the fish downstream and landed them there.

I was now beginning to see the grayling take the insects, and then I saw a big trout do so. My eye was at last becoming acclimatised, and I caught a grayling. The fish rose slightly at the moment of striking. Then, six or seven yards away, I saw a fine trout. I presented with precision and suddenly saw the white of its mouth. I struck too late! I tried again several times, but it was no good, the trout had become wary! I tried two others. I saw nothing of the first but a streak of lightning! The second moved quickly and slightly to the right. I struck. I had him! Sawyer was delighted. Then there was a period of calm. The fish seemed no longer to take the slightest interest in my artificial nymphs. Nevertheless, Frank, in order to prove his mastery, succeeded, after a short delay, in taking my big trout, though he admitted that he had not seen the actual taking of the nymph and had succeeded only thanks to his sixth sense.

I was amazed at the intense activity of the fish during a period of taking nymphs and by the astonishing possibilities of this kind of fishing. I shall never forget that afternoon, my excitement and the satisfaction of having discovered and learned something really new in the practice of fishing. I am eternally grateful to Sawyer who revealed his secrets to me with joy and enthusiasm.

That evening, in an inn at Amesbury, Sawyer explained the whole technique of fishing with a nymph, and here is his explanation:

In the first place, the conditions must be suitable: nymphs, larvae and fish must be active. The water should be rather low and the light favourable. On English chalk-streams it is better to wait till July.

Sawyer has spent more than twenty years observing the life of aquatic insects, particularly under the water and at depth. He has studied them in their daily life from the egg and the larva to the stage of the nymph. He has succeeded in watching their underwater movements, as they go from one weed bed to another, how they fold their legs along their bodies and use their tail as a means of propulsion, thereby obtaining the maximum of ease and speed in swimming. *Skues seems to have concentrated his observations mainly on the activity of flies immediately preceding the hatch, therefore when close to the surface.* That is why his patterns of nymphs have their *legs detached from their bodies*, which hinders their sinking. Sawyer maintains that when the Olives are on the move, the fish do not expect to see a nymph swimming with its legs dragging behind its head. The suppression of these hackles gives the artificial nymph a better outline and facilitates its presentation beneath the surface. It sinks in a more life-like way. Sawyer thinks that Skues fished close to the surface, at the stage of the nymph's inertia, while he fishes more often than not at some depth and even very deep.

The colonies of nymphs swim about like little fish, rising occasionally towards the surface, then diving for about a foot before sinking finally to the bottom. This may be repeated several times before the hatch. During the last two weeks of their existence, these insects move over a great area of the bottom, journeying from place to place, from one shelter or patch of weed to another. When you see a trout posted between two lots of weed, you can watch all the movements of the nymphs.

Sawyer has created a series of nymphs of varying patterns and weights, ballasted with extra fine copper wire, which facilitates the imitation of the various exploitable phases of these insects' behaviour. However, he has not been able to reproduce exactly the behaviour of the Blue Winged Olive (*Ephemerella ignita*) which, when about to hatch, swims towards the surface making movements from time to time with out-stretched legs. As soon as it approaches the surface, it begins to float just beneath it, making spasmodic movements in its attempts to reach the air. It is then that the movements of its legs and body attract the fish's attention. Even a faithful reproduction would not therefore have the resemblance to life which incites the fish to take. Sawyer considers that two patterns in various sizes are sufficient:

* *Type A.* The Olive and Iron Blue group, which are also taken by trout when they are established in the taking of spent Olive spinners, female spinners that float under-water when they have laid their eggs beneath the surface. Size of hooks, Nos. 15 and 14.

* *Type B.* Pale Olive (Light Pale Watery) and the Centroptilum group which is also very good. These two patterns have the characteristics of half a dozen species of Ephemeridae and the fish can be led into taking them in error. Hooks Nos. 16, 15 and 14. They can be weighted more or less according to the water one is fishing. In Austria, in certain cases, I have used Hans' patterns, on No.13, decidedly heavier than those Sawyer has created for the chalk streams. But you must not overdo it or you run the risk of making the artificial nymph sink vertically.

If you drop Skues's nymphs into a glass of water, they float, while Sawyer's im-mediately sink to the bottom. Their weight is calculated to overcome the resistance to sinking of the leader.

What I like about Sawyer is that he refuses to allow himself to be hypnotised by theories of over-precision. He is always in search of the simple, the practical and the essential and attaches importance above all to the *method of presentation* (the type of leader, the weighting of the artificial nymph and the exploitation of the various possible stages in the development of the insects). And, rod in hand, he can prove that he is right. For him, the nymph is a microscopic submarine which must respond im-mediately to the slightest command transmitted to it by his rod. And in the last resort, he says that with practice and patience one ultimately develops the blind man's sixth sense of anticipation, the height of mastery.

It merely remains for me to prove that Sawyer's method can be adapted to the majority of rivers containing salmonids.

Here is a summary of my experiences in Bavaria and Austria:

On a 24th July, I was with Kustermann, at Polling, on the little river where, before the war, I had taken fourteen trout in fifteen minutes dry fly fishing with a Tups. After luncheon, I went to the same reach and took, in a little over an hour, nine trout and one grayling with Sawyer's Type A nymph. The water was of medium depth and I was striking on the indications of the leader. On the 26th July, I joined Hans at

Gmunden. In the afternoon, I gave him a Sawyer-like demonstration, but of a much more modest kind! At my first attempt, I took a fine grayling, then a second. Then the light changed and prevented my watching my leader. About six o'clock, conditions became more favourable and the grayling seemed to be taking immediately below the surface. In a short space of time, I took six fish as compared to one taken by my friends who were fishing the rises with a dry fly.

The next morning, it was Hans' turn, and we went to Hamstockmühle where he caught ten fish by sight, all grayling which were not taking flies. His remarkable eyesight certainly helped him, but it was a splendid result!

Then we took the boat to fish the submerged island above the dam, a splendid place for observation when there is no wind, particularly towards the middle of the day. We were in a position to choose our fish, but they were very wary. We had to cast with absolute precision. We took six more! A splendid day's fishing from every point of view. For the next three days, we repeated our success wherever we went. Hans had quickly invented a new pattern which he baptised Type C Traun Nymph, a red silk body ribbed with yellow silk and heavily weighted. Hooks Nos. 13, 14.

On the 2nd August, on the upper Salza, after luncheon, I was taking a siesta under the shade of a pine tree. Opposite me was a large wall of rock, rising vertically. I was finally woken up by the conversation of Straub, Batchi and Emerl growing louder and louder. I grasped the fact that they were attacking two trout which seemed to be rising immediately under the wall. But, in spite of numerous changes of fly, the trout remained at liberty. Ultimately, these purists invited me to try my nymph. At the second attempt, my first cast having been outside the area, a third fish, the biggest, came out of a dark hole and threw himself on the Traun Nymph. Over two pounds! A good weight for the locality.

I could quote several other cases at Gschoder, each different and each more interesting than the last. But here is one that I consider remarkable.

Straub and I were walking along the road which borders the Salza and runs some nine feet above it. At this point, the river is fairly smooth and about three feet deep, the bottom covered with rocks. There were three fine fish perfectly visible, lying between ten and fifteen yards from our bank. The sky was clear but without too much sun. Straub chose the nearest and offered it a little Tups. In spite of impeccable presentations he had refusal after refusal. I gave him my rod and he placed the nymph a good yard upstream of the fish who went for it almost at once and the barb caught. It was the first time I had seen a grayling take in that place where I considered them almost untakeable. The second fish was missed and the third, alarmed by the casting, refused and disappeared.

I hope that this account, rather long perhaps, but in my view indispensable, will allow those interested in the nymph to benefit by the indisputable advantages of this method of fishing, which every good fly fisherman ought to try, having first furnished himself with the types of nymph recommended by Sawyer.

As far as I am concerned, it is the acme of the art of fly fishing.

The Monster nymph. Sawyer's Killer nymph is tied on a No. 10 or 12 hook with grey wool wrapped round the shank to form a very thick body. It can be weighted with fine copper wire. I have fished this nymph with good results for many years, especially on the Pollinger Bach, but last Fall (1971) on my way from Lech to the Pollinger Bach I found that my stock was totally depleted. My fly box contained the necessary hooks and some grey, red and yellow wools. I tied a couple of Sawyer-type nymphs, sealing the final knot with a dab of nail varnish. I must admit that they were horrible to look at, but during 10 days fishing in Austria and Bavaria I used them wherever trout or grayling seemed likely to be tempted. Most of that time the fish went for the lure enthusiastically enough, confirming results with similar nymphs over a four-year period.

At Polling, in the village itself, there is a shallow flat of water in which the fish can be seen moving. I found that when the nymph had sunk 12 inches or so – and sometimes as it penetrated the surface film – two or three fish would race towards it, competing for this unexpected titbit. Six trout were returned to that water and much the same experience had been noted on the Lech, Traun and other rivers.

I believe that if one had to accept the restriction of a single pattern of fly or nymph, this particular type would take fish under most circumstances. Monstrous or not, this woolly creation is a pleasure to use. I enjoy fishing it as much I do the dry fly and it is, of course, a reasonable replacement for any wet fly pattern.

No lure could be simpler. You may not approve its lack of style, but trout and grayling are by no means as fastidious. Please, do me the favour of tying one or two yourself and, at the next opportunity, try them.

Frank Sawyer's comment when he read of my lure was that 'the new nymph sounds a bit fearsome, but I can well imagine trout charging from all angles to take it. We need something like it here at the present time, for though the trout are moving throughout the day they are devils to catch or deceive.'

Fishing weedy streams

From the middle of June, and even during the last days of the Mayfly, the chalk-streams begin to grow weed which carpets practically the whole of their surface.

Before the weed is cut and also afterwards, if it has been correctly done, the trout lie near the channels, often narrow, between the banks of weed. They make first-class feeding and resting places. The fish often hide in the weed practically on the surface and slowly raise their heads to take the drifting insect with great delicacy as it floats, so to speak, almost straight into their mouths. You can hear a sort of sucking sound and the rings are barely visible. They take the insects with the ends of their lips, while their tails remain in the weeds, ready for immediate retreat into a protective hiding-place.

The rises are spaced out because the fish selects its prey like a gourmet, since the weed proffers a great choice of everything it likes best. To fish from the bank at this period is, in general, the most certain means to failure and of spoiling a fishing period that I consider one of the most exciting, most productive and, quite certainly, most specialised.

The best rises often take place in a narrow channel only some fifteen or twenty inches wide, or indeed on the very edge of a bank of weed. In the latter case they show only a half ring. Great precision is essential, but it is practically impossible to achieve by casting from the bank, unless the rises are immediately under it. Drag is, for the most part, likely to be premature or, rather, the normal drift much too short owing to the weed catching the line or even part of the leader.

If you do succeed, the trout will have disappeared into the weed before you have time to get it off balance or keep it on the surface. Moreover, you will have to make it cross many banks of weed. It is the moment to go into the attack by wading, provided you proceed with all the precaution and deliberation this form of fishing requires. For choice, select reaches with the greatest depth possible. You must fish directly upstream and very short. The thickness of the weed has the advantage of allowing you to get very close to the fish without alarming it. A fairly long rod and a rather short leader are necessary. You should place the fly twenty to twenty-five inches in front of where the fish is lying, taking care to gather the slack of the line in the left hand, so as to be in a position to strike at once. At the critical moment, you must raise the rod above your head and reel in with the utmost speed. An almost vertical, extremely rapid and energetic pull on the line puts the fish off balance and gives it no chance to regain its hiding place. You may often be almost up to the waist in water.

The length of the rod has the advantage of reducing the number of touches down behind during the false casts and of keeping the fly dry and floating. A metal net, attached to the belt with a cord of approximately a couple of yards in length, will allow of keeping the fish alive and avoid your having to return to the bank after every catch.

Fishing for big trout with a Mayfly

At the end of May, in Normandy, the wind blows most of the time. To succeed in taking big fish, you must be able to reach them as soon as they rise, at any distance and without being obliged to wait for a calm. Then, after the strike, you must fight the fish strongly without making concessions, owing to the banks of weed which are already thick and numerous. Adequate tackle, both strong and solid, is the best guarantee of success and the only means of reducing the average of lost fish which, in these circumstances, unfortunately reach a much higher percentage than normal.

* *Tackle.* Long, powerful rods of at least nine feet. For my part, I use a rod of nine and a half feet, nylon leader of ·010 in., or perhaps ·012 in.

* *Flies.* Divided-wing patterns are impossible to cast in a wind. Large Cahill or May, big spentwing or bivisible, or American flies of the spider type with fine hackles, very stiff and very long, of the extra stiff Plumeau type or, again, big Panama and Plumeau.

* *Hooks.* Big hooks are essential for security, because fish have to be held so hard. No.10 of the first quality. With ·012 nylon nothing is easier than to open the gape of the hook.

* *Tactics.* To succeed in landing big fish, though it is necessarily lacking in elegance, you must use force. It is far from easy. It is difficult and nervous work. You are often fishing at considerable distance and, for preference, those fish which most fishermen are incapable of reaching. The length of the rod facilitates holding the fish on the surface during the fight and the management of the line during gusts. It reduces the chances of tangling the line and the leader. It often saves you from taking the fly in your face during the false casts which are extremely difficult to control.

You must not be concerned with the quantity. On waters holding big trout you must only fish when you are absolutely certain, after careful observation, of being sure of presenting the fly well at the first attempt and, above all, you must take advantage of the rare rises of the very big fish.

Avoid presenting the fly when there are no rises.

In case of failure, try to animate the fly in imitation of a dying Spent. Long, supple wing hackles often vibrate in the wind.

* *Essential precautions.* Check the point of the leader, the gape and point of the hook, every half hour, and, after every catch, sharpen the hook if necessary with an Arkansas stone (a stone used for sharpening medical instruments).

Wear a Basque béret and cover your ears, or, if there is a wind, a hat with a wide brim as protection against the blowing back of the line.

Often, after a first attempt and refusal, it is better to stay where you are until you have caught the fish, if it is a good one.

Always keep ready reeled off the precise length of line so as to cast as soon as the fish rises again or the wind drops.

Before attacking the fish, observe closely all the banks of weed in the neighbourhood of the striking zone, where the capture will take place. Do not yield the fish an inch.

The great difficulty is to overcome the wind. You can achieve this by making a semi-horizontal or almost vertical cast, the back casts and forward casts well separated, the arm straight out and detached from the body to prevent the hook coming back into your face and to avoid getting knots in the leader. You must shoot plenty of line at the end of the cast.

The Aclou Reach

The finest and richest reach of the Risle is undoubtedly that of Aclou. I think it the finest in the world and better than the finest reaches of the Test, the Itchen or the Wylye. It begins at the road bridge and runs parallel to the railway as far as the island of Balicorne. If the fabulous Skues had fished this enormous and splendid reach I feel certain he would have called it the paradise of the nymph.

The river is wide. It begins with a principal arm of about thirty yards in length and, just above the wooden bridge, forms a secondary arm a hundred yards long, which flows into a huge cut thirty-five yards wide, which terminates at an old demolished dam whose pool still exists. The whole reach has been fished for years, but the enormous quantity of fish never grows less. Throughout its length, it is a practically uninterrupted stretch of banks of weed divided by innumerable narrow channels. Its depth is nowhere greater than four feet. The upper part and the beginning of the secondary arm have fast currents, the remainder medium or slow. I have never been there without seeing rises.

According to the season or the positions of the fish, you can fish it either with dry fly, wet fly, or nymph. It is an ideal ground for experiment! Despite its many advantages, the fish are often very difficult, particularly on the stretch opposite the railway building, and for two reasons: the first being that the trout are much fished there and have become very wary by the end of April; the second being that, owing to the clearness of the water and the light at certain hours, it is impossible to conceal your line except from fish under the bank.

A lodge of very large trout on the Risle

The currents in the upper part are perfect for wet fly at the beginning of the season, as are the currents lower down, but it gives less satisfactory results when the dry fly begins to be successful, and also because of the increase in weed. Moreover, the wet fly is only authorised at the beginning of the season and on condition of not abusing it, for mostly small fish are taken at that period. The bigger trout are still often on the bottom and seem to prefer to wait for the big hatches before coming to the surface to feed.

Owing to the width of the stream and the numerous back currents and currents of varying speed, fish in the middle or under the opposite bank require great expertness in casting.

The evening rise is a fabulous spectacle. The river boils. But the catch is nearly always very moderate for, in spite of the regularity and density of the rises, the fish will take only one in twenty or even one in forty dry fly. Moreover, the visibility is very poor. It is best to fish with your back to the light. By wading, you can make a very good catch in these circumstances. The law forbids fishing after the sun has set and you always have to stop at the best time. You must, therefore, not lose a moment of the last half hour. Luckily, during the day, by careful and assiduous fishing, you can always achieve success. Unfortunately, the frequent and numerous rises in the best places encourage fishermen to cast unceasingly, and the fish very soon learn to distinguish artificial flies.

There are often three or four of us fishing, sometimes even more, spaced out twenty or thirty yards apart, sometimes less. In spite of the continuous casting, the trout continue to rise, whereas in other places a few defective presentations will quickly frighten them off. Results would certainly be better if, after a number of attempts followed by refusals, one had the patience to stop and await the second rise of the following series.

The great interest of the reach lies in those localities where fishing with a nymph often gives excellent results, particularly in the smooth water opposite the railway house and along the bank bordering it. Here, more often than not, the trout are only interested in the insects at certain stages of the hatch, on their journey from the bottom to the surface, on their arrival at the surface or, again, while they are moving from one weed bed to another. Similarly, they may be indifferent to floating insects and then, a moment later, take them to the exclusion of larvae. At other times, only the drifting submerged fly, the drift ending in drag, will interest them. Periods of quiet rarely last for more than a quarter of an hour.

One afternoon, during the Mayfly season, when there was great activity, I was with that great writer on fishing, de Boisset, at the railway house. We had refusal after refusal. My friend, a great expert in aquatic entomology, and the possessor of a unique

collection of flies, including the famous Gallica series, created by him and manufactured by that master, de Chamberet, was looking for the precise fly. There was a
great variety of natural flies on the surface. Since it was the beginning of the Mayfly
season, his patterns corresponded exactly to the Ephemerae on the water, and yet the
refusals persisted while the fish were frequently taking a natural fly close to his
offering. Some of the fish were visible. The rises were minute, indeed many of them
merely dimples. I also noticed a few brilliant flashes of turning fish. Undoubtedly, the
fish were taking the nymphs before the opening of the shuck and the first deployment
of the wings. I took a Lemarchand (a wet fly with a few flat black hackles, a peacock
body ribbed with gold and silver tinsel, heavy hook No.9) and placed it two good
yards upstream of an eddy with a jerk of the rod point to make it sink; then a drift
with slack and still more slack; my eyes fixed intently on the point of activity; then
a half glimpse of the fish's belly followed by a slight eddy of the water; an instantaneous but very gentle strike; a tension of the leader, a bending of the rod, a jump, a
dive, an attempt to escape towards a weed bed – but unsuccessfully! Then another,
only partially successful this time; reeling in, running out; a run downstream, then upstream; a jump, a bewildered flapping of head and tail; these were the signs of defeat
and despair: the first manifestations of exhaustion! But at last the rod was master.
Aquaplaning on the surface, it made a last supreme effort at sight of the landing-net.
And then one pound twelve ounces of firm-fleshed fish, spotted with red, was
floundering on the grass.

In twenty minutes I caught six fine fish, and de Boisset, whom I had advised to
follow my example, had taken several more. Then, as the rings became better marked,
we had refusals once again. The fish had altered their method of feeding. We had
reached the floating fly part of the menu! My friend de Boisset's splendid Gallica were
then at the top of their form! But my Tups were certainly also on the *carte du jour!*

During the same period, Jacques Spier, sitting peacefully on a bench seventy yards
upstream, close by moderate currents and immediately opposite the fast currents, had
a splendid time with a Panama pattern.

The evening rise on a chalk stream

For many of us it is the most important moment in the day. The most promising, the
most exciting and, sometimes, the most disappointing!

After the first easy successes at the beginning of the hatch, you often begin to lose
your nerve when you see that refusals are becoming more frequent as the rises increase

in number. The situation is likely to be complicated by numerous changes of fly, which mean an appalling loss of time.

By fishing with method and pursuing a plan based on experience, the evening rise can become not only great fun but much more productive.

As soon as the day declines, check your tackle, then take up a position on the bank with the light behind you, which is the only way of watching the rises and the presentation and taking of your fly.

Present immediately on the first rise; do not attempt difficult fish, but try the greatest possible number. As soon as the percentage of refusals increases, which generally happens at the beginning of the evening rise, strengthen the taper of the leader, either by cutting it or, preferably, changing it for another shorter one prepared in advance: approximately six feet, terminating in ·010 in., maximum ·012 in., to which are attached two flies, one with a short, stiff dropper of ·014 in., some three feet above the other.

* *Flies.* The fly should be on the water as much as possible; the search for the precise fly is not recommended. Precision and accurate presentation at the first placing of the fly become secondary, false casts should be reduced to a minimum. The fly is fishing just as much when it is floating as when half submerged. Drag is often an asset. The secondary fly will compensate for lack of precision when the light seems bad.

First try the fish under the opposite bank, particularly if there are big trout among them whose rings will shortly become invisible.

At the height of the hatch, persistence with fish rising in a regular cadence will be more productive. In the case of two or three trout close together, try them one after the other, and endeavour to give animation to the fly. Above all, do not become fidgety, only deliberate mechanical working will produce the maximum result.

For the beginner, the moderate fisherman or one whose sight is bad in semi-darkness, the most simple and radical method is as follows: a six foot leader with a ·012 in. point and a wet fly with a sufficiency of hackles with which one can continually flog the water but without casting more than medium distances. Fish with a wet or semi-wet fly.

Old hands will prefer to try for big fish previously marked down, and to content themselves with working on a few of the largest, though running the risk of going away empty-handed, but with the satisfaction or consolation of having fished as connoisseurs!

Always keep a spare leader round your hat with one or two flies attached to it. When, because of the darkness, it is impossible to tie on a fly, it is often still possible to change a leader. Have two rods ready prepared.

These suggestions are neither laws nor fixed rules but, after a bad day, they will often help to make a better showing and make certain on arriving home of a smile from your wife whose first question is bound to be: 'How many did you catch?'

The usefulness of animating an artificial fly

The Aube, in its higher reaches in Burgundy, is a small stream containing very big fish indeed. Auguste Lambiotte one day caught a brown trout weighing seven pounds on a Panama fly.

I remember a trout rising at a bend under a high bank on a gravel bottom of eighteen inches. There was no tree or shrub behind which I could hide. It was no use trying to cast downstream, two previous presentations to fish in the same sector having put them to flight at once. There was a brilliant sun and, owing to the height of the bank, the shadow of my line and its almost vertical fall made surprise impossible.

Being exactly above the fish, which I had only seen at the last moment, I stood motionless and watched. The trout was active and very much on the alert. There were few flies, and it was searching for food in all directions. Moving in slow motion, I took the bull by the horns. I sent him a grey fly with a yellow body, dropping it with a parachute cast followed by partial drift, and the trout grew fidgety and irritable. I persisted till I thought I had brought it into a state of annoyance in which it would no longer be able to resist my lure. This produced an unforgettable sight. While to begin with the trout hardly moved at each presentation, its reactions gradually increased in intensity with every sight of my artificial fly. At the final presentation, when it saw my fly fall on the water a yard upstream, it failed to move as it had done previously. I was extremely anxious. Had I waited too long? Had the fish understood? There was my fly within its reach and it had not even moved its tail! The fly was now immediately over it and still it did not move! Then, suddenly, it leaped on it like a tiger. But now the trout had made me lose my nerve and I exploded with a strike which gave it its liberty, a liberty amply deserved. Bravo! God willing, it would give itself up tomorrow!

Two days later, towards the end of the afternoon, I again presented my grey fly with the yellow body and ate the trout with Lambiotte. It was thanks to my somewhat unsporting dapping, which was, however, the only possible method at that place.

Godart, the great expert, often ends his drift with a delicate drag. If he can see the fish and thinks it irritable, he begins again and sometimes gets results.

Here is the unique and effective method employed by a cobbler of the Eure region, one of the best fishermen of the district.

He ties his flies with a few hackles and any sort of hook. Of course he knows his fishing grounds perfectly, having fished them for years. Before going after a fish, he begins by wetting his fly with saliva, then presents it, placing it with delicacy and great precision, slightly upstream of the fish's position. As soon as his fly is in front of the trout he sinks it just under the surface with a flick of the point of his rod and makes it drift under water for a yard or two. It is his only tactic, but his numerous successes prove its worth.

Dapping, though not very sporting, is the favourite method of many professional fishermen. The rivers they fish are often too narrow or too encumbered with trees to allow of classic casting and oblige them to employ surprise. It is admissible in certain cases and can be very instructive, and even exciting.

I remember an incident on the Loue, in 1946, on the superb Fougère water which belongs to my friends, Dr Tisserant and Pierre Dufay of Besançon. Above a big dam, there is a canal which runs a turbine. It is approximately two to three yards wide and three to six feet deep. The current is slow and the banks are bordered with trees along the whole of their two hundred yards.

In the morning, at breakfast, Dufay said:

'It's a hot day, the sun's bright, our chances of success on the big river are very small, the trout will become active only towards the end of the afternoon and you know that grayling rarely rise at this season. Get your rod and come with me, I'll show you some very fine fish in the turbine canal. I don't know whether you'll succeed in catching any, it's a very difficult reach to fish, but the sight is worth the trouble. When we reach the place, make as little vibration as possible when walking and, above all, don't show yourself.'

We crossed in a boat, disembarked on the left of the dam, and took a little path leading to the end of the canal near the turbine. We were in a wood and there was a tree about every yard along the bank. After a few paces, I saw a trout in position. At the first false cast, it fled. Then I saw a rise ten yards away at the foot of a stump on my bank. It was impossible to reach it owing to lack of room to get my line out. I advanced about five yards, went down on my knees and tried a reverse cast, throwing out my line across the canal. It got caught up! I looked behind me, there was nothing to be done, an overhanging branch paralysed me. Dufay, who was watching me with a smile, said:

'I only succeed in catching fish here by dapping, you try it, if the fish is worth while.'

I crawled to a tree, then got to my feet and hid behind it. Two yards upstream was a big, fat trout with zebra stripes, as they are in the Loue, lying under the surface and rising a few inches from the bank. Moving very slightly it was inspecting all the insects that passed near it and making its choice. I withdrew from the bank and changed my fly, preferring a bigger hook because of the difficulty of hooking the fish with a vertical strike. I changed my Cahill No.12 for a No.10. Having shortened my leader, which was too long for dapping, I got back into position. The trout had moved back a yard, I feared it must see me; it was almost at my feet! I stood stock still, hoping it would move back into position. It let itself drift gently down with the current, then stopped. I had brought the knot of the leader back against the top ring of the rod. Suddenly, the trout went back to its first position. I placed the fly on the water in front of it and could see that it was interested, but it was suspicious and came back under my feet. I raised my rod. There was nothing to be done about it, I was too close. Again I waited. At last it went back to its position near the stump. I then dapped the fly without placing it on the water. The trout again showed interest and some signs of animation. If I could succeed in irritating it to the point when its excitement overcame its suspicion, I might have a chance of getting it to accept my fly. At the precise moment the Cahill was about to reach the position for a rise, I drew it back each time. At the first drift the trout remained absolutely motionless, at the second it fidgeted a little, at the third it moved a little; it was now showing definite anxiety to take the fly, but a ray of sunlight was dazzling the surface. Luckily, I noticed that a cloud was coming up. And now the sun was hidden and the moment seemed to have come. This time, I meant business. I placed the fly and let it drift down without drawing it back. Splash! A first class rise! I did not strike, merely raised the point of the rod imperceptibly. I sank the steel, immediately lowered the point of the rod, and had to give line, while the fish made straight for a bed of weed under the opposite bank. I now had to stop it, at the risk of breaking, for the fish was too heavy to get out of the weed. It broke surface, jumped and dashed down the middle of the stream. I brought the rod back and managed to turn it. It was now off balance and I knew I could hold it and bring it back. Dufay took my landing-net and went down on his stomach, so high was the bank. He brought up the net. A splendid fish! Over two and a quarter pounds. But it was only just in time! The hook was merely holding in the lip and on the point of tearing out.

When obstacles and conditions on the ground make casting impossible, fishing by deception is admissible, and trying to take the fish in spite of the drawbacks is often both more difficult and instructive than in normal conditions. It is also an excellent test of self-control.

The advantages of good sight in a fisherman

On the Andelle, the junction of two arms of the river create a counter-current with eddies, some four yards long and eighteen inches wide at the maximum.

At three o'clock in the afternoon, a trout was rising regularly at X (see diagram). After numerous attempts, I was compelled to abandon it. Visibility was very poor and I had repeated refusals, but I decided to come back towards the end of the afternoon, since the fish must be a good one.

About six o'clock, I returned and saw that the fish was feeding again. Moreover, I no longer had to fish blind and might even be in a position to discover the reasons for my previous failures. The trout was visible and was worth the trouble: over a pound in weight and very active. I could see its outline immediately below the surface. I cast: no result. I waited and watched very attentively. The fish broke surface. I realised that its head was downstream. There was a very slow and weak counter-current, with almost dead water in the centre of the current; the trout was only taking natural flies, which entered the dead water from the smaller arm in order to circle once or twice before drifting away on the current from the principal arm. But how could I place my fly without immediate drag? I tried different casts, all fruitless. The fish seemed to be rising for the most part some eighteen inches from the tree. I cast my Cahill, shooting it out violently against the lower part of the trunk. At the second attempt I succeeded: the fly hit the tree and rebounded nearly

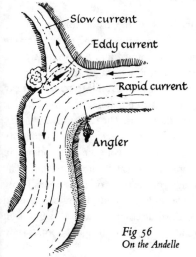

Fig 56
On the Andelle

eighteen inches; it landed, by an extraordinary piece of luck, at the very end of the current and was drawn at once into the pocket of dead water where it was immediately taken by a one and a half pounder, which was very soon in the landing-net. In the afternoon, my fly had been falling behind the fish and coming out of the dead water with drag, the fish probably never even seeing it.

An active fish which the fisherman can see is generally a fish taken.

When fishing, I have often noticed that my only average height often reduces my ability to see. How often have I not envied Auguste Lambiotte's six feet two inches, which allows him to see fish that are invisible to my five feet eight inches.

On the Risle, in the Mayfly season, in the centre of a big reach, some fine trout were rising regularly in the channels between the weed beds. The wind was complicating the problem and, in spite of some accurate casting, I was unable to get them to take. Immediately behind my casting position was one of those benches reserved for fishermen of a certain age. I climbed on to the bench and, after a few minutes, was able to observe a very big fish following the Ephemerae drifting down its channel. From time to time it selected one, and then returned to shelter behind a tuft of weed whose summit was about three feet beneath the surface. The fish could therefore only see me when it was moving to follow a fly. Fortunately I was slightly downstream of it.

At the next rise, I offered it a Cahill. It rose, examined it and refused it at the last moment as before, but I could now see the cause of its refusal. In the channel were two currents of different speeds: the nearer the more rapid, the farther the more slow. And it was in the latter that I had placed my fly, resulting in certain drag before the end of the drift. The fish was moving in its pocket to select the flies of its choice. Before climbing on to the bench, all these important details had been invisible to me. I now considered that I was practically certain to take this splendid fish provided it did not suddenly stop rising. In spite of several more rises, I waited till the wind dropped, which was necessary to allow me slack and precision of presentation.

The first presentation unhappily synchronised with the trout rising to a big Ephemera and then the wind rose again! As the fish was either resting or being active only when the wind was blowing, I was obliged to go on waiting. At last, my fly was presented at the right moment and without synchronising with a natural fly. It was immediately taken and I struck hard, raising my rod skywards and stretching out my arm to its full extent to get the fish off balance at the strike. After a first dive I held it on the surface and stopped it before it could reach the weeds. The fish was heavy, very heavy, and I had two banks of weed to get it across before the wide channel under my own bank. I jumped down off the bench and moved away from the bank, pulling in my line as fast as I could with my left hand, and letting it fall on the ground. The current by the bank was fairly strong, and, having got the trout on the surface, I only just succeeded in holding it with one hand while landing it with the other. I was on my knees and victory was only mine at the third attempt! It was a magnificent fish! Broad, short, small of head, tinted a wonderful golden green, its spots bright red.

Stalking

It often happens that fishermen taking up a fixed position, provided it is a good one, will have the maximum success provided they know how to select an adequate method. One of the reasons for their success is due to the fact that they end by becoming specialists through always proceeding in the same way. Among anglers of this sort, I can quote two of my friends: Jacques Spier and Paul Dormeuil.

The first was my hard-working and assiduous pupil and, as soon as he had learned enough, he specialised at once in the method that suited him best. He has the misfortune to suffer from asthma, due to having been gassed during the 1914-18 war. He is an excellent financier and a first class logician as well as being endowed with great calm. These qualities, though he started fishing late in life, have quickly made him an expert. From the very beginning, he preferred the bench or the fixed position. He knows how to select the most favourable spot according to the season, the time and the light. He takes up his position and watches. After having accurately located the fish, he works on them unhurriedly, one by one, taking care always to select the finest.

His casting has no pretensions. The leader and the end of the line fall clumsily, but he is very accurate and never fishes at a distance.

As for flies, he uses what happens to be in his box, with a preference for those with good hackles, which float well, such as the Panama, for which he has a weakness. During the many years that we have been fishing the Risle together, his daily catch is always among the best, and always consists of good fish.

Paul Dormeuil belongs to the same school, being under the necessity of avoiding fatigue.

I shall never forget an afternoon during the Mayfly, when he had taken up his position on a bench, near a little arm with a rapid current, at the Gabriel Island, about five yards wide and forty long at most. By evening, he had kept fifteen fine trout, of which the average weight was about a pound: one of the best catches of the day. He does not fish often and has never made any attempt to be classed among the experts.

The typical stalking fisherman fishes under the bank and only his own bank. I must admit that this method, as far as I am concerned, lacks excitement. I consider it rather boring, but it is effective and very productive. He conscientiously fishes his bank upstream, takes up his position for preference behind trees, watches the fish whose positions he knows and works on them till he gets results. He casts very short, always better than average, and sometimes with great expertness. His great advantage is derived from the fact that, on chalkstreams, many fish lie under the banks. He therefore has all the advantages of being hidden, the trout not being in a position to see the false casts, since they must come out of their hiding-places to see the fly drifting to their right. The faults in the placing of the leader are less apparent.

I think the example of my friend Pendleton ('Penny') has considerable interest for those fishing mountain rivers.

One day, on the Beaverkill in New York State, when I was only starting to fish, there were four of us, one July morning, when the fish were practically entirely inactive. We were flogging the water and fishing all the good places over some five hundred yards. The fish were taking nothing, and there was not a rise to our flies. 'Penny' had taken up his position on a rock, behind a hole of something like a yard square with a promising eddy. He was regularly placing his fly some three or four yards in front of him, letting it drift round the eddy for a yard or two and then casting again. 'Penny' always held his rod with his forefinger on the butt and cast short. He continued with this process for nearly two hours. He was presenting with great care a light Cahill and a Quill Gordon of a darker colour. His placing and drift were impeccable.

When we joined him at midday, he had caught four fine trout, all about one pound in weight.

He knew that the hole was a likely place for fish and, merely by continually passing flies across so small a surface, he had succeeded in interesting, irritating and finally causing the trout to rise. Several similar examples since then have shown decisively the value of this method when the fish are inactive, provided that the technique and patience of the fisherman are of the first order.

When trout are feeding

One day, on the Andelle, towards the end of the Mayfly, the fish were being difficult and capricious. It was during that period of hatches when the males predominate. Lambiotte, Dufay, Gaillard and I had taken only a few small fish.

Towards seven o'clock, I decided to go in search of bigger ones. They were lying at the tail-end of the current in the deep water, downstream of the big reach below the bridge. There were many flies on the surface, particularly dead ones, and there were but few rises.

I took up my position opposite a big tree where, during the course of the afternoon, I had tried for two big fish without success. The river was becoming a bit livelier. A few casts produced only very small trout which barely weighed a pound. Toward eight o'clock there was a change. The evening flies were beginning to flutter about, float or move across the surface. At last there was a fine little ring, preceded by a trout taking a fly, slowly, delicately and with great precision; it was one of the big ones starting to feed and, so impatient was he, beginning to eat his bread before the soup had been served! I watched carefully. And indeed there were three other diners!

Experience has taught me that the two best moments for attacking are as soon as the bread has been placed on the table during the first rise, when the appetite is still unappeased, and then after the dessert till the coffee and liqueurs. There were four regular rises and not a moment to be lost! I calculated the distance carefully, it was a few yards downstream(the trout were feeding close into the bank) and I presented my fly: there were several rises without result followed by a pause. They were clearly waiting for the next course! Suddenly there was great activity. I tried again, and was again refused. I watched. Oh, but this was no normal menu! It was like a buffet furnished with all kinds of dishes, hot, cold, in aspic, lobsters, roast beef, salads, cakes, ices and so on. And now the diners were moving continuously about, choosing their favourite foods! I tried again. I made successive casts without result. Clearly, my artificial chicken was falling beside a portion of lobster or a plate of ham and salad which were being rapidly swallowed! If I placed my fly beside a dish of lobster, it was a portion of roast beef that was selected! It was impossible to follow their movements. But now I understood. My only chance would be at the end of the meal, when the buffet would have been almost cleared and the greedy diners were hurrying to take advantage of the little that remained. Moreover, darkness would prevent their making a proper choice. However, I tried once or twice more in order to make sure. But it was no use. I therefore waited to give them time to forget and to recapture the advantage of surprise.

At last, towards nine o'clock, the activity of the diners had much diminished. This was the moment. And here was a glutton who wanted yet more! I cast and placed my fly in an empty plate just in front of his nose. Splendid! He was to pay the price of his gluttony and finish his career on our table that evening! He hurled himself on my fly and was compelled to quit the scene of the feast to be imprisoned in my landing-net.

That night at dinner my trout of two pounds, twelve ounces, was the only large fish we had caught that day.

* *Conclusion.* At the end of the Mayfly period, it is in the evening, when the hatch is coming to an end, while the last insects are drifting down and when visibility is very poor, that the big fish, though extremely wary, are most likely to make a fatal error.

In fishing as in shooting you must fire quickly

On the Risle, the two hundred yards of the canal, which works the Catillon turbine and is some six feet deep and ten to twelve yards wide, are full of big trout. The long, waving weeds contain abundant food while the current is but moderate and the water highly oxygenised, which makes this the favourite habitat of the big fish which always like to find their food with a minimum of effort. Hatches are rare and it is only during the Mayfly season, or occasionally at the evening rise, that these fish feed on the surface.

About four o'clock on an afternoon towards the end of May, as I was walking along this sector of the river, I saw a compatriot of Isaak Walton, dressed in a brown tweed knickerbocker suit, which revealed the impeccable cut of a Savile Row tailor, a sky blue Oxford shirt open at the neck to show a red and yellow silk scarf, a Phineas Fogg hat, Cording boots, and his left knee covered with a leather kneeling pad. He had a splendid creel with canvas pockets. Beside him was a big rod and a landing-net of amber-coloured thread and brilliantly polished aluminium.

This elegant figure was sitting on one of the numerous observation benches which are placed at intervals along the reach, and was in process of repairing his leader, made, of course, from Spanish gut. Vernes had warned me the night before: 'If you should meet my guest, Mr X, on the canal, leave the trout alone in that sector and fish else-where.'

I went up to him and introduced myself:

'Any luck?'

'No!'

At that moment, I saw a rise by the further bank and, what was more, it was a very fine fish that had got the better of me the day before by becoming unhooked in a weed-bed, all of which I explained.

'It's your fish.'

'Not on your life, it's yours!'

He refused. I insisted, but not very pressingly. Finally, he decided to go for the fish which, fortunately, was still rising regularly. He began getting out his line with interminable false casts but in the most perfect classical style. The rod moved back-wards and forwards like a slow metronome, describing the most elegant and graceful figures of eight; finally, he placed the fly with delicacy and precision, but the trout had ceased rising. He was refused. He tried again and was again refused. I could hardly bear it, that trout would have been in my landing-net quite some time ago! Fortunately, another trout rose and delicately took a *Danica* in the middle of a big tuft of weed, then rose again and avidly took another ephemerid. Once again, the fisherman gave a splendid exhibition of slow motion, his line going out inch by inch. Again he was too late! The trout had taken cover in the weed. It made me feel quite ill and I had difficulty in restraining myself from telling him the reason for his repeated failures. And what was more, there were two other splendid fish in full activity and within easy reach! But there was nothing to be done about it; British phlegm and dignified deliberation continued to be in evidence, and the landing-net was still dry!

'Your French fish clearly don't like English flies, why don't you offer him one of your Pont-Audemers; it seems they like them in Normandy!'

I required only this excuse to disobey my orders! I went quickly into action and gave our guest the consolation of landing two fine fish, one of them being the fish I had lost the day before. They were each two and three quarter pounds!

I now thought the fellow was in the right mood and that I was no longer in danger of angering him.

'Our trout have the temperament of their country and their habits are like ours. When they sit down to eat, they don't like having to wait to be served; like us, they throw themselves on their food as soon as it's on the plate!'

'Oh, yes! French appetites, eh? Ha! Ha! Thanks, I'm much obliged to you for your good advice.'

And, in all justice, I must state that that evening, when Vernes was writing up the day's catch in his fishing book, the fellow had profited by my advice and was able to announce with a wink: 'Six fish, totalling over eight pounds'.

The moral is that a fish must be tempted when it is anxious to take an insect. These rare moments must not be wasted, they last but a few seconds, rarely a few minutes. The fly must therefore be presented with a minimum of false casts and not a second must be lost, but this does not mean that one must fish precipitately.

Active feeding periods

Sometimes, outside the Mayfly and the evening rise, during approximately half an hour at the most, the fish seem to become possessed by the Devil! They feed like mad. At these times any fly will be taken. What struck me was that these periods of extra-ordinary activity generally took place between eleven and three o'clock, but that they were very rare.

I have seen them twice on the Andelle. On one occasion, Auguste Lambiotte and I were fishing two little tributaries about twenty yards apart at two o'clock in the after-noon. And at the same moment we each caught the two finest fish of the day. The period of super-activity did not last more than twenty minutes.

I achieved my record on the Pollinger Bach, in Bavaria, with Kustermann. This little canal, some three yards wide and three feet deep, is populated with common and rainbow trout with a few grayling in the holes in the lower reaches. A hundred yards from Kustermann's hut, where we were to have luncheon, at about 12.45, having caught a few fish during the course of the morning, Fisher exclaimed: 'Look, Herr Ritz, the fish have gone mad, the surface is boiling with rises!'

I repeat: three yards wide and at this particular spot about three feet deep; the cubic quantity of water is therefore very limited and can only feed a small number of fish. I caught, and we kept alive in Fisher's floating creel, fourteen trout of a reasonable size for dry-fly fishing in precisely fifteen minutes on a fifty-yard stretch. I stopped fishing and, from curiosity, cast a spoon which was taken, so to speak, at every revolution. At the fourth cast, I stopped, lit a pipe and watched.

The hatch was only a small one, but the fish were taking everything, on the surface, at the bottom, half way down; it was absolutely crazy! At ten minutes past one it suddenly ceased. I thereupon carefully tried several fish I could see at a place I had not been previously fishing: they all refused and fled. During the great moment, nothing seemed to frighten them and I was fishing without taking any precautions to conceal myself. Not one was missed, and all the fish were well hooked as they were feeding so freely.

The following year, believing that the days of the month when these periods are most intense are the four or five between the moon's last and first quarter, I had arranged to fish with Kustermann on the Ammer in Bavaria on the 3rd, 4th, 5th, and 6th August. Unfortunately, a violent storm and a sudden spate having occurred on the 31st July and the 1st August, the river only became normal again on the 4th, but the water of the principal tributary had become clear again on the 3rd. This tributary is more of a large mountain torrent than a true river and it has numerous holes. Wishing to make my observations as precise as possible I decided to fish first with a Devon Rublex ·317 ounces in the holes where the fish generally lie best. I knew from experience that when fishing with a Devon one has numerous failures owing to the fish being badly hooked and that more often still, the fish will follow it without taking. Should I be successful, however, the difference would therefore be well marked. With a fly, on the other hand, I ran the risk of falling on a series of isolated cases from which it would be difficult to establish precise conclusions. Late in the morning, I began to investigate the principal holes on the central reach of the tributary with my Devon. This is what I noted in my notebook:

Wednesday, 4th August: the Halbammer river, barometer steady at fine, wind north-west. My friend and I fished upstream a reach about a mile long. From midday to one o'clock the trout were taking very well, every cast was successful. About one o'clock, the fish ceased to take and we had lunch. About two o'clock, we began again, first going down to the two best pools, and then going upstream again to a reach we had not fished in the morning. Result very poor and even, in some pools, completely negative.

Thursday, 5th August: The Ammer river, barometer set fair, wind west. Two of us fished one of the largest pools on the reach where we rarely take a fish on a Devon, but which is fairly good with a fly. Tackle used Pflueger Supreme reel, Devon Rublex ·317 ounces. We began fishing at 12.30: several takes followed by failure. I attacked on the left-hand side of the waterfall: in spite of numerous casts and conscientious search of all the corners, not a take. At one o'clock, the fish started taking furiously: eight casts, eight trout in the landing net! At the same time, Kustermann took five fish. We had to stop in order not to empty the pool. At 2.45, we went back to it and began fishing again: twenty successive casts gave me only two takes which were both failures. At the same time, my ghillie, who had remained watching one of the best places for the fly a hundred and fifty yards upstream, reported that between 1.15 and 1.45, there was a considerable rise, up to twenty fish at once.

Friday, 6th August: the Ammer river, barometer set fair, wind north-west. We took up our positions by a big pool. I began fishing at 1.35, and took two trout; at 1.45, ten casts brought me ten trout. In all, during the next three-quarters of an hour I took fourteen fish without changing my position. At 2.30, there was complete cessation of all activity.

Saturday, 7th August: barometer set fair, wind north-west. It was the last day of our chosen period and the attraction must have been weaker. I decided to try a small and not very good pool which could contain but few fish. Up till then, we had never had any success there with a Devon and very little with a fly. I used a Devon Rublex. At 2.15, I began fishing and in spite of making numerous casts, I only took two small fish, but from 2.40 to 3.00 they were taking in the most extraordinary way! Six casts brought me five fish, the sixth having become unhooked. Ten fish altogether. It must have been all the pool contained.

To sum up: the first day, began fishing at one o'clock: eight casts, eight fish.

Second day: began fishing at 1.45: ten casts, ten fish.

Third day: began fishing at 2.40: six casts, six fish, of which one was lost.

It seems to me that if for three days running, with a difference in time of approximately forty-five minutes a day, it is possible to take twenty-three fish with twenty-four casts, there can be no doubt that the moon has an influence on the fish. They must have been taking the lure exceptionally well to have but one lost out of twenty-four. No fisherman who uses a Devon will contradict me.

Here is another observation from my notebook. Thursday, 26th August: on a lake in Styria, barometer rising, wind north-west, a very difficult place to fish, water very clear, no possibility of concealment. I was fishing from a raft, the fish seeing me all the time, casting lightly, using a spoon and a worm. The first catch was a grayling, then two fine trout, then two takes without hooking the fish between 5.15 and 6 o'clock. At 5.30, another fisherman, fishing with a fly, and casting from the bank, told us that he had lost, after a long fight, a common trout weighing more than four pounds.

These results may be considered exceptional because, for the most part, in spite of a large number of fish in the lake, complete failure is inevitable or nearly so, when the sun is in the sky, at least if there is no wind.

Years ago, in America, on the Mahopac lake, north of New York, I noticed the same phenomenon, taking eight black bass in twenty minutes with a plug, between 12.40 and one o'clock in July, in bright sunlight.

In Norway, on the Aaro, in September 1951, on a Monday, when I was fishing only for sea trout, I took on a spoon, with ·010 in, nylon, a twenty-four pound salmon between twelve and one o'clock! The following Wednesday, a salmon of twenty-seven pounds, still between 12.30 and 1.30!

Whenever possible, if the day is fine and the barometer steady or rising, I try to have luncheon by the water. It is often one of the best moments. Too many fishermen forget the famous proverb: When the cat's away, the mice do play!

It's up to you to decide whether you will follow my example, but there is one undeniable fact: it is always about the middle of the day that these intense though rare periods of activity take place, apart from the evening rise.

The taking of a very big trout

One evening I was after some very big fish with Pierre Creusevaut, on the edge of a big cut. Near the bank was a wide channel free of weed and, three yards further out, regularly spaced weed beds. I suddenly saw a little ring. I cast ten yards upstream near one of the weed beds, but without much conviction. The fish had been taking very badly for the last hour. The fly drifted down and reached the place of rise. Suddenly, it was taken two good yards downstream. I struck, the fish dived, moving downstream, skirting one of the weed beds. If I pulled on him now, as I had too much slack, he would take refuge in the weed bed before I could stop him. If he felt no resistance, he would try on the other hand to get rid of the fly. I took in line as fast as I could with my left hand while raising the rod. As soon as the line was taut, I attacked him strongly. I then saw an enormous trout, doing everything he could to get into a

The Andelle near Radepont (chalk stream)

mass of weed. Luckily, I was able to master him quickly and Pierre arrived just in time to land a fish weighing four pounds, an admirable specimen of a chalkstream trout.

This description may sound rather improbable, but it is absolutely authentic. The almost automatic manoeuvre by which I managed to avoid losing this fine trout was the fruit of numerous similar experiences.

The whole technique of catching big chalkstream trout consists above all in holding the fish with a very tight line and with strength, in remaining calm and foreseeing what the fish will try to do to regain his freedom.

Practical advice

1. HOW TO GET A FISH OUT OF A WEED BED

It often happens in weedy rivers that the fish succeeds immediately after the strike in getting into a weed bed. In such cases, the best tactics would appear to be the following:

(*a*) Try putting pressure on him at once with the rod raised and then with the rod horizontal;

(*b*) Take up your position in the direction opposite to the line and start again;

(*c*) In case of failure, give some slack, wait a few seconds and pull suddenly. Often, when the fish no longer feels the pressure, it lets go if it has bitten on the weed, or again, it will try to leave the weed bed if the line has not become caught up round a tuft of weed.

This is the best one can do, but ultimate success is not guaranteed.

2. LEVELS OR LINES OF VISION

The difference in the levels or lines of vision of the fisherman on the bank and the fisherman wading has an influence on the length of the cast, particularly on that of the first cast.

When fishing from the bank there is always a tendency to cast short.

When wading on the other hand there is a tendency to cast too long.

The less slanting the line of vision the greater the precision.

In casting competitions, Creusevaut asserts that the best results are obtained in the tests in which the casting is done from a platform. One must, however, realise that

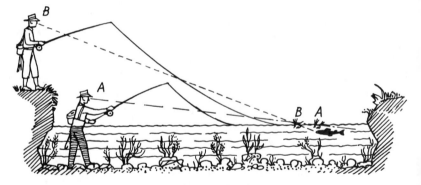

Fig 57 The more perpendicular one's line of vision to the surface of the water, the more accurate one's cast will be

the competitor is not casting as he would when fishing. During the false casts he maintains his fly above the target. Moreover, a final cast on an inclined plane accentuates the curve of the line at the moment of placing the fly, which leads one to suppose that it is moving slightly backwards. On the other hand, the higher the fisherman's eye above the surface of the water, the better he sees the fish. A fisherman of small stature sees fewer fish than a tall one.

3. HOW TO UNHOOK THE FLY
FROM A BRANCH ON THE OPPOSITE BANK

When fishing the opposite bank where trees or branches overhang the river, it sometimes happens that the fly gets caught up in a bough. If a light pull does not release it, it is often possible to succeed in loosening it and avoid a break and the loss of the fly by making a roll cast in the air, that is to say by making a roll cast as if the line were on the water. In order to do this, it is necessary:

(a) To bring the rod back to the position of one o'clock, slacken the line so that it falls behind the rod, holding the latter high enough so that at the moment of making the roll, the loop travels along the line in the air on an approximate level with the point at which the hook is caught.

(b) Suddenly lower the point of the rod to just beyond the three o'clock position. As soon as the loop begins travelling, raise the point of the rod to eleven o'clock. In case of failure, try it again two or three times.

On an average of once in three times you have a good chance of releasing the hook on condition that you have not sunk the point of the hook into the wood by pulling on the line before roll casting. Therefore, as soon as you feel yourself to be caught up, at all costs avoid pulling hard on the line or giving sharp jerks with the point of the rod. It is better to try the roll at once. Do not forget to inspect the hook and the end of the leader.

If you get caught up in a branch close to, the best thing to do is to tighten the line gently and tap on the rod above the butt. If the fly is within reach of the point of the rod, slip the top ring of the rod up to the fly and try to unhook it.

Always inspect the line, the leader and the hook.

Never pull on the line with the rod and, above all, do not jerk with the tip of the rod because there is a danger of deforming the rod tip and even of breaking. It often happens that, at some later period, the rod will break or become deformed in the actual process of fishing and the fisherman will unjustly attribute the accident to a fault in manufacture.

Never pull on the rod to free the hook from weed, either forwards or backwards. It is death to it.

Pull directly on the line at the rod tip.

4. PRECAUTIONS AGAINST CERTAIN DANGERS

Since fishing trout and grayling is not quite the safe and peaceable exercise the profane imagine, it may be useful to indicate and classify the various accidents which can overtake the fisherman.

Beside the water

* 1 *Barbed wire.* Tetanus. Get inoculated.

* 2 *Loose stone walls.*

* 3 *Dangerous bulls.* Climb a tree or take to the river.

* 4 *Snakes.* Look where you put your hand when climbing out of the stream. Be careful when searching for a lost object in grass or brambles. Carry anti-snake venom.

* 5 *Hornets.* In holes in old willows. On a lesser scale, horse flies (Loue), midges (Aube). In northern countries, midges and black flies. Provide yourself with repellants.

* 6 *Overhanging banks.* Due to spates (Doubs, Aube, Ain, etc.). Take care where you put your feet.

* 7 *Avalanches of rock.* In the gorges of the Ain or in mountain streams, luckily fairly rare.

* 8 *Wet boards.* On bridges and dams. Walk very slowly, particularly if wearing rubber boots.

* 9 *Rotten boards.* On bridges.

* 10 *Frost.* Everywhere.
* 11 *Water rats' holes.* Risle, Andelle, Charentonne.

In the water

Generally speaking, wading always has certain dangers which require care and attention. The first and imperative rule is that you must never take a step forward without being certain that your remaining foot is solidly based on the bottom of the river. Those whose age or physical inaptitude makes them less active, should carry a stick attached to them like a bandolier which will serve as a third leg in difficult places (wading staff).

* 1 *Quicksands or mud.* When taking to the water from the bank and about to place your foot on what looks like a solid bottom, you will frequently be surprised to discover that it is far less solid than it seems. Indeed, you may well be in danger of drowning, breaking your leg or getting a soaking at least. Try the bottom first with a stick.

* 2 *Variations in depth* when wading in a river subject to sudden variations in level owing to a dam upstream.

* 3 *When fishing upstream in rapids* and wearing waders and you come suddenly to deep water which is not negotiable, you may well find it impossible to return to your point of departure owing to lack of visibility due to eddies or the pressure of the current.

* 4 *When fishing in gorges* where, for lack of paths, you have to cross fords to return to your point of departure, there is danger if the river is subject to sudden spates following on storms or if the water quickly becomes rough. Never move without knowing precisely where the fords are.

* 5 *Chalk overhangs.* In rivers with chalky waters, such as the Loue and the Ain, there is danger of overhangs suddenly giving way beneath your feet.

* 6 *Granite slabs.* Yonne and Cure. It is impossible to stand on the smooth sloping slabs.

* 7 *The blue clay* of the Ain and Canadian Pacific rivers. Often covered with a thin layer of sand. As slippery as ice.

* 8 *Holes.* You must be careful of them everywhere. Never move forward without looking, particularly over unknown bottoms.

* 9 *Waders* with lacing hooks. Avoid them at all costs, because the line may become entangled in them.

* 10 *Rocks* which a drifting boat may hit.

* 11 *Ricochetting bullets in the hunting season.*

Dangers from tackle

* *1 A fly* in the eye, the ear, or the face of a ghillie or companion. Look behind you to see that you have room to cast, particularly in a boat.

* *2 Hooks* in the finger while manipulating them. In the ear, the face or the eye in a high wind. Be provided with wire cutters.

* *3 Fishing for salmon with a fly.* Using big salmon flies in a wind, particularly with people fishing salmon for the first time and lacking experience in casting with two handed rods. Very dangerous; risk of losing an eye. Wear ski-ing glasses.

* *4 Gaffs.* Falling, getting caught up while crossing obstacles or merely in using them. Always have your gaff furnished with a sheath.

* *5 Walking through woods.* Never hold the leader. Getting the line caught in a branch will drive the hook into your hand.

* *6 Spoons or devons* which come back and hit you violently on the head after touching an obstacle.

* *7 Loss of tackle.* Landing net sunk near the bank. Place a mark. A red or white rag attached to a post.

* *8 Pockets.* For fly boxes, tackle, etc. Should be deep if on the stomach (fishing waistcoats). They must close properly; or when bending down things will fall out.

* *9 Protecting your rod.* Always walk with the point of the rod to the rear, whether in the open or among trees, so as to avoid a break.

* *10 Don't place the rod on the ground.* Particularly when greasing the line, putting on the leader, etc. Your friend will inevitably step on it, or if he does not, cows or horses will.

* *11 Don't let your line or leader trail on the ground.* Your dogs are certain to get entangled. Every year, my dog-loving friends give me several rods to repair, and this has been going on for many years!

* *12 When wading in the wind,* always turn your back to it before opening your box of flies.

PART VI * HOW I HAVE SEEN THEM DO IT

A day's fishing on the Ain with Simonet

Maurice Simonet plies his trade as a cobbler at Ney, a little village in the Jura, near Champagnole. But, over and above this, he is private keeper on one of the best beats of the Ain. He is also an exceptionally good fly fisherman.

He is an attractive character. A solid Comtois, well set up, with a good-humoured expression behind his bushy grey moustache. His grey-blue eyes, hidden under thick eyebrows, light up with a gleam of irony when he talks. In all weathers and by all conditions of water, he still, at sixty, perambulates both by day and by night the $3\frac{3}{4}$ miles of river under his care. It flows through a wooded gorge among a chaos of rocks. He is the terror of poachers!

He was one of my first instructors in 1933.

In 1945, Auguste Lambiotte, Dr Tixier and I decided to return to the Ain and watch Simonet and his methods of fishing.

Of all the fishermen whom I have been privileged to watch on the water, Simonet has impressed me the most. It is impossible to make a comparison between him and Godart, because the rivers they fish are so very different, but I think that for moderate distances, Simonet is unbeatable, while Albert Godart is unapproachable for long distances.

To watch Simonet fish is to be conscious of the magic of dry fly fishing by wading in all its splendour.

In general, trout in mountain rivers are easier than those in chalkstreams owing to the smaller number of insects and hatches, but the Ain presents the angler with more difficulties to overcome than our best chalkstreams. The water is clear, the currents fast and the trout of the Ain very wary.

It was in July that we watched Simonet. The river was low and very clear, there was a nasty wind blowing, the sun was bright overhead and insects very rare on the water. These conditions on a river of the Comté, though they could not have been less favourable, did not impress Simonet. Having fished the same river since 1903, he has learned how to succeed whatever the weather. In 1945, he estimated that he had caught during his career as an angler approximately one hundred thousand fish, of which two-thirds were trout and one-third grayling!

* *His tackle.* He uses a 9 ft. rod which facilitates the back-handed and semi-horizontal

casts. The butt and centre of the rod are of ash and the tip of black bamboo. The weight is about 10½ oz, 9½ oz at least. I do not know if you realise how much strength is required to manipulate such a rod for eight hours a day with fifteen minutes rest to eat. It's almost unbelievable!

After my last visit, I had a 9 ft. split cane rod made for him at the Amboise factory. I wanted a light rod with reasonable speed, in spite of its length, which presented a nice problem. After a good many trials with Plantet, we succeeded in manufacturing a rod which was entirely to Simonet's satisfaction. I fear, however, that this model will find no other takers!

His reel is an ordinary one but with a very big drum to recover line quickly. His line has a double taper.

For flies, he uses but two patterns. A ginger brown hackle with a red body and a blue dun hackle with a yellow body of the spider type, which he ties himself. The cocks in his backyard provide him with the hackles. Hook No.12. Tails fan-shaped and bent downwards. He believes in the exact body-colour for dry flies, particularly for grayling.

His leader is made of nylon Rafale type of 9 feet to 10 feet in length with a taper of ·010 inches to ·009 inches.

He uses waders, of which he gets through a good many, but only for fishing in cold waters. Otherwise, he fishes in ordinary trousers and has managed to avoid the rheumatics!

He greases his line once before beginning to fish. Never oils the flies. He always keeps his fly dry by false casts.

For a creel he uses a big zinc box, without holes or cover, so that the fish may remain dry, even when he is wading in deep water. This box is called a *bouille* on the Jura rivers. A big ring fixed to the strap of the box holds a round landing-net with a stiff wooden handle which he slips through the ring. The landing-net is thus immediately at hand while the handle can be used as a wading staff by leaning on the loop which is very strong. The handle is 31½ inches. The loop 19½ inches.

* *His cast.* He reduces it to the simplest form. He casts semi-horizontally or back-handed, both executed with absolute perfection; his placing of the fly on the water has unequalled precision. He does not use left-hand pull, for the simple reason that with a 9 ft. rod it is useless. I made him try one of our 8½ ft. rods, but he was not at ease with it. His forward cast begins when his line is still curved like a hairpin. This is correct with a very long rod. He very rarely uses the overhead cast and always ends with a little shoot.

* *His tactics and ideas.* Simonet prefers casting upstream for rapid currents and across

165

for slow ones. Short casts as much as possible. His placing of the fly on the water is delicate, light and quick, after a careful approach and without ever alarming the fish. He walks as lightly as possible to avoid vibrations. He gets as near as possible to the centre of the river. He can thus cast back-handed for the right bank and semi-horizontally for the left, in order to present the fly before the leader.

He wastes no time over refusals. His approach and presentation being impeccable, he very seldom has refusals owing to making errors. If the fish has not risen at the third presentation, it is because it is at that moment untakable. He considers that the loss of time occasioned by continuing to try stubbornly for an acceptance is not worth the labour.

He always holds the line under the middle finger of his right hand to get a more rapid strike. He likes long rods because they allow him to hold the fish's head out of the water more easily and to get it off balance at the moment of the strike and also prevent it from diving beneath the surface.

He lands most trout, except big ones, very quickly. They slide across the surface and, as soon as they are within reach of his landing-net, it goes straight down into the water.

Lambiotte has often timed him and has discovered that there are very rarely more than six seconds between the strike and the landing.

A badly embedded hook always ends by tearing itself out. If the fish is really badly hooked and likely to become unhooked, the danger will certainly not be diminished by going slowly at the business!

He much prefers fishing by sight. A fish seen is a fish almost caught! He looks carefully for fish under the banks, particularly when fishing grayling. In sunlight, he wastes little time on smooth and open waters. Though every good place must always be tried, whatever the conditions. He believes that the quivering of the caudal and dorsal fins of a trout indicate wariness, even if the fish does not move from its position. In such circumstances he considers it useless to present the fly.

When the fish are bulging and tailing and taking just below the surface, he still maintains his average. He merely changes his tactics and makes the fly pass almost over the trout's nose, when he has once tried the normal method. He believes that a deviation of a radius of 20 inches, whether to left or right, whether upstream or down, will result in a refusal. He remembers a big trout which continually ignored his fly till, at the fifteenth presentation, it almost hit the fish on the nose!

Simonet's strength lies in:

1. His sight, which allows him to see almost imperceptible differences in the colour of the water and thereby to detect the presence of a fish at a given place. He marks it

and very quickly succeeds in seeing it and determining its precise position. I have met anglers with this gift in Austria, Bavaria and America, but never with it so developed as with Simonet;

2. His perfection of approach and his great stability while wading. The Ain has often a very slippery bottom. He walks about the bottom of the river as if on a highway and appears to have eyes in his feet! He never makes a false step and never creates a vibration by tripping over a stone;

3. His accuracy of judgment as to the area of drift in which he must place his fly, followed by precise and infinitely delicate placing, allows the fish to see his fly, which he keeps very upright on the water, only at the last moment. His false casts are never within the fish's area of vision, even in shallows of less than 10 inches;

4. The perfection of his backhand casting;

5. His faculty for limiting his movements to the indispensable and the productive;

6. His perfect knowledge of the river, of which he knows every stone;

7. His instinct for conservation and his strict adherence to the rules of the sport. When he catches a fish of under the legal size, he takes the leader in one hand and the fish in the other while holding it in the water, removes the hook and waits till he is quite certain the fish is alive before letting it go.

The day I watched him fish there were frequent circular gusts of wind, but they did not prevent his placing his fly with precision and delicacy.

By the end of the day, when the evening rise began, I felt inclined to give up fishing, for I felt that I had still so much to learn!

That day, Simonet had kept fifteen fish and Lambiotte three. Yet, I consider the latter unbeatable for his average catch.

How Edouard Vernes fishes

My good friend, Edouard Vernes, the most excellent of hosts, is the happy possessor of two treasures whose combination makes a very rare whole for an angler: the finest of trout fishing and the most skilled of fisherwomen. It is always a pleasure to me to watch Mme Vernes performing with such ease on the admirable reaches of the Risle, searching for the big trout which, more often than not, succumb to her mastery. But that is not the whole story! The gambols of her pack of fox terriers, that follow her everywhere, are the delight of MM. Pezon and Michel. The number of rods broken every year by these enchanting animals, past masters at the art of entangling themselves in a line and breaking a rod tip, increases considerably the turnover of the repairs effected at Amboise.

It is thanks to Edouard Vernes and his fishing that, since 1930, I have been in a position to perfect my numerous prototypes of fly rod, and I want to thank him for his inexhaustible kindness.

The extent and variety of the Valleville fishing, which contains innumerable trout, make it a trial ground unique in the world as well as the finest chalkstream fishing in Europe.

Edouard has taught me much about fishing chalkstreams. The pages of his fishing diary show that he is nearly always the day's champion. He knows his water as Culbertson his bridge, and seems always, during hatches, to be in the places where the fish, particularly the big ones, are most active. He selects his locality according to the season. But he prefers above all places with the minimum of light.

His years of experience have given him many landmarks. For instance, during the Mayfly, he avoids the rapid waters of the narrows and currents, knowing that the big trout, still too weak to stem the stream, will not be active in those parts till later. For preference he chooses the artificial river, a narrow canal, which is both deep and slow.

He keeps a list of the positions of all the big fish, so that they can be regularly watched. And though, from one year to the next, there are sometimes changes, thanks to his sense of the water he finds them again very quickly.

He thinks the best period is before the 15th May, approximately from the 5th to the 15th.

He prefers fishing upstream, except for distance casts which he makes across the river. He never fishes with a tight line, always with a bit of slack, gets very quickly on to a fish, and attacks at once, provided he has seen exactly where and how it rises, otherwise he prefers to wait till he is sure. If the fish continues to rise beside his fly, he will present five or six times, and then come back later.

His maxim is above all a sporting one. A trout he sees rising is a trout he has got to take. He limits his false casts to the minimum.

During periods when flies are rare on the water, he fishes by preference at a distance, at the precise moment of the rise, when the slightest error will result in a merciless refusal, but takes every necessary precaution to ensure success.

During the Mayfly, he uses nylon with a point of ·010 inches. During the fly fishing season, there are often eight or ten rods on the river which, during the twenty years I have been fishing it, has given me unrivalled opportunities for observing a variety of techniques.

Edouard is a most perspicacious observer whom nothing escapes, and his extraordinary memory produces immediately that precious piece of information that can be so vital when one is hesitant or at a loss.

His strike is perhaps a little hard, but this is due to his being accustomed to fishing rivers encumbered with weed.

He despises the wet fly and the nymph; he is a hundred per cent purist of the dry fly and a great lover of nature, passionately devoted to the preservation of his fishing.

Three days on the Andelle with Albert Godart
15th to 18th May, 1947

The champion long-distance fly caster with a fly rod of 3½ to 4oz is also one of the best fishermen in Europe.

In 1947, Auguste Lambiotte invited Godart to fish on the Andelle, at Radepont, during the Mayfly season, from the 15th to the 18th May, so that I might have the opportunity of watching him.

He has been fishing from childhood, having begun with a hazel stick. At that time he used to play truant, unable to resist the bank of the Semoy, near Bouillon, his natal district. At fourteen, he had already taken thousands of trout.

In order to arrive at precise and exact conclusions, I had to take into consideration the fact that Godart, a professional champion, who makes his living by giving lessons and selling tackle, had a certain natural anxiety to impress those watching him fish. He is so expert that he need not have bothered.

* *His cast*. He likes casting long and straight. Godart's cast is typical because, during the back and forward trajectory of the line, the tip of his rod, between eleven and two o'clock, follows a slight curve high, low, high. This movement allows the line to deploy while rising fairly high, in particular for long casts. A slight pull with the left hand adds the necessary correction. Most anglers do not practice this cast. Those who do not know how to take advantage of shortening the line, by a pull with the left hand at the moment it loses speed, touch down behind.

Godart insists on the maximum looseness of the grip so as to preserve suppleness and eliminate jerks. He holds his rod with thumb and forefinger and only grips it with the other fingers at the precise moment of transmitting power and speed (the beginning of the back and forward casts). He thus eliminates the fatigue which always results from a too-powerful grip.

To extend the line and drop it on the water, he accompanies the movement of his wrist with a fairly strong pressure downwards of the thumb, the rod ending below nine o'clock, practically at eight o'clock.

He rarely dries his fly with amadou or other means. In general, he dries it with false casts. The back and forward movement is begun just before the leader is completely extended, thus forming a loop of a foot at the maximum. This produces an effect like cracking a whip and dries the fly. One can see a little cloud of droplets of water. Very precise timing is necessary.

He always holds three or four coils of line in his left hand and shoots them at each presentation, except for short casts. He reduces false casts to the essential minimum.

His straight cast, with the rod coming down perpendicularly, gives him great precision and he places his fly within a maximum radius of 20 inches from the fish's head, even for casts of 20 yards. His casting is rapid and the line whistles a little. The trajectory of the line is very tight.

His side casting is as perfect as his straight casting. As he casts, one has the impression that he is aiming with the point of the rod.

I look on Godart as the king of long side casts. At the last competition of the C.C.F. in Paris, I watched him from very close to, when, before going up on to the platform, he was trying a rigid rod with a heavy line on the ground. His backward and forward hauls started from his feet in order to obtain the maximum of power over the minimum of distance. When he went on to the platform and was using a borrowed rod, which was much more supple, he immediately altered his whole style, going much more with his rod and nevertheless achieving remarkable casts.

* *His views.* He does not believe in the elbow against the body.

He does not believe in the curve cast, his dexterity allowing him to do without it.

He does not hesitate to finish the fly's drift with a slight drag.

He never hurries. If a fish ceases to rise, he waits for it to start again.

He prefers the fly to fall vertically. He believes that the trout, seeing the artificial fly fall from the sky, takes it for a natural one, which excites it and incites it to take it. He considers that this method of placing is the most delicate. He sometimes likes to give an appearance of life to the fly with a slight movement of the rod tip, a speciality of Belgian anglers. He says he can see the fish very well when it rises to look at the fly.

His striking is delicate, the rod rather low and, when at distance, almost horizontal, while he moves the rod point upstream.

* *Tackle.* His preference is for short rods of 8 to 8½ feet maximum, stiff, with a fine, almost untapered line to obtain extra light placing. He has completely adopted nylon for his leaders; these are of three yards in length with a point of ·009 to ·011 inches. He sometimes goes as low as ·007 inches. He often dyes them brown with tea.

* *Flies.* He prefers American dressings. Very much likes the ginger hackle with the yellow body. Will take fish with any pattern provided it has visible hackles with good hooks, but insists on impeccable dressing. Attaches much importance to the size.

* *Observations.* The principal reasons for his great success are:

1. His remarkable aptitude for seeing exactly where a rise takes place and not losing sight of it;

2. His mastery in casting which gives him unequalled precision, particularly on long casts;

3. His excellent eyesight, his calmness and that particular angler's sense that only professionals who have spent the major part of their lives since childhood on rivers can acquire;

4. His mastery in side casting;

5. The abnormal size of his thumb, giving him a grip that is probably unique in the world. When Godart was at the zenith of his powers I do not believe there was another caster in the world capable of beating him in long casting in the dry fly style.

I remember that one year, before the last war, at a C.C.F. Competition, I had the opportunity of examining his right hand. It was covered with dried blisters and even raw places, owing to the power of his grip.

I am of the opinion that one may well take example from Godart's method of casting, particularly when fishing from the bank for distant fish, but that one should not limit oneself exclusively to it. To obtain great precision with this particular cast, one must be a very expert caster, a master of timing and have a strong hand. Its principal advantage is that it raises the line high at the back. The placing on the water with this cast, however, limits the length of the drift without drag.

His method of drying the fly is my favourite and also Simonet's, but it requires an iron wrist. One gains much time, but it is tiring and can be dangerous if the rod is not of superior quality or if one's timing is not exact.

The vertical placing of the fly partly destroys the effect of surprise, but this depends on the exact field of vision of the fish.

* *General conclusions.* There are no magicians in fishing, particularly for the fish of the Andelle! They are great gentlemen who have a right to the angler's respect and refuse to be hustled.

Godart was supreme on long casts in the narrows. The first and second day, on the smooth waters of the lower reaches, when the fish were delicately taking insects flying at surface level, he succeeded no better than we did. But the third day, having carefully studied the conditions, he spent the afternoon on one of the Château tributaries, fishing by sight, and obtained excellent results.

Godart is a great master, a phenomenon of dry fly fishing, and I wonder whether we shall ever see another caster of his quality.

How Tony Burnand fishes

Tony Burnand, a fisherman? Yes, of course! But above all a flutterer, a butterfly who prefers hovering by the water to alighting on it, who appreciates delicacy of touch in fishing as much as he does in literature, happy to place his fly on the reflection of a cloud or a flower, more sensitive to the copper glow of the rings at the evening rise, than to the importance of the fish that made them, more taken with the frame than with the picture.

He does not belong to that category of irresistible fishermen for whom a trout seen is a trout caught. He misses many, but by and large makes up for it.

From the point of view of casting, his hobby is the side cast because he is obsessed with drag which, however, he knows how to use artfully to make shy fish rise. It is not for nothing that he has fished for several weeks each year the rivers of the Massif Central and of the Pyrenees, where the dragged fly succeeds.

He says he uses only one pattern of fly, always the same: a fly of varying shades of grey and of varying size, a completely neutral fly, which succeeds when used small in the morning and very large in the evening. In fact, he always carries ten boxes full of all sorts of patterns which he tries for amusement's sake, fortuitously, convinced that the fashion in which they are presented counts for much more than their shape or colour.

He also has his faults. He is impatient, has a craze for moving up and down the river, and succeeds in getting himself into an appalling state of nerves when things go against him: wind, vegetation, leader, fly, reeds, etc., and this happens frequently! Like all anglers who have acquired a philosophy, he neither boasts of his successes nor grumbles at his failures, since he is always happier by the water than anywhere else. He says that he is as happy casting in vain throughout a whole afternoon, as he is at catching dozens of small or moderate fish taken without difficulty, and therefore in his eyes without merit. Indeed, he is sufficiently disinterested to bear no grudge towards the big fish that has broken him or become unhooked, provided he can feel that he has mastered it to the point of bringing it to his feet or that he has been more clever than the fish has. But if he should entangle his fly in vegetation, either by land or river, several times running, he gets into a cold rage in which he might well break his rod in small pieces and give up the idiotic game for ever!

From the point of view of tackle, he began, like all French anglers, by breaking his wrist with long, heavy, soft rods. The day when tempered bamboo rods first became available to us, he became their keen disciple, but as he grew older, he adopted a compromise formula: a light, strong, supple rod, with which he likes to cast at distances which he himself calls absurd. Tony Burnand finally adopted the P.P.P. Zephyr Burnand type, which I made especially for him.

He came rather late to fly fishing, by means of the little spoon cast with a fly rod. If he gained a peculiar vigour with his right arm, he also acquired an unhappy tendency to excessive roughness in his movements and a poor appreciation of the timing necessary to fly fishing. It was his initiation into the little spoon on the fly rod which nevertheless brought him little by little to find his road to Damascus. His increasing contacts with skilled fly fishermen, from every region and every social level, gave him the chance to perfect his technique.

What was particularly useful to him was the fact that he fished extremely varied waters, both in France and elsewhere, which necessitated his adapting himself instantly to all types of river, wide and narrow, clear and weedy, turbulent and smooth. He thereby acquired not only dexterity, but a useful sense of water, though he has never been able to control the enthusiasm which makes him cover miles of river, starting again on the same reach two or three times, while more placid fishermen are flogging only a few hundred yards of water.

Burnand is not the man to insist on a big fish, nor is he a man of one fly or of one method, dry, wet or semi-wet, nor, finally, a man of single rises. He belongs to the quick and impatient type, he wants to get results quickly and is not willing to solve a problem he judges to be too difficult. He is more inclined to fish the water than rises, will try rapidly one after the other every corner in which there might be fish, will cast two or three times and then pass on to the next. As he has a sense of water, a correct cast and indefatigable enthusiasm to attack every fish he sees and even those he doesn't see, he succeeds in catching a good number, of which he puts back a considerable proportion because not only does he dislike carrying them, but he dislikes killing them.

He always uses a weight-forward line, an automatic reel, but also, and it is his only real peculiarity, he uses an excessively long leader, twice the length of his rod, thanks to which his placing is rarely rough even if its precision is easily impaired by the slightest breath of air.

In action he is moving continually and with elegance, his rod making graceful arabesques in the air with the line while seeking a tempting lie.

His style is very classical, with a good left hand. He throws the line in a figure of eight and has a tendency to start the forward cast while he still has a loop at the back. He could be more precise at his first presentation, but this is due to the extreme length of his leader.

He likes talking to the fish as much as to his companions. According to circumstances, he flatters them or insults them. He is capable of meeting every kind of adversity without becoming discouraged.

Auguste Lambiotte, an exceptional fisherman

Auguste Lambiotte is one of the best amateur anglers. The regularity with which he gets results is remarkable, on whatever river he may be fishing. He has one advantange, his great height, which gives him the maximum of vision of the fish and a great facility in wading (his height and weight allow him to reach many fish that would be impossible for most of us). He holds the record for the Traun, with a brace of three and five pounds into the bargain.

His method of fishing is based on speed and the obtaining of results. He never allows himself to get lost in the thousand and one futilities into which we are all too prone to fall. When he wakes up in the morning, he carefully prepares his plan of battle for the day, consulting his annual records in which he keeps all his observations and results as well as those of his friends. He pays particular attention to the conditions of light according to the hour of the day, and seeks places sheltered from that obstacle which is the wind. His first day, on returning to a beat for the first time in the year, is largely devoted to a general inspection during which he seeks out the best places for fish and marks down the positions of the big ones, particularly the most inaccessible, which he will continue to attack until they make the fatal error.

His tactics consist of determining the exact placing of each presentation, which must be immediate and impeccable (the fly well dried, floating high and in front of the point of the nylon, both fly and leader carefully oiled). His speed, which is accompanied by remarkable precision, allows him very frequently to surprise the fish which will have seen nothing till the dry fly begins to drift practically on to its nose. To achieve this, he uses the side cast as much as possible, with the minimum of false casts, dropping the leader in a curve, most of the time at average distances. He casts long only by exception, preferring to use the time he would lose in seeking places where the fish are active. His fly is constantly at work.

His strike, which is nearly always instantaneous but gentle, is one of the main reasons for his success.

His unceasing concentration and self-discipline have made of him a machine of great precision but with nothing of the robot, since his intelligence, complemented by great good sense, directs all his operations. And, to complete his armoury, his enthusiasm and terrific keenness keep him constantly active from the beginning of the day until dusk, when he often continues to try for the last of the last! He likes difficulties and has a marked preference for water which makes him give of his best, such as the Aube, for instance. For him, the Normandy chalkstreams are merely

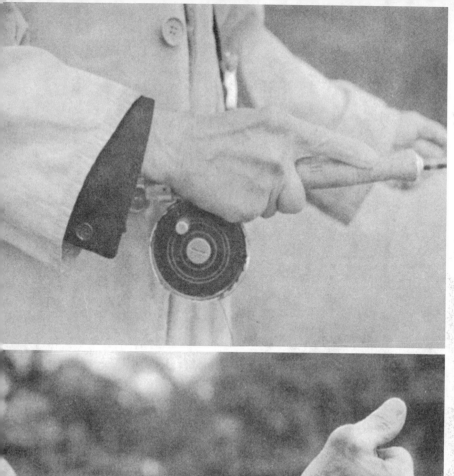

Deformed hands after decades of fly fishing
: *Herr Campagna's index finger   below: The thumb of Albert Godat, the world champion*

Madison River in Montana typifies western U.S. rainbow trout streams

above: On the McKenzie River in Oregon
below: The great fishing platform on the Aaro

amusing. He seems always to have found the exact fly, which he rarely changes, since his percentage of acceptances is almost incredible.

* *Tackle*. He uses a Master 8 ft. 3 in. in two pieces, which I invented specially for his technique, which demands a machine that can be used for a great variety of purposes, and has the maximum of oscillation and unvarying precision.

He uses only weight-forward lines, long leaders Rafale type and an automatic reel.

* *Flies*. He has a very nearly complete collection of those used on our rivers, but for 95 per cent of the time he contents himself with a few well-tried patterns which have been proved over the years. The grey with the yellow or green body, a Panama, a light Cahill in two sizes, an Iron Blue Dun. Of the smaller varieties, grayling flies, he uses a Lunn's Particular with straight wings and one Spent which he uses for difficult fish but only rarely, since he nearly always succeeds in taking them by surprise. He attaches great importance to the precise dimensions of the natural fly of the moment.

During a day's fishing, he always makes a greater number of presentations to different fish than anyone else without in any way disturbing his companions' fishing. He has often offered me a fish which he thought might be interesting.

Here are his own views and the reasons for his great mastery.

Like many leaders of industry after their forties, he looked about for some form of relaxation to the feverish life of a businessman. To be of any use, this relaxation had to be complete. He found it in dry fly fishing (though he is an excellent wet fly fisherman, which was how he started). Moreover, he believes that his favourite sport is an excellent method of judging his general physical and mental condition and that, the day he discerns a lowering in his average, it will be time to reduce his business activities and devote himself more to golf!

Each time he sees a fish rise, he feels that it has done so for the sole purpose of defying him and he immediately enters into competition with it.

He won his spurs on such uninteresting rivers in the Nievre as he could reach from his factory in company with his inseparable companion, Dr Tixier. The fish, constantly being harried by local anglers and poachers, were rare and presented him with difficult problems. But his training as an industrial leader had taught him from his youth not to admit mediocrity or accept defeat. From the start, he applied his principles to fishing. He made rapid progress and achieved the mastery which has made him the complete fly fisherman. At that time, he was unable to take his holidays at the best periods of the year. Between March and October, therefore, he was compelled to search for a fish over six or seven hours and several miles of dull fishing on which there was practically no hatch, and, when he had found his fish, he had to present it with a fly in such a way that it would be sufficiently interested to leave the bottom.

Dry fly water on classic Beaver Kill River

His eye had to be constantly on the water, ready to mark at once by stumps, weed, etc., even the most distant rises. This early training had a prime influence on his method of fishing and he is still affected by it today in spite of his sixty-six years, and even on the well-stocked rivers of Normandy, probably because any modification of his methods might diminish his sense of relaxation.

He takes a great interest in his friends' results, not in order to make sure that he has triumphed over them once again, but because he believes that you can always learn something, even from people less skilled than yourself. His pride is not directed at his friends but at himself, it is a pride concerned solely with maintaining his form.

For him, the first necessity is to hunt down fish everywhere, and then act quickly and with precision. He fishes both with his legs and his head.

I do not mind prophesying that, next year, he will also take to fishing with a nymph as Sawyer conceives it, a form of fishing which every great fisherman should know.

The American school

The American fly fisherman came into being about 1860, and drew his inspiration from the English school, using principally tackle imported from Great Britain. But he soon realised that English flies bore no resemblance to the insects of his own country. The conditions on the rivers in the neighbourhood of New York or in Pennsylvania have nothing in common with the rivers in the South of England. The Beaverkill, the Œsopus, the West Branch, and the Tobyhana have rapid currents and few weed beds. The climate is colder in winter and hotter in summer. The insects are large and smaller in number. There are big deep pools and you fish mostly by wading.

The practical sense of the Americans quickly decided them that modifications in tackle were required: flies that floated better and were very visible, more rapid and lighter rods.

Three pioneers of American fishing were principally responsible for the evolution of American fly fishing: Hewitt, for general influence, George La Branche, a veritable acrobat, whose book, *Dry Fly Fishing in Fast Water*, will remain the masterpiece of American fishing literature, and Theodore Gordon, who created the principal patterns of American tying, of which the celebrated Quill Gordon is a perfect example.

Later, when the influence of the Middle West (Rockies) fishermen and the Pacific fishermen began to become manifest, a new type appeared, particularly among the young. They became a combination of dry fly, nymph, bucktail and streamer fishermen, owing to the number of big fish, many rainbow trout among them, which lie in big holes and are rarely takable on the surface.

It is from the American method of tying flies that I believe European fishermen have most to learn. In dry fly fishing, the American has one rule: he demands a very visible fly which can be placed very straight. I may add that they are past masters of the bucktail and streamer and of submerged drift with a nymph, which is different from Skues's nymph fishing owing to that fact that the fish are less selective in American rivers. It is above all precision of presentation, so that the nymph passes close to the fish, that is important. The American often fishes very deep with wet fly, nymph, etc. In the Pacific rivers, which are wide and rapid and contain not only ordinary trout, but rainbow and steelhead, tackle must be powerful, indeed I would say that in general a very light two-handed rod of ten or twelve feet would seem necessary, but the American prefers the one-handed rod. It is therefore essential, for making distance casts, to shoot very long.

The American rod-maker, Winston, has searched for the extra light and has created the Winston Hollow Built, a hollow rod of split bamboo that is a marvel, the 10 ft models being as light as the standard 9 ft.

For a long shoot, steelhead fishermen used to carry on their stomachs a flat basket on which reposed the part of the line to be shot. Today, an ingenious machine, a big fixed drum, carried in the same way, permits casts of over one hundred feet in length, with a forward taper line with a short, thick taper prolonged rearwards with a backing of monofilament nylon spliced to the taper. This is used with single-handed, light rods.

Al McClane, Fishing Editor of *Field and Stream*, is the perfect type of the new generation of American anglers, an analysis of whose methods is, in my opinion, of real interest. They are all first-class casters, great sportsmen and capable of initiating themselves very rapidly even into grayling fishing which is very little known in the United States.

I do not instance the great Knight, the father of solunar tables, one of the great rods of our epoch. In my opinion, he represents the mixed, though highly evolved, school, and he would be a less striking example than McClane.

In 1950, Bumby Hemingway, son of the great writer, a perfect representative of the Far Western angler, came to try the trout on the Risle and showed himself to be extremely proficient from the very first day. He has exactly the same technique as McClane. Both these fishermen are great sportsmen, accomplished anglers and ultramodern.

* *How Al McClane fishes*. I have known most of the Fishing Editors of *Field and Stream*, such as Dan and Ray Holland, Ted Trueblood and finally, young Al McClane.

The last spent his youth on a farm in New York State where his early years as farmer-fisherman soon initiated him into all the secrets of the life of the river. He has Indian blood! Still very young, he was far from being a dry fly purist. Very powerful, but supple as a cat and extremely keen, he has all the natural gifts of a born fisherman. Wounded and decorated during the last World War, he fed his company, while in the occupation forces in Germany, on the fish he caught, using such tackle as he could find.

In 1948, he came to the Risle and the Andelle to learn about chalkstream fishing.

The first day, we prepared our rods on the bank of the Aclou narrows, my favourite reach. While I was still making my first false casts, he had already hooked a fine trout on an American nymph (belly striped yellow, black back)!

What strikes me most about him is his change of expression whenever he sees a fish rising! There is a glint of murder in his eye, though no one puts a fish back into the water more quickly and with greater pleasure than he does. He refuses to use a landing-net or a gaff, even for salmon, except in very exceptional circumstances.

He is a great specialist in fishing with the streamer or bucktail (minnow fly) and the deep nymph.

In the United States, on rivers such as the Beaverkill, Ausable and the Delaware, which flow through the little mountains of New York State and Pennsylvania, he prefers using the nymph in slow currents, judging that once he knows the feeding habits of the fish in any given place, he can catch more fish by this method than most anglers could take on a dry fly. He is of the opinion that a few patterns of flies suffice, but that their size is very important, as is also good colouring which should be related to the colour of natural insects. He attaches much more importance to the exact likeness of a nymph because a trout can observe it from much closer to. He fishes turbulent currents and rapids, where the big trout shelter in pockets behind rocks or on the bottom, with a nymph. It takes the greatest skill to be able to manage a nymph properly in these places. But the big fish that lie in them practically never take on the surface during the day. At nightfall (in the United States there is no legal finishing hour), he fishes with a big wet fly, streamer or bucktail, casting somewhat across and downstream. The darker it gets the better are his chances of success. He strikes by sound. He takes many big brown trout in this way. Fish of five pounds and above are not uncommon.

His style of casting is impeccable, it has a rare elegance and grace. For him, short casts are always more effective than long ones. He casts slightly sideways with the forefinger on top to give accuracy. He is capable of casting over forty yards, but he thinks that long casts are unnecessary. He contents himself with casting between thirty to forty feet. For long casts, or on chalkstreams, he often substitutes his thumb for his forefinger on the handle. In these circumstances, he thinks it more important to watch for fish than to fish the water.

He likes long rods with supple action. Long, because when fishing with a nymph, the line must be held high in order to retard the drag during drift. Rods of 8½ to 9 feet, of approximately 4½ to 5 oz. The length of the rod depends on the width of the river.

He prefers standard reels with silent action.

The dry flies he uses are: Light Cahill, Quill Gordon and Blue Spider.

His nymphs are mounted according to the insects on the water to be fished. But he always has an assortment of grey, brown and black ones.

His preferences in wet flies are: the Leadwing Coachman, McGinty and the March Brown.

He uses leaders of at least nine foot of nylon and suited to the rod. He prefers the Rafale P.P.P. formula.

Light weight-forward lines for dry fly and medium weight-forward lines for bucktails.

He wears very long waders reaching to his arms. I have always seen him with water above the waist. This allows him to reach fish which are never fished.

All his very big fish have been taken with flies of the streamer or bucktail type. He believes it to be a science and has proved it to me more than once.

One must learn to distinguish, according to the water, the favourable places for these various types of fly. For instance: the food-bearing currents over large, quiet holes where the big fish can lie quietly during the day, till, half-an-hour after sunset, they start being active. If a bucktail is then worked in the current, zig-zagged here and there, and withdrawn as little as possible from the water, it will often achieve results. During the middle of the day, if it is worked in the bottom currents in a similar way, but allowed to trail to the bottom without any drag, at the mercy merely of currents, counter-currents and eddies, it will often take a fine fish. Drag and the frequent removal of the fly from the water awaken the fish's suspicions, and then it is all over!

This is the basis of this form of fishing in the United States. The reason for it is that big fish always take a certain amount of time to make up their minds to take and the fly escapes them at the precise and propitious moment.

McClane prefers to reconnoitre a big fish rather than try to find it by ransacking the water at random. He is persuaded that the common fault is continuous casting, that is, never leaving the fly long enough to behave naturally and respond to the pressures of the currents on the bottom, particularly in places where there are minnows.

On the Risle, in July, in the deep water at the top end of the fishing, a reach we normally only fish during the Mayfly or the evening rise, owing to almost complete lack of activity at any other time, he gave me an astonishing demonstration of how to let a big nymph drift in the middle of the river an inch or two from the bottom. But I have always wondered how he managed to detect a take.

PART VII * REMINISCENCES

Chief Moose Heart

At the end of August 1921, I was fishing black bass in the lakes of the State of Maine.

One evening, in the hardware store at Mount Kineo, the usual meeting place of the fishermen of the district, one of the locals said to me: 'Since you're here, you ought to go and fish with a fly in the waters north of the lake near the Canadian Frontier, where the landlocked salmon gather in shoal before the frost. I guarantee you won't regret it!'

Fortunately, I had with me a fly rod, bought for five dollars from a pawnbroker in New York. I had cut and refashioned it. It was my first attempt at working in split bamboo. The rod had been transformed and was powerful, supple and, so far, virgin. Here was the opportunity of trying it out! I sought information and discovered that it took one day to get there, one day to return and that I could have two days' fishing. A big canoe was essential for crossing the lake which was always subject to storms. It was necessary to take food and the most important thing of all was to have a good guide.

Someone said: 'Ask Chief Moose Heart, who's smoking his pipe by the stove, if he'll go with you. You'll have the best guide in the district. He wins the canoe races on the lake every year and he's a famous fisherman, but his wife Carabou is expecting her sixth child and I am afraid he may refuse to leave her.'

I turned and saw a young Indian, about thirty years old, with ebony hair hanging in long locks, a superb specimen of his race, with no trace of degeneracy, wide shoulders, a powerful body and narrow hips, dressed in a black and red check shirt, doe-skin trousers and moccasins embroidered with coloured beads. On his head, he wore a black felt hat with a large brim covered with the bright and variegated hues of innumerable salmon flies.

An expedition with an Indian chief by canoe into the wilds, and an opportunity to try out my rod, what a piece of luck! But would he agree?

My heart beating, I said to him:

'How's the fishing?'

He looked at me, smiled and replied: 'Sometimes good, sometimes bad, it depends.'

Fortunately, the American came to my assistance and said: 'Chief, the Frenchman wants to go fishing.'

He looked me up and down, then addressed me in Canadian French: 'You want to catch fish on the lake?'

Thinking that we had better get down to brass tacks, I said: 'I want to try out my fly rod.'

I took my treasure out of its case to show him. I saw at once that he was interested. I put it together and handed it to him. With an expert hand, he made it bend two or three times, turned it about in all directions and then ran his eye along it.

'A good stick to take silver fish.'

Was I going to be lucky? I was now pretty certain that he coveted my rod, because he didn't give it back to me but made the other men present try it. The conversation began again: 'You French, many fish in your hunting grounds? I, Paris with Buffalo Bill, much beautiful women, much drink, good firewater, French *pinard*.'

'I'm Swiss, Chief.'

'Cheese with big holes, I been Zürich too, no speak, no understand, much mountains touch sky!'

'You like fly fishing, and I see that my rod pleases you; I made it myself but it has not caught anything as yet. I should much like to try it on your silver fish! Will you take me to where I can catch them?'

He looked at me for a moment before replying, hesitated, and said: 'Not possible, awaiting little chief.'

'If you consent, I shall stay there only two days, I merely want to try out my rod.'

'Pity, good stick, but can't catch fish before little chief arrives.'

It was no good! Death in my heart, I dared insist no further. Yet, there was a gleam of hope! He had taken up my rod again and was examining it. Well, it was worth the sacrifice.

'The rod's yours if you'll come with me and see that I get some fish.'

His eyes suddenly brightened; he got to his feet and went to the door. How tactless of me! I must have insulted him! I had heard that the Indians, and particularly the chiefs, were proud and independent.

'Wait, I come back.'

At that moment, the American winked, smiled and put a finger to his lips.

The door banged; doubtless he was going to find a friend. But the American said: 'You're in luck! I know him, and you can thank your rod! He's been wanting a rod like that for a long time, but with all his children and his wife, who's constantly pregnant, he's still waiting to save up enough dollars. He has to content himself with an old steel Bristol. Last year, he broke the tip and replaced it by two umbrella ribs bound together!'

182

After a wait of half an hour, Moose Heart came back smiling.

'See the medicine chief, allowed to go for three moons only; if you agree, be at landing place tomorrow morning six o'clock!'

The next morning, I met Moose Heart who was waiting for me by a huge canoe. He was looking at the sky and seemed anxious.

'Bad weather, cross lake very quickly, dangerous!'

He took my precious rod and rolled it up in blankets. The canoe was full to the bulwarks with tents, sleeping bags, pots and pans, two huge axes, a long pole and a tarpaulin covering the whole. He handed me a paddle and off we went!

During the journey, we talked and became good friends. This was the moment to ask the great question.

'Chief, do these silver fish only take a fly when it's cast? Do you think you can make them take by trolling?'

'Impossible. Where we going to fish, must cast.'

'I've practised fly casting in New York, but I've only fished with black bass rods!'

He looked at me but did not seem surprised.

'Fish take well, easy, me accustomed make beginners fish. Paddle harder, quick, storm coming, still an hour crossing lake.'

The wind rose, the storm broke, the waves grew higher and licked dangerously at the sides of our frail craft. We paddled like madmen, shipping a little water, while the rain whipped our faces and soaked us. Finally, towards midday, we drew near the land.

Moose Heart showed me to our left the mouth of a splendid river bordered by birch trees, its strong current washing furiously against the rocks in its bed.

'Leave paddle, me pole rapids.'

He stood up, seized the huge pole and punted the canoe, choosing with wonderful dexterity the best channels between the rocks.

About two o'clock we ate and then, after going about another three miles, I saw a magnificent pool. The Indian signed to me to put my rod together.

'Look, here many fish for beginner, get up in bows.'

There we were in position, all about us landlocked salmon were rising and jumping; I could see their backs and their fins breaking the surface. I went into the attack, casting and casting again without success. Then, suddenly, I felt a formidable take on an enormous fish, who shouted: 'Oy!' I turned about, startled, and saw that my Silver Doctor was anchored in Moose Heart's ear! He smiled and, without a word, tore the hook with a sudden jerk from his ear, detached it from my leader and stuck it in his hat, which he then pulled down over his ears.

'Quick, put on another fly! Fish there, to left, big fish!'

Much concerned, and not knowing what to say, I obeyed him. After several more failures, I asked him whether he had not a better fly in his hat and offered to exchange several of mine, but he refused and looked at me, smiling.

'All flies good for tenderfoot.'

After two desperate hours, in spite of my incompetence, and innumerable missed strikes, I succeeded in taking five fine fish, the smallest over two and a quarter pounds, and one over six pounds. I was tired and soaking, it was five o'clock and we still had to make camp before night. We stopped and went down the river to a little clearing among the birches, three hundred yards downstream.

That night, smoking our pipes by the fire, Moose Heart said:

'Tomorrow, fish beaver hole, many very fine big fish.'

Taking off his hat and showing me my Silver Doctor, he went on: 'Pretty hat; see also Parmachene Bell, ear; Palmer, nose; Zulu, cheek; Black Beauty, neck. Perhaps one or two for hat tomorrow!'

When woman wills

In 1924, I was returning to New York with Elizabeth in the *Berengaria*. In the evenings, after dinner, smoking a cigar in the big saloon and listening to the music, I noticed, sitting always in the same armchair, a man of some sixty years of age who, so it appeared, was also an amateur of cigars. Elizabeth, much more social than I, soon got into conversation with him.

'Mr Leonard, you have the same name as the famous rods!'

'They are my favourites and the only ones I use for salmon fishing but, alas, I'm merely a modest bearer of the same name!'

Salmon! My dream, my ambition! To fish salmon with a fly in Canada! I immediately offered him my largest Cabana!

'Thank you very much, it's my favourite brand. Unfortunately, I finished my last box two days ago and have had to content myself with what I could find on board.'

'It's a Cabinet, English selection 1920, perhaps you'll allow me to supply you during the crossing; I've got a box of fifty.'

Great success! I'd found the sensitive point.

'Where do you fish salmon? With the fly, of course.'

'I own, together with the President of the Telephone Company of New York, all the fishable part of the Romaine, on the north bank of the St Lawrence, opposite the north shore of the Anticosti. I shall be there in a month's time from 10th June onwards.'

It was enough for one day, I felt I had to go carefully! These Atlantic fishings were much sought after, the good ones were very hard to come by and very expensive; lovers of fishing competed for them and guarded them jealously. To be invited was a great privilege. I would cultivate my man. But, in all sincerity, I must admit that, by the third day, I was somewhat remorseful. I was torn between my conscience and my appalling fisherman's covetousness.

My cigar smoker, a charming and delightful man, was far from suspecting my unavowed intentions! Moreover, I lacked the courage even to drop a hint to him!

But, with women, you have to be prepared for anything.

The day before we landed, we were having a farewell drink together, when he suddenly raised his glass, and said: 'To the success of your first day's fishing on the Romaine!'

Was I dreaming? Had I heard aright? I looked at him, not knowing what expression to assume.

'My dear Ritz, since the very first day, Mme Ritz admitted everything and said: "My husband's mad about fishing! When you mentioned the Romaine I was watching him and his eye grew troubled, and he had the very expression I've always noticed in him when he reaches the river bank and begins fishing. You must forgive him, he's sincere but it's stronger than he is! Please do me the pleasure of taking advantage of it and smoking all his cigars, you'll be rendering me a service, our cabin will smell less of smoke".'

Then he added: 'I shall expect you on the 15th July, fishing will be coming to a close unfortunately, but we're full up till then.'

It was one of the very few occasions in my life when I got drunk. Towards midnight, my wife led me down to our cabin. It was a terrible night. Never had I caught and lost so many fish. When I woke up in the morning, I discovered that I was still wearing my dinner jacket!

When I arrived in New York, I marked off every day with a cross on the calendar. At last, there was no more than one day to go! We left at six o'clock by car for Montreal, then on to Quebec, where we were to take ship down the St Lawrence as far as the Romaine. The next day at noon, we arrived in Quebec, at the offices of the shipping company. We were told to be on board as soon as possible, as sailing was fixed for six o'clock. By the side of the quay was moored a big steam yacht, which had once been Czar Nicholas's and now plied backwards and forwards from Quebec to Labrador, stopping at Anticosti and Newfoundland. She supplied all the principal Indian villages and the post of the Hudson Bay Company during the summer months.

At ten o'clock, the yacht dropped anchor in Mingan Bay, a tiny village where there were only an agency of the Hudson Bay Company, a church and a few tents in which the Indians lived.

A motor boat came alongside and Mr Leonard greeted us. An hour later, going down river close into the bank, we disembarked at the camp: a miniature village, a big cabin, in which lodged a dozen guides, the cook and butler, another less big in which was the fishing-room, the dining-room and the shower baths, then six little huts each of one room. There were mosquito-proof doors everywhere. The whole camp looked over the St Lawrence and was surrounded by birch trees and carpeted with moss.

My friend introduced us to Mr Dobbel of Montreal. The other members of the syndicate had been in the boat that had passed us at Anticosti. Mr Dobbel, an old Canadian sportsman, had one arm; his left hand was replaced by a hook; the result of an accident while hunting bear. Leonard was in despair. For the last two days, though the condition of the water was excellent, the salmon had not been taking the fly, but he hoped, if we went to the upper pool, that we should still find some fishable fish.

After luncheon, we unpacked and put on our fishing clothes: long trousers, their ends in the top of lumberman's boots, shirts with sleeves drawn tight at the wrist, grease on face and hands, felt hats with large brims and mosquito veils, mine with a movable opening for my pipe stem.

We each got into the middle of a big canoe with a guide at each end and went up the Romaine. There was a wind and the black fly had not yet manifested their presence. After two hours, we reached an island some hundred yards long and twenty yards wide.

Mr Leonard made us disembark.

'Wait for me here, I'm going up another three hundred yards, there's a little pool with a waterfall from a tributary; perhaps I may find some salmon there that have just run up.'

Suddenly, the wind dropped and we were subjected to a terrible attack from those cursed insects with their heavy solid bodies and little wings, which prevent their flying in the slightest wind.

They alighted on our clothes and then ran all over us, looking for a chink through which to reach our skins. On my wife's sensitive skin, the little holes they made left their mark for several days. It was appalling! Elizabeth, who never loses her head, started running up and down the island. I at once followed her example. It was impossible to stop; if one halted for a moment, the attack began again. After twenty minutes, Leonard luckily returned full of excuses.

'As soon as I saw the wind drop, I thought of you. I've come back as quickly as I

186

could. I'm terribly sorry but there are no salmon! Tomorrow, we'll go up to the higher pool, it's our last chance!'

At night, millions of mosquitoes began murmuring their war cry, and their buzzing, as it grew louder and louder and shriller and shriller, seemed to fill the whole night.

The next evening, after another day of failure, we came back early to camp. Leonard was concerned and I took care not to let him see my disappointment. At dinner he said: 'I've got good news for you, though it's something of a makeshift. You'll have two days fishing, Saturday and Sunday, on the other side of the Mingan. As you've got your camping equipment with you, I would advise you to come back with me tomorrow to Mingan, and camp there till Saturday. There are a great many sea trout about. Most of them over two pounds. The record is somewhere about fifteen or sixteen pounds. You should have some good fishing at each tide.'

The next day, having arrived at Mingan and said our goodbyes to Leonard and Dobbel, we went to see the agent of the Hudson Bay Company, Mr Edwards, who, having furnished us with supplies, advised us to set up our camp near the beach some fifty yards from his cabin.

Half an hour later, all arrangements had been made. After a quick luncheon out of tins, we set off for the mouth of the Stick, with our fly rods and a big bag.

I put the rods together. Edwards had advised me to put three wet flies on my cast. Elizabeth had refused to take my trout rod and insisted that I should take along her little 11 foot salmon rod. I put on her usual leader in the ordinary way. She wouldn't have it! 'I want a stronger leader, with two little salmon flies. I'm going to catch big ones.'

'You're wrong, these are the right flies!'

But she wouldn't listen. I gave her a Silver Doctor and a Jock Scott on No.3, contenting myself with a Coachman, Parmachene Belle and a Red Spinner.

The trout did not keep us waiting long; after a few minutes I had a strong take followed instantly by a jerk, and there I was with two fish on! After a few seconds my third fly broke the surface and I saw another trout jump out of the water and get hooked. On her side, Elizabeth was also in trouble! We were taking fish so rapidly that we threw them behind us on the sand, but I saw that they had such extraordinary vitality that many of them quickly made their way back into the river. I had to dig a hole in the sand. Suddenly, I heard Elizabeth cry: 'A big one! A very big one!'

Her rod was bent to breaking point; finally she succeeded in bringing an enormous sea trout to the shore. We had neither gaff nor landing-net. I went into the icy water and succeeded in seizing the fish by the gills. It certainly weighed more than ten pounds!

187

Elizabeth looked at me slyly, none of my fish weighed more than three!

'Put me on three more flies.'

I was furious! When women are determined it's no use trying to have the last word. I tied two casts together, having shortened the first one to gain time. Finally, I started fishing again. My wife had gone a few yards upstream to a place she had noticed where there was a junction of currents. The water there was alive with fins, we were catching fish unceasingly.

Suddenly my wife called to me. I went to her and, after a hard struggle, she brought a parcel of five trout to my feet. She had simply let the first, and then the second fish swim till she had achieved a full house!

Half an hour later, the pace suddenly slowed, then came to a stop, not another take. The hole in the sand was full of fish of all sizes. I did not count them, but that night the whole village crowded round our camp while we distributed them. Afterwards, Elizabeth was thanked by the chief, a fine looking young man and the only one of average size, all the others being barely five feet high. Then, of course, we had to smoke the pipe of peace. It gave me indigestion and I coughed all night!

Finally, on Saturday, at eight o'clock, a motor canoe arrived, piloted by a man named Laflèche, a Canook Franca, a brown little man with a broken nose and short bandy legs; his eyes were cunning and did not look you straight in the face. He was the chief fishing guide, and was already drunk.

By ten o'clock, we had reached the river and went up it for a couple of miles to a big hundred and fifty foot waterfall.

By eleven o'clock, I was standing on a rocky platform on the right of the fall, with my wife on the opposite bank.

I cast and cast again: not a take. My wife had already caught a salmon. I watched her for a moment, then cast again: still nothing! I changed my fly. It was lucky I did so, my hook was broken! I tried again and heard a click behind me. I looked round and realised what was happening; I was spending my time breaking my flies on the wall of rock at my back. It was clear to me that I was a novice and a bad caster with a two-handed rod! But that fool Laflèche might have told me. I looked at him in fury. He seemed to understand and contented himself with replying: 'Me, always silent, fishermen don't like advice'.

Finally, I hooked one and, after an insignificant fight, a seven pound salmon was not too badly gaffed by my fellow who then proceeded to kick it on the head and throw it into the canoe. While this was going on, Elizabeth was catching her third. I was not very proud of myself.

'Twelve o'clock, Mister, time for lunch.'

He signed to my wife to get into the canoe. Anyway, we should begin again all the earlier in the afternoon. We only had another day and a half and I had caught only one small salmon! When we sat down to eat, Laflèche departed, saying: 'I'll fetch you at four o'clock, the salmon don't take before then'.

Surprised and disappointed, I stupidly allowed him to have his way. Elizabeth, having realised that the chief guide needed to digest his excess of drink, began fishing again at two o'clock.

As I was smoking my pipe, I saw through the window my wife in the canoe at grips with a big fish which obliged the canoe to go downstream to land her at the bottom of the rapids. I rushed to the guide's cabin in search of Laflèche.

'Useless before four o'clock, the fish don't take.'

'Come on, get up! I want to fish!'

My man was still drunk but capable, however, of paddling, and I was soon in the same place as in the morning; but I was certainly having no luck and never had a take. Elizabeth teased me: 'Two more and one lost! Hurry up, come over here!'

Something, however, had begun to interest me. I had noticed that she was not casting, but was holding her rod as if fishing by sight and was leaning forward as if examining the bottom.

Laflèche protested: 'There's no room for two with Madame, better here!'

Instead of getting to his feet, he lit his pipe. But I insisted and we joined Elizabeth, who had just hooked another fish: a big one again!

'Charles, go and look in the hole under the pointed rock near the fall, I'll join you there.'

What a sight it was! It was a fine hole, as big as a room, in which salmon of all sizes were swimming about. I counted one, two, four, ten! I stopped counting in a state of intense excitement. I dropped my Silver Doctor into the hole without achieving the least sign of interest or even alarm.

'It's not four o'clock', said Laflèche by way of consolation. 'Wait!'

'What about all those Madame has taken?'

'They didn't take!'

Fortunately, at this moment, my wife came up.

'Charles, take your fly off and replace it with a double hook. Give me your rod; look, do you see the big one on the right?'

She let the fly sink and, as soon as the salmon passed near the line, she struck hard and handed me the rod. What a brute! He went off towards the current, got into it, and I had to give him line. My reel began to empty itself. I jumped into the canoe and had to make the same manoeuvres as my wife had had to do for her last. The Indian was with me, landed me on the beach, went into the water and gaffed a splendid twenty-three pounder!

Elizabeth came running along the bank.

'Charles, Cowichan, who knows the river well, secretly warned me: "The salmon have been in the big pool since the beginning of June, and for the last eight days have no longer been taking a fly. You have to foul hook them. Laflèche is too fond of fire-water!"'

Then, Laflèche arrived: 'Wind falling, weather changing, tomorrow black flies.'

But, fortunately, on the following day, Laflèche's friends were still absent and we spent an unforgettable day. At one moment, I was on the left and Elizabeth on the right of the waterfall, each of us with a salmon going down the current. Our lines crossed, both our reels were rapidly emptying, every second counted. We tried to free our lines by getting into the canoes, but the current made this manoeuvre almost impossible. My canoe drifted next to my wife's in the middle of the rapid:

'Take my rod and give me yours!'

I went down my bank and Elizabeth down the other side; we reeled in and the gaffs soon came into play.

By the end of the day, we had a splendid catch. Exactly two dozen, but my wife had caught two-thirds!

On Monday, we returned to Mingan where, on the Wednesday, the Quebec boat was due to call. The tribe was impatiently awaiting us and greeted us with joy. There was a great distribution of salmon. A party was organised that night in honour of the American woman. She was adopted by the tribe after a wild dance by torch-light to the sound of tom-toms.

High tension

In 1930, I took the Glos fishing on the Risle with some friends. It consists of several channels of which two feed the turbines. There were many trout, but also many anglers, of whom two, Willy Savariau and I, were rather too active for so restricted a beat. During the Mayfly, we were so numerous that one might have thought we were taking part in a fishing competition!

At that time, I possessed a fine assortment of Hardy and Payne rods and had procured them for most of my friends.

One Sunday, one of my companions announced the arrival of a friend who was to show me an excellent and inexpensive new fly rod which he had bought at the liquidation of some American stocks and which could be acquired in quantity.

Robert, the friend in question, whom I knew well, a charming fellow who was always optimistic both in business and in life, knew nothing about sport or fishing, and I had no illusions as to the quality or pretensions of this wonderful rod he was going to show us.

The following Sunday was a beautiful day, it was very warm and, before luncheon, my friend arrived dressed in a bowler hat, a black coat, striped trousers and city boots!

At luncheon there was a great argument about rods:

'Charles, your American Payne has cheated us! Fifty dollars for a rod and they're pretty fragile ones too. Robert beats you by ten lengths! Take a look at this rod, it's unbreakable steel, and only costs five hundred francs! Why on earth, with all your knowledge and the ten years you spent in the United States, have you never tried a metal rod?'

And they showed me the rod! It was a really cheap article in four sections, lacquered black with a massive cork handle. I pretended to examine it with interest.

'It's clearly very good, Robert, I shall be delighted to try it. Do you know how many are available? I'd be prepared to buy fifty of them, it'd be a good investment.'

I was perfectly familiar with the wretched thing. When in Canada I had broken two the same day!

At about three o'clock, we all set off, each of us going to his favourite corner. I took Robert to the Island, near one of the turbines. I put his rod together, took two trout with it, gave him some rudimentary instructions and went to the point of the island to look for a fine trout I had seen that morning.

Robert, whom I was watching out of the corner of my eye, was continuously flogging the water, entangling his leader round the rod tip, getting caught up in branches, breaking his leader and coming to ask me for another. I noticed that the rod tip was already out of shape, but said nothing. I put him on a big Plumeau.

He went back behind the turbine where, in a strong current, several fish were rising fairly regularly in spite of his too evident presence!

At last, my big fish began rising. I had just gone into action when suddenly I heard a shout! I ran up and found Robert sitting on a bank. His bowler hat had fallen into the water and in his hand there remained nothing but the handle of the rod!

In order to deploy his line he had climbed on to the bank and his rod had hit the high tension wires with a great crackling of sparks! Luckily for him, the handle was of cork.

Black market

In 1941, the factory manager at Amboise telephoned me that some prototypes of salmon rods were ready and that I would receive them the following day. I proposed to try them out on the Allier, where I was to meet M. Césario, the great angler of the district.

A telegram from Brioude, announcing the death of an imaginary uncle, had allowed me to obtain an Ausweiss to go into the free zone! The *feldwebel*, who was examining papers at the demarcation line, asked me why I needed several fishing rods for a funeral! I replied: '*Petri Heil!*'

He smiled and stamped my papers.

'*Ich bin auch ein fischer!*' (I'm a fisherman too!)

At eight o'clock, I reached the inn, where I found M. Césario drinking a great bowl of coffee.

'How do you do, Monsieur Charles! I got your message, but only just! The Boches were after the messenger! Hurry up, we must get off as soon as possible, the salmon have arrived. I sell them all in Vichy. Yesterday, I caught two: twelve thousand francs! I can't satisfy the demand!'

We left at nine o'clock. He towed my bicycle behind his motor-bicycle.

In the morning, my companion took two salmon of fifteen and seventeen pounds in the lime-kiln rapids. In the afternoon, he fished the Cheval Mort bridge. I contented myself with watching the Telebolic rods in action: all went well. The first one tried was perfect, only needing a slight modification to the butt. I took notes. The third day we finished the trials and, taken all in all, Césario was satisfied. That was enough for me, but I've never known anyone fish with such strength as he does. He is not a professional for nothing!

That night at dinner he said: 'Tomorrow, I'll find a salmon for you. I know a place where there are always one or two at the beginning of the season.'

We started very early. When we had reached a place where the road runs above the Allier, he said: 'Stop. This is the place. But we must be quick before another fisherman appears; this place is seldom vacant. We'll take the path to a rock that juts out into the river'.

But I saw a local getting ready to fish and, to add to our bad luck, he took a salmon with his third cast. Disgusted, we went back to our machines.

'We'll go three miles downstream, to the island. Don't worry, I'll keep my promise.'

As went on our way I remembered that, before leaving Paris, Tony Burnand had recommended me to make the acquaintance of a Monsieur X, a gentleman farmer of the district, who was an excellent fisherman and a charming companion. He had warned him that I was coming to those parts.

Césario led me to a place where there was a splendid chance, the surroundings were ideal for anyone who was not too hardened, plenty of space, and little risk of losing your fish. There was a good sandy beach, a moderate current, little depth but easy working conditions and not much risk of getting caught up on the bottom.

I mounted my rod, Césario put me in position, explaining where the fish was and the exact drift of the lure. I was ready, when I heard: 'Hullo! Hullo!'

I turned about to see an elegantly dressed fisherman running towards me. He said: 'Are you Monsieur Ritz?'

'Yes, how do you do.'

'Good morning, Césario, how are things?'

'You've got a fine rod', he said to me. 'Since the war, one has not been able to find anything like that in the shops of Brioude or Vichy. May I try it?'

'Of course, with pleasure!'

He felt the rod's balance, bent it, went to the water's edge, made an impeccable cast, began turning the handle of the multiplying reel and thereupon had hooked the fish that Césario had been reserving for me. I'm not envious by nature but I was far from pleased!

Césario was shouting: 'Hold it! Don't give it line! Haul it in!'

He was already in the water with his gaff. The poor salmon did not have much of a run for its money. Once it was landed, there was much whispered discussion between the two of them, then more loudly an argument as to the precise weight. They compounded at sixteen pounds.

My companion took out his note case and gave the gentleman farmer only half the black market price of the fish. Probably because the rod belonged to me! At least that was what I thought I heard! The whole thing was done so quickly under my nose that I never got a look in!

That night, the Paris train freed me from this nightmare!

Fishing by night on the Traun

In 1938, when the fishing on the Traun belonged to Dr Duncan, and its population of trout and grayling had reached its maximum both in quantity and size, I had the opportunity of spending an unforgettable night on the deep water above the Marienbrücke Hotel with Kustermann and the famous Hans Gebetsroither.

It was the end of August, and I was with Kustermann in his hut on the Ammer. We had enjoyed a splendid week of fishing, having caught numerous grayling as well as a huchen of fifteen pounds which Kus had taken in Hell's Hole on a Rublex. His brother had come to join us for supper, with a bag full of crayfish and two duck killed two days earlier.

From eleven o'clock onwards, the rain fell in torrents, and did not cease till morning, which is rare in the Ammer region where, in general, it rains just before the evening rise.

Kustermann, at breakfast, after his fourth cup of coffee, said: 'The river will be unfishable for at least two days. I'm going to telephone to Marienbrücke, the Traun must still be normal, it's full moon and, if Hans is free, we'll do the evening rise on the deep water opposite Höplinger. If the fish will rise to big Sedges, we shall have a splendid time!'

At five o'clock, we arrived at Frau Höplinger's Gasthof Marienbrücke, where we found Hans, who told us that the trout and the big grayling had been rising very well the day before and advised us to be ready by seven o'clock at the latest.

Having carefully verified the temper of the hooks, cut and re-tied the knots at the ends of the lines, which is an excellent precaution to avoid any danger of breaking at the line knot holding the leader, I mounted three rods, one as a spare in case of trouble, with two big dry Sedges, one above the other. One had to try to reduce risks to a minimum. On the Traun there is barely one good evening rise in three.

We punctually embarked in Hans' boat. There was still too much light to fish the holes where the big ones lay. I got into the stern of the boat, Kustermann three-quarters of the way to the bows and Hans in the bows with his enormous pole, and we went slowly upstream along the left bank looking for the first rises.

To begin with Sedges were rare on the water, and only gnats from the end of the evening hatch were interesting the fish. As usual, we got mostly refusals and only caught one or two small fish which we put back. Hans then suggested that we should go downstream under the right bank and anchor fifty yards from the deep water and watch.

As soon as we were in position, there was a splendid rise at the extreme limit of the range of Kustermann's rod, and he went into action. But the fish was cunning; in spite of Kus's swearing, the fish was rising constantly beside the fly. A last oath confirmed a missed strike.

It was now beginning to grow dark, and Hans, who was constantly watching downstream, suddenly cried: 'Let's go! I've just seen three rises, one of them above the position of the big trout I saw yesterday evening!'

He raised the anchor by some three feet and let the boat drift slowly, only using his pole from time to time to guide the boat and keep it straight, but with great precautions in order to reduce vibration to the minimum. Finally, he stopped the boat.

'Herr Ritz, take the ring on the right, the others are grayling rising.'

I had seen nothing and Hans grew impatient.

'Hurry up, that trout only rose four times yesterday evening. There it is again, but this time three yards further upstream.' I saw it. I cast too long, and let the flies drift for three yards before taking the leader off the water as delicately as possible. The trout rose again, I presented again, very slowly raised the tip of the rod, my arm rigid to eliminate wrist action.

'Strike!' cried Hans.

But, before I had time to react, my rod bent almost to breaking point. The fish had struck on its own as it dived: this is very rare, they nearly always spit out the flies instantaneously. The reel was emptying very quickly. I tried to stop the fish, but in vain. The rod tip plunged into the water.

'Raise your rod, Herr Charles!'

Emotion always creates a certain intimacy for, normally, no one is more reserved and more formal than Hans!

I tried to raise the rod, but my wrist wasn't strong enough. All the line had run out from the reel; luckily, I had fifty yards in reserve. I did not dare estimate the size of the fish but I had the impression of holding a salmon on a trout rod. At last, the fish stopped for a moment. I tried to reel in but it was as if I was caught up on the bottom. Suddenly, the fish went off again and this was followed by a terrific shock and then slack.

'Broken on a rock, as usual.'

It was the only consolation I got from Hans.

Night had fallen, visibility had become very bad. The boat was surrounded by insects, the Sedges were all about us. I heard Kus slapping his face to get rid of the Sedges that covered it. The surface of the water was a mass of live and dead insects.

It was now the turn of a fine grayling, which Hans saw twelve yards to our left. At his second cast, Kustermann struck and within three minutes had landed a splendid fish of two pounds.

'Yours, Herr Ritz!' Hans cried. 'A trout eight yards straight downstream from the boat!'

As usual, I had seen nothing. I cast without result.

'Herr Ritz, you're dragging too soon and your flies are going too much to the right, take in one turn of the reel!'

I obeyed and there I was with a trout on.

A fish in deep water generally begins by going full speed downstream until the moment the tension of the line obliges it to come to the surface, jump and try to free itself, before diving again. When near the boat, it will obstinately refuse to be brought to the surface and it is then that the rod often has to make its maximum effort. The big fish are so powerful that you have to hold the rod with both hands.

Hans tried three times to land my trout but it dived each time. Finally, he succeeded. It weighed over two and a quarter pounds. A splendid *lachsforelle*, which had come from the lake. It was one of those exquisite fish, silver coloured and marked with black crosses, which have exceptional vigour. A fish such as this, weighing two pounds, fights much more strongly than a four pound trout in a chalk-stream.

Hans, in order to see better, was kneeling in the bottom of the boat which was anchored ten yards from the shore, lit by the rising moon. We had two fishing zones, one facing the moon, the other away from it in complete darkness, where we could distinguish the rises only by the noise.

Between the boat and the bank, Kustermann saw two fish rising three yards from the shore, on a good bottom practically without current. Hans got as low as he could and, looking towards them, said: 'Take ten turns of the reel, and place your fly slightly to the left of the reflection of the light from the house opposite.'

Kustermann took a splendid grayling of over two pounds. And as we went on fishing we took four more grayling and three trout, but none of them was as much as three pounds.

Suddenly, Hans seized the anchor chain.

'Herr Ritz, take your competition Parabolic and check your hooks quickly. If you've got Sedges on No.8, change your fly.'

I only had one, which I tied on at the bottom.

'We'll go towards the big rock in the centre, I think I saw a ring. If I did, watch out: there's a big *lachs* there; I believe him to be a good six pounds, but he doesn't rise every evening. He's an old cannibal. And, believe me, if you hook him, you'll have a rough quarter of an hour.'

We raised the anchor and I was wild with anticipatory excitement! Hans moved the boat very slowly, going upstream with a paddle, and gradually approaching the centre of the river (the water is too deep to use a pole) in order to drift down within range of the rise. While this was going on, we were watching the place, having gone down on our knees to see better. There he was, rising again! A tiny, almost imperceptible ring. Hans was surely being optimistic, but he reaffirmed that it was an exceptionally large fish!

Now we were in position; on Hans' advice, I took fifteen arm's length of line and cast. I was very excited. The thought of missing the strike paralysed me. And now my flies had finished the two yards of drift Hans had prescribed. Very slowly I raised the tip of the rod. It quivered and I felt a formidable tug. I tried to strike. I was probably hooked but I nevertheless gave two little jerks of the rod tip to consolidate the barb. The reel sang!

'You've got him! Watch out! Hold your rod up, get into the middle of the boat, I'll raise the anchor. We'll try and get away from the rock. He'll certainly try to get back to his hole under the rock and that'll be the end, as usual.'

For once Hans' pessimism was not confirmed, and the fish went down the river at full speed towards the bridge over the dam.

'Follow him, Hans, I must get in some line. If he goes on and decides to change direction before I can slow him down, the resistance of the water on the line may break me.'

But the line stopped running out. Was I broken again? My throat constricted. No! Fifty yards to the left there was a terrific jump; an enormous *lachs* jumped twice and then shot down to the bottom. The boat had now drawn nearer and, finally, I was able to get him off the bottom by reeling in. He dashed off again but I stopped him, and then he began swimming in circles round the boat, but refused four times to allow himself to be brought to the surface. My wrist was hurting and I was compelled to hold the rod with both hands. There was no help for it! I pulled as hard as I could. Either he would come to the surface or I'd break. At last he seemed to be weakening and allowed himself to be brought to the surface. Hans shone his torch and, suddenly, we saw a mass of silver, still fighting desperately. At last, after a quarter of an hour of agony, Hans' huge landing-net plunged into the water. The *lachs* lay in the bottom of the boat, enormous, powerful, with wonderful markings: it was an old male.

Hans yodelled with joy: 'La-i-tout! La-i-tout! Bravo, Lieber Herr Charles!'

We were all three in ecstasies! Kustermann and Hans gave me the accolade of victory! We caught several more trout and grayling and, at ten o'clock in Frau Höplinger's kitchen, we had the happiness of inspecting a splendid catch: twenty trout and grayling with a total weight of forty-six and a quarter pounds and a *lachs* of six and a half pounds. That was our best evening on the wonderful Traun.

Grayling are no fools

In 1938, I arrived in Munich and went at once to the Rosenheimer Strasse to meet Kustermann, who was awaiting me to go to his camp near the Ammer.

After dinner, Fisher, the keeper, sat down to enjoy Kustermann's famous coffee by a splendid fire flaming on the great hearth.

As usual, we talked only politics the first day; after which the subject was absolutely forbidden! I gave him news of France and asked him if the Nazis were going to make war. He put a finger to his lips.

'Hush, I'll answer that one later.'

The next day, at about three o'clock, Kustermann, who had just taken a trout and a big grayling, right in the middle of the river at the exit of a big pool, signed to me to join him. Having made sure we were sufficiently far away not to be heard, he said in a whisper: 'I'm very annoyed. Constant pressure is being put on me to join the Party and, what's more, we've got a Heil Hitler who's coming here to fish on Thursday! You know the fat fishmonger whose shop is close to my flat on the Victualienmarkt, well, he's a fervent Nazi! I was obliged to invite him. I've been trying to get out of it for a year, but I've had to give in at last, otherwise I might get into difficulties. One has to watch out with those chaps! If he asks you any questions, tell him that you are Swiss, neutral and take no interest in politics. We'll each fish a different reach. You'll go upstream as far as Paradise Pool, I'll put the fishmonger on the Canal of Despair and he'll discover that my grayling don't care a damn for Nazis! As for me, I've got an assignation with those brutes by the bridge that got the better of me today. The one lying near the stump must be a pretty good size!'

On the Thursday, at nine o'clock, we arrived at the little bridge across the Ammer, near the sawmill. We put on our waders, mounted our rods; Fisher, my inseparable ghillie, filled two ruck-sacks with all the rest of the paraphernalia, and prepared the trap of his enormous *lagel*. I had brought some chewing gum, a wise precaution against uttering compromising words! I offered some to Kustermann but he refused saying: 'Dangerous! The Nazis would think that I was sympathising with the Americans!'

Suddenly, a Mercedes arrived. The door opened, a mustard coloured uniform appeared filled with a mass of flabby flesh, crowned with a little shaven head! The Nazi put on his cap, clicked his heels, turned his enormous stomach towards us, and, raising his arm, said: 'Heil Hitler!'

The introductions were made. Charles Ritz, Gauleiter Herman Grossman! Then, after a *Petri Heil!* to the new arrival, Kustermann invited him to don his fishing clothes and told him that he had reserved him the best beat for the morning.

'I haven't got any fishing clothes, and never take off my uniform!' he replied smiling.

'Moreover', he added, 'as soon as your fish see my Swastika, however cunning they may be, they'll know what they have to do if they don't want to become inmates of Dachau!'*

* Dachau was, at that period, one of the principal camps for political prisoners.

And he laughed loudly.

He mounted his enormous rod, a 10 foot Stork, wished me *Petri Heil!* and off they went.

Fisher, who had said nothing till then, hung his *lagel* over his shoulder.

'We must hurry, Herr Ritz, we must take more fish than Herr Herman. Beware of him. He looks genial enough, but I'm afraid of him, particularly as I'm not a Nazi.'

At midday, we gathered at the bridge for luncheon. Kustermann arrived first and, a few minutes later, the Nazi followed. He was not looking too pleased.

'*Heil!* The grayling aren't taking, I've caught nothing.'

We showed him the *lagel* which contained a dozen fine grayling.

'You've been fishing the best place! I'll go there after luncheon.'

At six o'clock, it was the same story, Herr Herman was empty-handed and seemed both unhappy and disappointed.

'Your damn fish are fools! They ought all to be in Dachau!'

Kustermann winked at me.

'Herr Herman, I told you that your uniform would not do for fishing! Really, the grayling are no fools! They take care not to open their mouths when they see a swastika!'

The trout cable railway

On the Salza, at the end of the Weichselboden Lake, there is a dam at whose foot lies a big pool between two rock walls, with a narrow path on either side. There is no back space for casting. Nevertheless, from the right bank, it is possible to make short casts, since the rock wall slopes somewhat backwards. The pool was stuffed with grayling, common trout and a few rainbow trout, of which many were of large size.

The day after our arrival at Gschöder† I took Dr René Toupet to the dam. It was two o'clock in the afternoon and the sluices were practically closed; they are opened every morning from ten to midday to empty the lake and create a strong current to drift down the rafts of logs to Hieflau, the end of the Salza, where the railway is.

The fish were active. We took several grayling and trout. But the big fish were only rising in the centre of the pool, in the deep water. Impossible to reach them. We marked a trout which seemed to be the biggest. All our attempts ended in getting hung up behind or in breaking hooks against the rock or the roof of the dam-keeper's lodge.

Toupet, always perfectly calm, kept watching the trout which was swimming on the surface and gently sucking in all the insects passing in its vicinity. 'René, if you

† Gschöder is the hunting-box of Prince Elie de Bourbon-Parme, one-time owner of the Château of Chambord.

want that trout, I think that between us we can take it, but the procedure is rather like poaching.'

I explained my plan.

'After all, what's the harm? The attempt is worth it and we can always put the fish back!'

I went to the car and brought back two rods and two multiplying reels. I joined the ends of the two lines and attached to them a strong cast with a big Tups. Toupet, with one of the rods, crossed the dam to the opposite path. I paid out line and there we were, face to face, with a cable railway. We tightened the line and were ready. We had agreed that whoever was nearest the fish should strike and reel in the line, while the other would pay it out.

As soon as the fly was near the trout, we tightened the line and dangled it temptingly without placing it on the water. Suddenly, the fish saw the fly and showed considerable interest. After two unsuccessful attempts at presenting the fly, the trout meanwhile constantly swimming in circles in search of insects, the Tups landed in the right place. The trout went slowly to it and took it delicately. A slight pull and a rainbow trout was in a position to appreciate for the first time the advantages of a cable railway!

Unfortunately, he fought very badly, being very long and thin, certainly a sick fish: three pounds only instead of at least four and a half.

We kept it. At dinner that evening it was inedible.

Two marks for heroism

The Pollinger Bach flows through the centre of the village of Polling where it widens out to make a little lake. The butcher throws all his offal into it. The big trout in those parts have elected to inhabit this piece of water. Where the stream flows out there is also a quantity of rainbow trout. These fish have become gourmets, have grown fat and are always ready to show their appreciation of a varied menu, even including bread!

One fine morning, my friend Jacob Wochinger, who introduced me to the Traun, suggested that we fish the village water.

We began by the current and, furnished with bread, took up our positions on a little bridge so as to have a long drift for our hooks which we had baited with bread pellets.

Our enthusiasm languished after half an hour. It was really too easy.

'Charles,' said my friend, 'it'll soon be time for the morning hatch. Come on, we'll take a look at the lake, there are a few fish from two to four pounds, but one has to mark them and cast with great precision! They're gorged with offal, rarely rise and are very wary owing to the shallowness of the water. Casting is difficult owing to the trees.'

After half an hour's wait they began rising.

'Do you see that stump opposite, about eighteen yards away, there are tiny little rings under it: it must be one of the big ones!'

I quickly cast a Tups Indispensable to the spot, the fish took it slowly and delicately. I struck. A silver shape broke the surface, leapt into the air and fell back with a noisy splash. A splendid fight followed: the fish went upstream, then down, jumped, dived, jerked with head and tail, the line cleft the water, throwing up fountains, but my tackle held; the rod was master, and three pounds of living silver were brought to the landing-net! After a pause of ten minutes, the rises began again. This time, the fish of my choice was still farther away. I began deploying my line, extending it carefully, meanwhile watching the single narrow gap in the branches behind me, which was my only hope of reaching my target without getting caught up. Nevertheless, I suddenly felt that I had hooked a tree. But not at all! It was a big fish this time: the hook had caught firmly in a village boy's head!

Wochinger rushed towards the child.

'Idiot! I told you not to stand there.' And, indeed, several children had been hanging round us from the start. I cut the leader; the barb was firmly embedded. I was considerably concerned, but the boy said not a word. A brave child! Wochinger scolded him at length and said: 'Let's take him to the barber'.

The latter seized the fly with a pair of pincers and, with a sharp tug, detached it and put on a little iodine. Much concerned, I gave the victim two marks. His little pink face smiled broadly!

'You're mad, Charles, fifty pfennigs would have been ample!'

Reassured by the boy's evident satisfaction, I went back to my trout. It was still feeding peacefully. I set about making a careful presentation, but my first cast was too short. I tried once more. The boy was standing behind me again.

'Idiot! Go away!' Jacob shouted. 'Hurry up! I'll spank you if you don't do as you're told.'

It was impossible to make the child go. Wochinger went over to him. I followed him hoping to prevent the wretched child getting a smacking. I remembered how, when I had started in the hotel business at the Frankfurterhof in Frankfurt, the head waiter, whenever one of the fourteen-year-old apprentices had committed a fault, used to line them all up and smack their faces in turn.

'Why do you stay there?'

'Herr, I want to earn another two marks!'

Last hopes

After the war, I had but one desire: to see my dear Traun again and to fish it with my inseparable companion, Hans, the head keeper. But how was this desire to be realised? It was impossible to obtain a visa for Austria!

One day, I made the acquaintance of an American Captain whose duty it was to organise sport for the occupation troops in Germany. I immediately went into the attack.

'Are you a fisherman?'

'Yes, indeed, I like fly fishing.'

In under an hour, I had infected him with Traun fever and, what was more, had obtained his promise that we should go there and fish together. But when? We were already in high summer and September was approaching.

A few days later, as a result of an urgent telephone call, I went to his office.

'Can you leave tomorrow? Come with me.'

He opened a door and I found myself in the presence of his General in the next room. 'Traun, grayling, trout! Yes! Munich, Salzburg, Gmunden, Marienbrücke!'

But I was told that we had only a day and a half for fishing. The General had to catch an aeroplane for Washington.

The next morning at seven o'clock, we left Orly, stopped for two hours at Frankfurt for a conference, then going by Munich, we finally landed at Salzburg at midday. We lunched with the officers of the garrison in Hitler's big Conference House. At three o'clock, we left by car for Gmunden. A Buick and a jeep were loaded with tins of food, camp beds, and so on. During the journey, I sat with the Captain on the back seat.

'You know, the General is a black bass fisherman and only a novice with the fly. He only agreed to come on my absolute guarantee that he would take trout or grayling with a fly. We couldn't have done it without his aeroplane! Whatever you do, look after him and don't leave him till he's caught a fish!'

I realised what I was in for. I could only hope that there were still salmonids! A returned prisoner, who had been in the district, had told me that the river had been poached with hand grenades! Moreover, the Traun fish are far from easy for a novice! However, as far I was concerned, I had nothing to lose! But for the Captain, it was quite another story, and I began to feel sorry for him!

At five o'clock, we arrived at Frau Höplinger's, who wept with joy at seeing me. Hans was a prisoner in France, but was due to return soon; the other keeper, Willy, was there. We unpacked quickly and set off for Astecker for the evening rise. A boat for the General and myself, it would allow him to fish close . . . I felt confident, the *lachs* were still there and the river was normal. The Captain took up his position on one of the dams of the waterfall and it was not long before he had taken a splendid lake trout followed by a big grayling. I had the boat anchored in the best place, at the junction of two currents. The day was beginning to fade and we were surrounded with rises.

The General went into the attack, got tangled up, broke, hooked the keeper's cap. My best advice was fruitless: rise, rise, rise, miss, miss, miss. Always too late. He could never make up his mind to strike soon enough! There was nothing I could do and it was exasperating. I began to despair. The Captain had reached his half dozen. The General was still unsuccessful. Five fish had certainly been given the necessary time to spit out the Sedges. The General remained impassive, almost silent, but I felt sure he was not pleased! I noticed that the Captain was no longer announcing successes and was returning them discreetly to the river. I understood very well! The poor devil must have been beginning to curse me!

At dinner, the General was calm enough, and we still had a chance with the grayling at Steyermühle. But we had to leave next day at five o'clock in the afternoon. If only the weather held! The glass was beginning to fall seriously.

A restless night! Grayling, trout, the General, the Captain, complete failure, storm, I saw them all! I got up twice to look at the sky. It was overcast.

At eight o'clock, I had breakfast with the Captain. The General, who was tired, was to come down at ten o'clock. The barometer had fallen lower still, rain was certain. Provided it held off till the afternoon! My companion was morose.

'If only you could arrange for the General to catch a grayling, I should begin to enjoy fishing!'

'Don't worry, I'll arrange it. You can wade and I'll take the General in the boat.'

At eleven o'clock, we were comforted by the sight of numerous hatches at Steyermühle, but the nasty black clouds were already over the Traunstein. We needed to make haste. It was easy enough to say, but my pupil revealed himself no better than with the *lachs*, while the Captain showed himself to be an excellent grayling fisherman.

After numerous failures the General insisted that I should fish myself. At the third grayling I offered him my rod, which he accepted. The fish jumped and became unhooked. Fortunately, he brought the next one to the landing-net!

'Please don't bother about me any more, I've come here to catch one of your grayling, and I'll take it on my own.'

The first little shower fell. We took the opportunity of lunching under the trees.

Then we tried wading. The rises were now less numerous. We were on a wide expanse of water with a gravel bottom. One hour, two hours went by, and still no result! And, to put the lid on it, a storm broke! It was the end, we had had it! We took shelter. The Captain was a sorry sight, he took his rod to pieces but the General, who had remained at the downstream end of the reach, continued fishing.

The ghillie said: 'Watch out, sir! If the General goes any further downstream he'll fall into the hole at the end of the current'.

I seemed to have got myself into a hornets' nest.

The rain was falling in torrents. I waded out into the water to join the General when, suddenly, I heard him shout! Much concerned, I made my way towards him.

He had caught a grayling. It had been the last hope! He came back soaked to the marrow but happy as a king!

Top brass

Paris, 1945. Von Rundstedt's offensive had begun, the Americans were encircled at Bastogne, and Brussels was threatened.

On a Thursday, I got a telephone message.

'General Bedell Smith is expecting you to luncheon at Versailles. General Rogers will pick you up at the hotel at 11.30 tomorrow morning.'

The following day, a Friday, having passed through a dozen offices, we reached General Bedell Smith, who then took us in a huge bullet-proof Cadillac to his villa, hidden in the wood not far from the hotel. The house was surrounded by M.Ps., armed with sub-machine guns; they were lurking in every bush; one might have thought one was in the Maquis! The cook and the servants, bright eyed little Phillipinos, were awaiting us at the entrance. We went into the drawing-room where I noticed book-shelves containing nothing but German books. During the Occupation, the house had been inhabited by a senior officer of the Luftwaffe.

I gave the General a completely equipped fly rod, which had been manufactured specially for him, and showed him a map of Bavaria.

'Here is the Ammer and my Munich friend Kustermann's fishing. He's got a fishing and shooting box near Oberammergau. I've been fishing grayling on that river since 1930 and I advise you to try it.'

'I'll certainly see Kustermann and try to take some of your grayling.'

After an excellent luncheon, we returned to the drawing-room. Bedell Smith opened a cupboard and took out of it a veritable collection of fishing rods and sporting guns: split cane from Payne, Leonard, Hardy and several splendid rods without trade-marks, as well as guns by Purdy and Holland & Holland. I gathered that during his rare moments of leisure the General also had his hobby: he made most of his own fishing rods and, what was more, was an expert tyer of flies.

General Rogers, who remained silent most of the time, seemed anxious and pre-occupied. Suddenly, he decided to ask a leading question.

'What's happening at Bastogne?'

'I may have good news in forty-eight hours. Now I must go back to work.'

Then, one summer's afternoon, an officer arrived in Paris, gave me a Browning and cartridges from the General and informed me that the Ammer fish had made the acquaintance of Bedell Smith's flies. Kustermann and his family were well. His camp was occupied every week by the top brass of the Allied Army.

The following year, at the Mayfly, Bedell Smith arrived in Paris like a whirlwind and told me he had two or three free days.

We went to stay with Vernes on the Risle and then to Lambiotte and Gaillard on the Andelle. What a splendid fishing companion! He has both the enthusiasm of youth and the modesty of age. He takes loving care of his tackle, and the sight of a fish rising fills him with excitement. His numerous fly boxes contain a wonderful collection made for him by the famous Lunn. His favourite is Lunn's Particular.

In the morning, after breakfast, in the guide's house, our meeting-place on the Andelle, while he was carefully arranging a cast, I saw a crow perched on a tree and seized my ·22 American rifle. The window was open, I aimed, fired, and missed.

'Perhaps it's not shooting accurately. Have you got a target?'

And a few seconds later, there he was flat on his stomach on the gravel in front of the house, giving us a perfect demonstration of American Infantry shooting.

Finally, there we were, on one of the arms by the Château, looking for a promising rise. I saw a fine trout feeding well:

'Yours, Beedle! But take care, don't show him anything before you present your fly!'

His first attempt was too short. He cast again; the line was lying in the grass at his feet and became entangled round his Canadian boots, while he performed an Indian dance to get rid of it, still continuing his false casts. He was pale, his nerves were at high tension. Finally, he regained his self-control and an impeccable presentation assured him success. I congratulated him and gave him the accolade. His expression at that moment was regal.

'Charles, what a great moment! My first fish on the Andelle, and what a beauty!'

While we rested on the grass, he told me of his beginnings as a fisherman.

'You know, Charles, I get more excited when I see a trout rising than I did on the day I had a bone to pick with von Rundstedt's Army!'

Olsen and the lovely Caroline

Jack Olsen came from America to fish with me. After two days he wrote the following article for *Sports Illustrated*. The title: 'Ritz Isn't Ritzy, but he has a cast system.' I reproduce it here by courtesy of Mr Olsen and *Sports Illustrated* as I find it such an excellent description of his stay on that greatest of European chalk streams, the Risle river...

Charles Ritz, *hôtelier*, trout fisherman, gourmet, author and miniature railroader, whipped his line high into the air and fired a cast 25 yards, smack on the upper lip of a brown trout, which thereupon did perish from the earth. 'I don't believe in all this admiration for experts,' Expert Ritz mused as he walked briskly along a French chalk stream looking for another victim. 'Trout fishing is simple. But the men who write about it want to become so important, and the people throw them so many compliments, that they get like the Sphinx. They add all kinds of gimmicks to make their systems more mysterious, more fantastic. Now, I want to take all the mystery out of fly casting. I want to put an end to all that foolishness.'

The 74-year-old Ritz paused as a freight train, pulled by a diesel and a steam engine in tandem, rattled by on the Rouen-Le Mans line along the stream. 'People can say who am I?' he went on in a Continental accent ranging somewhere between Victor Borge's and the Little Old Winemaker's. 'Well, I'm just a man with his father's name. They tell me I'm supposed to be distinguished, but the only time I can be distinguished is when I'm drunk. Thank God, I'm not an expert. Experts make simple things complicated. That is how they survive.'

The chairman of the board of the Hôtel Ritz in Paris is a dink of a man – 5 feet 6 inches, 145 pounds in his waders – with gray-black hair cut *en brosse*, darting brown eyes, brown-rimmed bi-focals, an olive-brown complexion and a pencil-thin black moustache. With his natural rapidity of movement, his merry eyes and his swarthy coloring he puts one in mind of a tiny French mouse, a description with which he disagrees, 'because I am Swiss.' On behalf of his clientele, he has become an expert winetaster and student of foods; on behalf of himself, his tastes are simple, running to meals of spaghetti and beer. 'The Ritz is not ritzy,' he once pointed out – to which could be added, 'Charles Ritz is not ritzy.' He lives in a tiny room on the top floor of the hotel, leaving space for his six miniature trains in an adjoining room. Across the hall is the considerably more sumptuous suite of Coco Chanel. Ritz likes to boast that he is the liveliest resident of the floor. 'Every night when I go to sleep,' he explains, 'I fight the legions of Julius Caesar and make love to the girls of the Lido. That is the noise you hear: '*oui, oui, oui, non, non, non*' all night long.'

A 5-pounder from the Traun

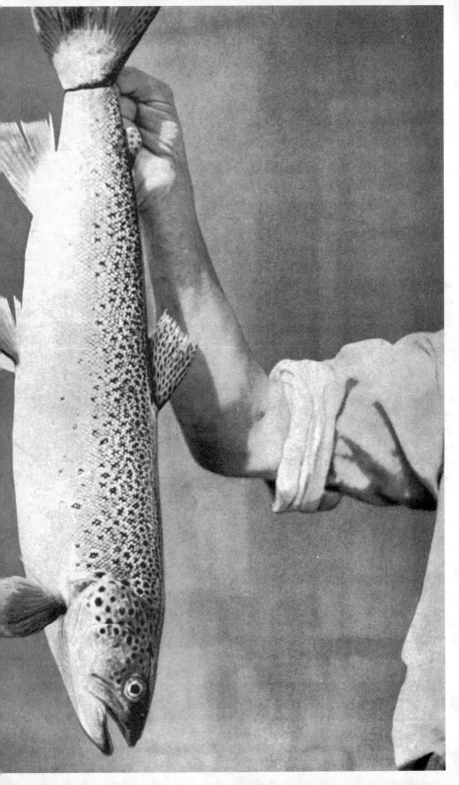

above: General Bedell Smith, a first rate fly fisherman
below: The author with a steelhead trout from the Stamp River on Vancouver Island

The range of Charles Ritz's activities is encyclopedic; he is easily bored and must keep on moving from interest to interest. As the only living son of Cesar Ritz, founder of the hotel, the young Charles could have nested in the tight security of the Ritz chain for life. Instead, he has been a shoe peddler, a designer, a movie-theater entrepreneur, an importer, a customer's man in a brokerage firm, a writer, a tackle manufacturer, a sergeant major in the U.S. Army during World War I and a dozen other things, only returning to the relative stability of the family's hotel business about 10 years ago. But of all the multitudinous interests of his life one has remained constant: trout fishing or, more accurately, fly casting ('I tend to lose interest after the fish has been hooked'). He has written two books on the subject: *A La Mouche* in 1939 (in collaboration with Tony Burnand) and his magnum opus, *A Fly Fisher's Life*, which has been published in half a dozen countries and continues to sell steadily. 'As the world is run now few people can fish as far as Monsieur Charles fishes,' Ernest Hemingway wrote in the introduction. 'No matter how it is run even fewer people could ever fish as well.'

Ritz's long career as a hunter of trout began in 1911 on a stream in France. 'I was 20 years old, and a friend gave me a rod and took me out,' he recalls. 'I horsewhipped the river all day long and got a handful of blisters and no fish. Then my host came along and took four or five trout, and I said to myself, "This is not for you. This is something devilish, you poor sucker, keep away from this damned stuff, see?" Then around 1920, when I was working in New York, another friend took me to the Beaver Kill. The first trout I caught, it took the fly all by itself. I didn't even know what was going on. I dragged it on the sandbank and fell on it.

'Now all of a sudden I knew everything, I was an expert. I figured it was just a matter of knowing where the fish were. I noticed the fellows were catching trout every evening in the Junction Pool; so I had another conversation with myself. "Now you're gonna get all the fish," I said, "because you're gonna get to the Junction Pool and get the best position before anybody else." Two hours before the evening rise I took up my position. When the night hatch began, up came a fellow two feet away from me and he got 'em all and I got nothing. So that was the real beginning. Between that time and now I had to go through a lot of suffering. Where I finally learned how to fish for trout was on the Risle. When you can take fish there you can take fish anywhere. I first tried the Risle on May 21, 1927, the day Lindbergh landed at Le Bourget. Since then I have fished all over the world. But after you've been on a piece of water like the Aclou Reach of the Risle, any other place is lousy.'

I was staying on the same floor of the Ritz where the '*oui, oui, oui, non, non, non*' was alleged to go on all night when written word came that I was invited to go to the Risle for a day with Ritz, who was already vacationing on the river. A while before the great day my telephone buzzed, and a faraway voice, faintly identifiable as that of the *hôtelier* himself, told me: 'I just wanted to remind you to wear a tie when you come up here. Let me suggest a tie and tweeds. We're having lunch with my host and hostess, and she won't let you in without a tie.'

'All right,' I said to M. Charles. 'But what are they running up there on the river? It sounds like the Ritz.'

'It's worse!' he said, laughing.

At 7 in the morning Ritz's friend, Guy Duchange, an electronics-equipment manufacturer, picked me up at the hotel for the 80-mile drive westward to the Normandy village of Valleville, where we would find the Risle and Ritz. '*Bonsoir!*' I said ebulliently, because I always get light-headed before a fishing trip and also because I had been told that the French appreciate one's trying to speak their language even if one is a Berlitz reject. '*Bonjour,*' my new friend corrected gently and then continued in French, which turned out to be his only language.

Nothing daunted, I began to study the road signs as we made our way past Long-champ and St. Cloud and onto the Autoroute de l'Ouest. I saw a familiar one at last; it showed a smiling, happy tiger and was captioned: '*Mettez un tigre dans votre moteur.*' I stowed the phrase away in my mind, and after we had finished a roadside breakfast of croissants and coffee I patted my stomach and remarked with seeming nonchalance: '*Maintenant j'ai un tigre dans ma moteur.*' It was my first joke in French: a poor, ungrammatical thing but mine own. Duchange smiled politely and began telling me, in rapid French, about the fishing on the Risle. It is, he gave me to under-stand, the fishing place the most beautiful of the world. His friend, Charles Ritz, is the fisherman the most beautiful of the world. One would have a lovely day on the stream, is it not? One was not to regard badly the dark clouds descending the road; after he rains the fishing is well because the river it becomes then the tomb of all the flies. Comprehended I?

'*Oui,*' I said.

Charles Ritz waited for us by the river, and we went straight to the Aclou Reach: 200 yards of classic chalk stream full of many mysteries and few solutions. On this stretch the Risle moves at an even pace through waving fields of submerged weeds and watercress. At its extremes it is only four feet deep and some 35 yards wide. The trout lie in pockets and fingers of water between weed beds, gobbling up a proliferation of sedges, gnats, mayflies, stone flies, duns – all the fly life of a typical chalk stream. The trout get so much food that they become lazy, disdaining any offering that is not within easy reach; hence there is a premium on casting accuracy. Once the trout is hooked it must be horsed across the weeds to the limit of the leader's strength, else it will stick its head into the greenery and wait for the fisherman to break off.

I tried my best to follow the gamekeeper and the elderly Ritz, who keeps his legs in shape by daily isometrics, as they headed upstream through a tapestry of Norman green: olive and chartreuse and lime-colored vegetation in the water and verdant pastures all about and here and there a copse of elm and linden and chestnut trees, all dotted for relief with buttercups or *boutons d'or*, yellow irises in full bloom marching down to streamside, purple clover, brown-and-white dairy cattle and chubby, rust-colored chickens. We passed decaying wooden footbridges, ruins of tiny factories that date to the nonelectric times when the river's waterpower ran the mills, eel traps sticking out into the water like crumbling piers. It was a Monet painting in the wild state. Swallows darted overhead, feeding on the same flies as the trout, and from deeper in the woods a familiar sound kept repeating itself at short intervals: cuckoo! cuckoo! cuckoo! It suddenly dawned on me that these might be alive. To the gamekeeper I said, 'Are those real cuckoos?'

'Either they are real cuckoos,' said this local wit, 'or it is 137 o'clock.'

Taking in all this audible and visual grandeur, I made a snap decision: not to fish. Years ago I had played bridge with Charles Goren, and my ego had suffered bruises and lacerations. I would not repeat the error now by fishing with this other expert Charles. 'Come now,' Ritz said, 'you need not be ashamed. Let me show you.'

He lifted the line over his head, false-casting slowly, until far across the stream a ring of water exposed a trout's position. Within seconds Ritz dropped a perfect cast on top of the fish, which, however, was not having any. 'See how easy it is?' he said. But I had observed several points. Ritz had used about half the normal number of false casts to get out enough line to cross the stream. His cast was so flat and so fast that he shot all the extra line held in his left hand plus another six or eight loops that he had held in his mouth. He had cast twice as far as my own personal record with more accuracy than I could have achieved with a ·22. 'Would you like to try now?' he asked.

'*Non*,' I said.

Instantly he put the rod in my hand, clamped his oversized hands on top of mine and began teaching me the 'high-speed, high-line' casting technique perfected by himself and several of his close friends. The system is built on a strong upward snap as the rod moves from about 10 o'clock to about 12. When the rod reaches the trigger point the wrist straightens out, the forearm jerks upward and the elbow rises about three inches, all of the motions seemingly with one aim: to punch a hole in the sky with the fly. As Ritz explained the technique, the elbow lift and the sharp wrist snap and forearm movement are the heart of the cast, with everything else flowing from that. But as an old caster of bass bugs, worms and hellgrammites, accustomed to using all the muscles from the *abductor hallucis* of the big toe to the *occipitofrontalis* of the forehead, I was a hopeless student. 'Come on now,' Ritz implored. 'De-tense yourself! De-contract your muscles! You're trying to squash the rod, that poor little fellow. Listen, for heaven's sakes, this isn't difficult. You've got to succeed if you want to make me happy. Do you like me?'

I said that I liked him.

'Well, succeed for my sake, because then you'll be doing the finest thing for me. Hold the rod loosely. Imagine you have a pretty girl in your arms instead of a fly rod. De-tense yourself! She's not going to respond to you like that, is she? You must learn to take it nice and easy in all things.'

A merciful thunderclap fell over my ignorance of girls and fly rods, and we repaired to a gamekeeper's shack, where I asked Ritz how he had developed his high-speed, high-line technique. 'At first I didn't know what I was doing,' he said. People would tell me, 'Your line is so fast, we've never seen a line so fast in the air, and we've never seen one stay up as high and as long.' I paid no notice. I said, 'That's nice.' Then one day my friend, Pierre Creusevaut, the champion caster, said to me, 'Your casting is jerky. It lacks elegance.' But nevertheless I was faster on a fish than Pierre. 'Why is that?' I asked myself, and I realized that I am naturally jerky in all my movements. I began to analyze my casting, and I found that I was packing all my effort into one jerk.

'Then I went to a casting tournament in Zurich to see Jon Tarantino, the American who may be the best caster in the world, and I saw that he was doing the same thing: a short pull but a very fast one. So I said to him, 'Let's go to my laboratory: the Risle.' I took him there and he put on the finest exhibition of fly casting that I have ever seen, using the same controlled jerk. Now I was aware of all the mechanics except the short lift of the elbow. I watched Pierre Creusevaut casting for salmon in a film, and I saw the elbow lifting at the same time that he straightened his wrist and jerked his forearm up – *zic*! It was all done in such a short space that no one knew what he was doing, including Pierre himself. That was the last piece to fall into place in the high-speed, high-line system. It's not a big discovery. It has always existed. But no one ever explained it. Now, by using this system, by simple mechanics, brass tacks and logic, the mystery can be taken out of fly-fishing.'

But isn't it true, I asked sagely, that neither the establishment of trout fishing nor the anglers themselves want to take the mystery out of trout fishing? Isn't the mystery part of the allure?

'Perhaps,' said M. Charles. 'There are many eekons in trout fishing.'

'Icons? I said.

'Yes. I don't want to disturb anyone, but some of the ideas are ridiculous. Such as matching the hatch. Of course, there are times when you should have a fly as alike as possible to the flies in the water. But the casting and the accuracy and how you present your fly and how fast it gets there and how it swims are all more important than matching the hatch.

'I've never been interested in flies. Flies annoy me. I don't want to spend hours changing flies all the time. Once I had 3,000 flies. Every time I fished I took with me a whole cabinet of them. And when I had taken a fish with a certain fly I'd run up and down telling everybody, "I've got the right fly! Here's the fly. Take it and fish with it!" I was an easy victim at first.

'But I don't want to take away from the fisherman the pleasure of his flies. The fellow who ties beautiful flies, I like to look at them, I like to have some. But if I'd spent my time on flies I'd never have found out what I did about high-speed, high-line. So I use nothing but the Tups Indispensable, the Panama, the Lunn's Particular, the Bivisible and the Black Gnat. I use only these flies because I'm lazy. I put one on and I say, "Damn it, now the fish has got to take this fly!" Sometimes I feel it would be better for me to change, but I leave the fly on anyhow, because I believe more in technique, getting on the fish as quickly as you can, letting the fly arrive there so fast that the trout doesn't know where it comes from and he's taken by surprise and he says, "My God, that thing's gonna escape if I don't grab it." I don't say I'm right, but with this system I don't have to waste my time fooling around with flies.

'But trout fishermen are believers. They believe in the leader, they believe in the line, they believe in the rod, the reel, balancing the rod with the reel, matching the rod to the fisherman, matching the hatch. That's all nonsense. The fly-fisherman should learn how to cast. He should adapt to the rod. But fishermen waste time and money matching the rod when they don't understand movement and muscles. With our system the fisherman can feel when he's got it right. There's a certain feeling, like when you hit a golf ball well.'

Over lunch I met the other dramatis personae of the Risle. There was Auguste Lambiotte, whom Ritz calls the Giant of Flanders, a tall, white-haired Belgian industrialist who links up with Ritz for trout-fishing vacations as often as possible. Together, the Belgian businessman and the Paris hotelkeeper are streamside models of old-world courtesy. If Ritz spots a feeding fish, he says to his friend Lambiotte: 'I offer this fish to you.'

'*Non, non*,' protests the Belgian, '*je vous l'offre!*' Sometimes they argue the point until it is too late and there is no fish left to argue about. '*La politesse* is more important,' says Ritz.

The proprietor of the Aclou Reach of the Risle is Edouard Vernes, head of a French bank and a dry-fly purist, who has been buying up angling rights and property along the river for decades until he now controls some three miles of breathtaking fishing water. M. Vernes is one of a class of Frenchmen who speak English not merely with a British accent but with an upper-class British accent, intoned in slow, careful sentences with long pauses in between. He walks along his stream with head down, heavy pipe clenched in his teeth, wearing an English-style tweed jacket, the kind with one little pocket above each big pocket, clasping the rod behind him with the tip sticking above his head so that he gives the impression of being a well-tailored, Eton-educated Martian. Until he speaks, M. Vernes has a tendency to awe one and make one nervous. But he turns out to be, like Ritz and Lambiotte, a most kindly man and a gentle needler. At lunch Vernes waited for Ritz to finish telling a story, then said to me: 'One day during the war a nervous pilot came down the river firing all his machine guns. You should have seen Charley! He went flat on his stomach and turned the color of that plate there!'

'Now, just a minute, my dear Edouard,' said Ritz, taking the bait. 'I was *not* afraid! I was merely anxious to live.'

Vernes laughed and gave Ritz a bone-shattering clap on the back.

'But I do remember a time when we were on the Cherbourg express on the way to the river,' said Ritz, 'and the American planes came over, and we all had to jump out and run for the weeds. Everybody was hungry in those days, and most of the passengers were on their way to Normandy to try to find meat and eggs. While all the bullets were spattering around, a hare got up in the field. Every Frenchman on the train jumped to his feet and tore after that hare.'

I asked Ritz and Vernes what had happened to the Risle during the German occupation. 'Surprisingly, very little,' said Vernes. 'The Germans were disciplined about restricted waters. There was only one exception. Towards the end of the war Ribbentrop's son was posted here with the Hitler Jugend. He would shout, "I want to eat trout!" and he would come to the river with rubber boats and grenades. But he was the only one. I was more concerned about a gasoline pipeline the Germans ran from the Paris area to supply the airfields around here. Our people treated it like a – how do you call it? – a self-service. And sometimes mysterious accidents happened to the pipeline. *Pouf*! We do not know how these happened. Acts of God. But I used to tell certain people, "Watch out what you do to that pipeline! It goes across the Risle, and *you might kill the trout*!'"

To hear Charles Ritz tell it, M. Vernes has never used anything but dry flies in his entire life. One can imagine his shock when, shortly after the liberation, Vernes spotted an English major, who was also a lord, fishing the Risle with his batman. 'I saw him lifting the line out of the water and placing it a few feet further downstream each time,' Vernes recounted in his English accent. 'And suddenly I realized he was fishing with a – eh – a wuhhhhhhhm!' Into the single blasphemous word 'worm' Vernes put all the shock and horror of a Hitchcock movie, pushing out the sound as though it pained his voice box.

'What in the world did you do?' asked the bemused Ritz.

'I walked straight up to him, and he was ashamed, and he said, "Oh, you saw!" "Yes, indeed I did," I said, and I gave him a good fly rod and some flies to use. I don't know why he was using a – eh – a wuhhhhhhhm. He turned out to be a good fly-caster.'

After lunch the fishing contingent on the Risle was augmented by the arrival of a Bavarian nobleman, Prince von Quadt, who pulled up in a Mercedes after a 100-mph dash from Germany. 'He is a very nice young man', Ritz said of the friendly Bavarian, 'and I have only one reservation about him. He fishes like a tournament caster, and he is not interested in a trout unless it rises a mile and a half away.' Working earnestly, his rod flailing the heavens, Prince von Quadt took three small trout. But nobody took the prize trout of the day, nor did I believe, at first, that such a trout could exist in the Risle. Ritz and I were walking along the stream when we came upon the prince's chauffeur in a high state of excitement. 'There is out there a huge trout,' the chauffeur said in German, one of Ritz's many languages. We looked at the pool and saw nothing at first. Then there was a slight swirl of water on the other side as the fin of a big fish came into sight. Plainly, no fish that big – at least two feet long and eight to 10 pounds in heft – could be a trout in these waters. 'Pike!' I said, drawing on knowledge gained in the New World.

Ritz said nothing.

Then the big fish made a dash across the river to our side, pushing a conspicuous ridge of water ahead of him. He made a single, tail-slapping swirl and disappeared. Ritz gasped. 'That is not a pike!' he said, 'That fish is feeding exactly like a big brown trout. He is chasing minnows from one side to the other. A pike would not feed that way.' Now the fish rose again, and all we could see were spots.

Ritz called down the river to Vernes's wife, Michou, a formidable, outdoorsy woman who is always followed by a cloud of tiny dogs (she sometimes hooks them in the ear when casting). 'Come, Michou!' Ritz called in French. 'There is a big cannibal trout up here.' Madame Vernes, the same gracious hostess who insisted that even fishermen must wear ties to her luncheons, clomped up in her no-nonsense fishing shoes and her no-nonsense brown stockings and her no-nonsense tweeds and studied the fish carefully. Then she trudged off toward the gamekeeper's house. 'Where are you going?' asked Ritz.

'To get the shotgun.'

Madame emerged from the house in a few minutes, spraying orders all around. 'Stand back there!' she shouted to me in English. 'Out of the way!' she snapped at the German chauffeur in French.

The fish surfaced, and Madame fired one barrel. The trout descended a few feet and swam slowly upstream. Madame let go the second barrel, and the fish merely accelerated its departure until it was out of sight. One suspected that Madame had not allowed for refraction, but one was not going to say so. Madame was disconsolate. 'I know that dreadnought very well,' she said in a British accent like her husband's. 'I had her on two years ago, and she just towed me downstream and broke off. She's been around here for four years. We want to get her out because she's bad for the fishing.'

'Do you have a name for her?' I asked.

'If it will please you,' said Madame, 'we will name her Caroline.'

Somehow I found it more than pleasing, after enjoying the Verneses' hospitality over a big Normandy dinner, to realize that the prize fish of this prize river now bore such a wholesome, American name. And as much as I admire Edouard and Michou and the Giant of Flanders and the free-swinging Prince von Quadt and, most of all, Charles Ritz, I hope that they fail in their sworn ambition to remove Caroline from the Risle. In my fantasies I see them imploring me by urgent cable to bring my American know-how and skill back to the Risle. There I will make a perfect high-speed, high-line cast, and after a clean but bitter struggle I will haul the lovely Caroline out of the clear green depths of the chalk stream.

I only hope that they don't notice the – eh – the wuhhhhhhhm.

Confessions of the author

As you read this book, you may well think that I am in a position to find the precise solution for every individual case and apply that solution instantly. The truth, however, is quite otherwise!

The charm of fly fishing lies in one's numerous failures and the unforeseen circumstances that must be overcome.

At sixty-six, I was happier than ever each time I saw a chance of getting a fish to rise to my fly. At eighty I still have a great deal to learn.

I have no pretensions and if, after some little success, I believe myself to have done rather well, it only needs a fish or two to defeat me to call me to order. Then, I go back to work, trying to learn and correct the faults and weaknesses which, only too often, cost me the loss of a fish.

I am lazy and often have to spur myself to serious concentration, for I no longer have the passion for actually catching fish. I lack patience, too, and my fly often fails to stay long enough on the water. My professional bias, indeed my passion, for perfecting tackle and studying the mechanics of casting are also handicaps. If I think that my cast or presentation is imperfect, rather than leave my fly to complete its drift, I will take it out of the water at once and begin all over again. I cannot help it! In circumstances such as these, I am absolutely convinced that my fly will be refused. It is a ridiculous mistake; a fly is fishing so long as it is on the water; and every fishing day several fish see my fly escape at the very moment they are about to take it.

I devoted twenty years to perfecting my strike but, even today, I often strike too late, simply because I am too conscious of my faults and liable to be taken by surprise by a too-obliging fish.

More than all else, I like watching other fishermen, and examining their tackle. In helping beginners, I often learn as much as they do.

To watch a master is more important to me than to fish myself, and I do not hesitate to go hundreds of miles to interview one and watch him fish.

Trying out tackle, particularly with Pierre Creusevaut, is a constant preoccupation and, to prevent my hand acquiring too-individual habits, I constantly change my rod. I often go suddenly from a little 7 foot rod to a 9½ foot. I get no satisfaction and have no faith in my chances of success, if rod, line and leader are not in perfect harmony.

As far as leaders are concerned, I am a maniac. I make them all myself; one of my pockets is invariably filled with ten little reels of ·006 to ·020 inches nylon. If the wind or weather changes, I alter the dimensions of my leader on the spot.

As far as flies are concerned, I always begin grayling fishing with Choroterpes, Tricolores or Tups. For trout, if visibility is poor, Cahill. And for good visibility: grey with green or yellow body. I always hesitate to change my fly, except when it is absolutely necessary. Laziness again!

As far as hooks are concerned, I always check the points and sharpen them carefully on an Arkansas stone, as well as rectifying the gapes with pincers whenever it seems necessary, which means more often than not after landing a fish.

I rarely oil my flies and then only with silicone. I believe if I missed a fish owing to some defect in tackle it would kill me!

I have no definite physical position for casting. According to circumstances, I vary between a slightly loose elbow to the arm raised above the head. My style has nothing of the suavity and elegance of so many other people's. It is abrupt, powerful and very rapid. The line whistles but there is a reason for this: I cannot bear a fly not to be absolutely dry, and drying it with amadou after every catch, or after several presentations, bores me. I therefore whip my rod hard to keep the fly constantly dry. In rapid currents, I often use the parachute cast or the cast upstream at 45 degrees. Above all, I try to drop the leader in a curve so as to present the fly before the nylon. In order to cast anew, I take the fly off the water with a roll. I always make very long shoots. I only keep my elbow to my side for the horizontal side cast.

It is in a high wind, when up against difficulties, in bad light or in long casts that I have most confidence and succeed best. I can generally manage the strongest winds, thanks to the storm cast. My rod sometimes reaches half-past-two but I practically never touch behind, whatever the conditions, probably due to the importance I attach to the working of the left hand. The line rests on the thumb of my line hand (see photograph, facing p.15). Most of the time, my rod works to the limit of its power; but I never deform a rod and have only broken two. Only supple rods give me satisfaction.

I use only weight-forward lines of the greatest possible lightness. I always gather the line in my left hand when recovering it; this dries it quickly owing to the warmth of the hand.

I like going up and down the river, and this often costs me fish. I always believe that there are more rises somewhere else and have great difficulty in making myself stay in one place. When I do manage to do so, I often achieve the best results.

When I can see and observe the fish, I quickly decide whether they are active or passive and, according to circumstances, I am inclined to be confident or persuade myself in advance that I shall suffer a refusal. My judgment is not too bad in these circumstances, but it is on the whole a bad habit, for the experience of seeing numerous fish I have failed to try caught by my companions has proved to me that I have been wrong.

Before presenting my fly, I study the currents and their speeds carefully, in order to choose the right cast. If a water does not please me, and it is often a question of the countryside, I seldom fish it even if it offers good prospects. I do not like fishing short, and hate fishing my own bank. I am always keen on the trout under the opposite bank and it often makes me lose a lot of time. I like wet fly fishing and fishing with a nymph, which is the most difficult type of fishing and the one about which I still have most to learn.

I hate landing-nets and use them as little as possible. The only one I can tolerate is the American type: short, light, all of wood; I am often obliged to kneel or lie flat on the ground to land a fish.

While wading, I am always more or less frightened and never risk it in strong currents, because I am too light. I often use a wading staff.

People who like keeping their fish attract my profound contempt. I prefer returning my fish to the water unless they are exceptionally large.

I do not like fishing alone and generally seek a companion.

I constantly verify my own ideas and am always on the look-out for the new and the better.

I am constantly fighting the intoxication of the temporary success of having brought off some minor triumph.

Before closing this chapter I must put on record an incident that weighs heavily on the heart of Charles Ritz, fly fisherman. Confession, they say, is good for the soul and so it may be, but Heaven forbid that my frankness should see me branded a bait angler. However, at 3 p.m. one bright summer day, after an excellent lunch at Steyr, in Austria . . .

We had been told that there was good fishing below the bridge. A large wet-fly pool held at least fifty rainbows. Below it, grayling could be tempted with a well placed dry fly and for this my choice would be a Tups Indispensable, Lunn's Particular or a Black Gnat with upright white wing making it clearly visible.

I fished the pool slowly and conscientiously. One trout fell to a Monster nymph (see page 139) and I lost two others before deciding to fish for grayling. No luck: I returned to the head of the bridge pool, intent on giving the Monster another chance.

Concentrating on the task in hand, I was barely conscious of people gathering on the bridge upstream until a man cupped his hands to his mouth and shouted to attract my attention. Some fifty people were there, the water below them boiling with surface feeding fish. But this was no hatch of fly; two boys, having the time of their lives, were throwing bread to the rainbows.

There seemed no point in demonstrating the sweet action and power of my new rod to the assembled company and I might as well have cast shirt buttons as artificial flies to the fish they were watching. I started to retreat. Another shout. I looked up and understood that I was to *cast and take a trout*, but by this time I was in no mood to have my downfall witnessed by so many people. The solution was obvious: bread. I took off my hat, held it upside down and yelled, 'Brot, Bitte!'

At the second attempt a piece of bread dropped into my hat. Danke schön! I broke the bread in half and put one piece on the point of the Monster. The spare bait I stored in my hat before replacing it on my head. And to cut a long story short, after releasing three fish I quit, bowing out to a roar of applause.

However, the entire incident had been witnessed by my dear friend O'Neill Ryan, resting on the bank, his face like thunder.

'I expected better things from you,' he said. 'Did I have to travel this far to see Charles Ritz become a beggar in order to catch trout? I just wish you could have seen yourself – arm outstretched, hat in hand. 'Brot, Bitte!' Horrible! Wait until I tell this story to the boys of the NYAC (New York Anglers' Club).'

To think that I waited until I was eighty before wandering from the straight path of the purist! Perhaps I am reverting to childhood, to the days when I fished Lake Lucerne for Swiss sardines. Bread, I recall, was an excellent bait.

My one consolation came later that afternoon. Our ghillie told us that for many people the bridge is the shortest route from the city to their homes. The trout know that at office closing time bread and other food will be dropped to them and at that time of day they never take a fly. The joke is to persuade a visiting fisherman to try for the fish and when the poor man has been well and truly snared, deride him for repeated and inevitable failures.

'I've been a ghillie here for twenty years,' said Hans. 'You are the first fly fisher who had the courage to use bread and not worry about the purists' reaction to such . . . what would they call it? . . . *sacrilege*!'

Health

As I am now eighty years of age – and still fishing – it may not be inappropriate to include a chapter on Health in what is essentially a book on fly-fishing techniques. Fishermen equipped with good tackle and poor health have the odds against them, though some 50 per cent of the illness experienced during the latter part of our lives could be avoided.

Much of the ill health that comes with advancing years involves the heart, the vertebrae or the weight-bearing skeleton. Some is due to prostate trouble, while other setbacks are the result of excessive eating, drinking or smoking; sometimes all three.

I advise you to consult a medically qualified osteopath immediately following a sprain, a bad fall or the sudden appearance of rheumatic pains. If a bone has been displaced an experienced osteopath will quickly confirm this. Do nothing and you may find that after a few days the pain will go, giving the impression that all is well, whereas the nerves have recovered from the initial shock but the bones remain in an unnatural position. Such troubles are often revealed years later when it is too late for anything to be done and one must learn to live with acute pain.

Avoid chiropractors – osteopaths who are not medically qualified. Too often they have only limited knowledge and in many cases their manipulative techniques leave much to be desired.

Men approaching old age often suffer from hip trouble and find it difficult to walk properly. This too can be avoided. Years ago I suffered with slight pain in my right hip and immediately consulted Dr Douglas, an osteopath who diagnosed displacement of the hip bone. At that stage the matter was not serious, but had I not acted so promptly I might have been lame later in life. Dr Douglas had only to stretch my leg a couple of times before the hip went back into place. From that day, more than ten years ago, I have had the same treatment twice a year. It lasts only a few minutes – time well spent as an alternative to walking with a cane.

A new school of manipulation has been established in France under the guidance of Dr Robert Maigne, who takes care of me. It combines osteopathic manipulation with the most recent advances in medicine. Dr Maigne tells me that he is not opposed to cervical manipulations, which require great care and which he does almost daily, but he does object to the chiropractic theory that most ills can be cured by manipulative treatment.

Osteopathic treatment for minor troubles over the years has kept me in extremely good physical condition. I have sent many friends and employees of the hotel to osteopaths, with great success. A good specialist will tell you at once whether he can help or not: some cases require manipulative treatment, others medicine. But manipulation and medicine are not the only means of recovery.

From the age of fifty we may experience pains which cannot be relieved except by massage and then only after a series of treatments. One reason for such pains is the accumulation of poisons or chalky deposits in various parts of the body. A good masseur concentrates on these hypersensitive spots and the pain associated with them should disappear as the treatment progresses. A balanced diet also helps.

Other troubles arise because the muscles and ligaments controlling the skeleton are worn out, like strips of perished rubber. The bones are no longer held tightly in place and any unbalanced effort, strain or shock may further damage the nerves or tissues involved. Lacking the elasticity of earlier years they do not recover so readily.

The extensor muscles of the trunk and legs are often most easily damaged because from childhood days they have had to counter the weight of the body, standing, crouched or sitting. Their function is to prevent the body from falling forward and the legs from collapsing – countering the pull of the flexor muscles, their partners through life.

There is, of course, a natural balance between the flexor and extensor muscles, like cables holding the mast of a yacht in an upright position. Pain registers when there is a lack of balance between them. As a means of maintaining both in peak condition I have practised isometric exercises for many years – the same exercises observed by leading athletes throughout the world.

Isometrics involve maximum contraction of each group of flexor muscles, followed by contraction of the corresponding group of extensor muscles. This I do every morning, six times and for six seconds each exercise. They can be carried out while lying on a bed, on one's back or stomach, or in a hot bath if the bath is long enough.

If I may mention another personal experience, on one occasion I had what seemed to be an acute attack of rheumatism in my right shoulder. I could not lift my arm above shoulder level and all movement was reduced by at least 30 per cent. My osteopath, who could do nothing for me, suggested that a rheumatologist might succeed with injections, possibly of cortisone. I decided to have massage treatment before submitting to anything more drastic. Six months later the pain disappeared and I could again hang from the trapeze bar in my room, with both feet clear of the ground.

I must assume that if I had not given time and thought to these problems when I was younger I would now be a lame man. Instead, at eighty years of age, I can drive a car, run, play golf, wade in rivers and, of course, cast to rising fish. I could still go up and down mountains if necessary, but I decline because this is not good for one's heart.

With age we tend to become more nervous. Stress situations place a greater strain on the heart and this condition can get steadily worse. It happened to me, but recognising the symptoms I taught myself to relax; not to rush, not to hurry, not to become upset about relatively trivial matters, and to rest whenever possible for at least thirty minutes after my mid-day meal. I have always slept for eight hours each night and will not take sleeping pills under any circumstances. If I wake during the night I read a book for a while, preferably a detective or spy story – serious works are not conducive to deep sleep.

As to my diet, I have reasonably good digestion and will only eat foods that do not leave a bad taste in my mouth. I never eat to excess and normally choose from vegetable soups, meat, fish, potatoes, rice, macaroni, carrots and a limited number of sauces. To drink, red wine or water. I also drink at least two pints of water before going to sleep.

One out of every ten men over fifty years of age has difficulty in urinating and this may make a prostate gland operation necessary. If you experience this kind of trouble don't hesitate, consult a urologist without delay. He will probably wish to examine you once or twice a year before deciding whether to operate or not, but if you have to undergo the operation there is nothing to worry about; it is painless and will incapacitate you for no more than a fortnight or so. If you delay, you run the risk of further complications.

Finally, the older you get the more important it is to try and walk for at least one hour a day. I have several guests, men and women well over eighty years of age, who follow this advice with great benefit. However, I cannot over-emphasise my belief that at any stage of life good fishing and good health are inseparable. The trouble involved in taking care of oneself when young is amply repaid in later years.

PART VIII * SALMON AND SEA-TROUT

Sweden

THE GREAT PARADISE FOR THE TROUT FISHERMAN

We all dream of taking a very big trout with a small rod. We insist that our tackle dealer should give us a reel big enough to contain safe backing. During the whole of our fishing lives, we are continually in search of this marvellous experience and the Paradise in which one may secure it. Any one of us who succeeds in doing it is envied by the rest; he becomes a hero, he is spoken of for years. The monster's photograph never leaves his pocket book, it becomes dirty and its edges torn. He is always on the look-out for an opportunity of showing it. He'll even pay for a round of drinks in order to be able to tell the story of the great fight for the hundredth time. The locality in which he caught it becomes legendary, almost a place of interest to tourists! In the days of our grandfathers, more big trout were caught and they were less talked about! Today, we content ourselves for the most part with thinking about the giant rainbow trout in New Zealand, South America or Alaska, the steelheads of Oregon and British Columbia, and the famous marbled trout of Yugoslavia.

But the great Paradise still exists today. Its secret is jealously guarded by the few people privileged to enter it. I tried for more than ten years, but in vain, to gain access to it. At last, in May 1952, thanks to my good friends in Goteborg, I received a letter telling me that I would have the right to fish there from the 12th–24th September. At last! I could test myself against the giant sea trout of the Em, which is the most extraordinary river of big trout in the world.

On the appointed day, I arrived at eleven o'clock in front of a big white house. I had hardly opened the door of the car when two pretty young Swedish women in pale blue dresses, aprons and white caps, seized hold of all my paraphernalia and hurried off with it! Then my host appeared. A tall man who looked completely English: the Chevalier Ulfsparre, followed by a splendid looking woman with all the air of a great lady of the court of Louis XIV. She will always be for me the queen of hostesses. I was then presented to H.R.H. Prince Wilhelm of Sweden, to M. Gabrielson, the maker of Volvo cars, to M. Magnus, a client of the Ritz, and several other men among whom I had the pleasure of recognising my friend Arvid Carlander, the champion tunny fisher. They were all accustomed to fishing the Em.

The fishing is some seven kilometres in extent, but it is in the last thousand yards in

above: The steelhead or sea-run rainbow trout
below: The Malangfoss 'Salmon Aquarium'

The head keeper of the Soca fishing for marbled trout in Yugoslavia

above: A stretch of the Aaro, where salmon must be held, come what may
below: A stretch of the Em (main pool for sea trout)

Fishing on the Tweed

particular, as well as in the river mouth on the Baltic, that most fish are caught. The upper reaches are encumbered with weed and the banks too difficult of access. Wading is risky, and the pools are few and far between.

The Em resembles a Normandy chalkstream, but with numerous rocks and more rapid currents. There are also slow currents and smooth water. As for the fish, they are to be found practically everywhere. Wading is difficult. One needs a third leg owing to the big stones on the bottom and the poor visibility. The water is transparent, but dark, as in many Northern rivers. The Em is fished in April and in September. It contains 90 per cent sea trout (fish of less than five pounds are rare) and 10 per cent salmon. There are also pike which will sometimes take a fly and white-fish, like pollan, which make excellent eating, as well as chub.

After luncheon, I went to the fishing-room and saw on the rack big two-handed rods of thirteen and fourteen feet. I decided nevertheless to fish with my 9½ ft. rod.

On the 12th, 13th, 14th, and 15th September, I caught nothing, merely losing three fish of which two were big ones. I fished in the mornings before breakfast, then from ten to twelve-thirty and in the afternoon from five to seven. At last, on the 17th September, the fish became more active, and, in the morning, before breakfast, I took my first trout in Lawson's Pool. Then, in the Sea Pool (at the mouth), at my second cast, my reel began emptying at full speed and I had the impression of having on the end of my line the fish one can only find in Paradise! I was all alone and was wondering where and how I would take my fish with my pocket gaff. At nine o'clock I went back to the house, painfully carrying my two fish which weighed 13½ and 20 pounds on the scales!

During the following days, I took another six trout, making eight in all, on my Parabolic with nylon tapered to ·014 in.: they weighed 9, 10, 13½, 17, 17½ 17, 18 and 20 pounds. Average 15 pounds.

Here are a few words on the technique of fishing the Em.

* *Rapids. Moderate currents. Deep water.* You fish with a wet fly as for salmon. The artificial fly should as far as possible drift down the current well ahead of the leader and without drag. Whenever the current forms a loop or pocket in the line, you must mend the line by moving the rod tip in the opposite direction, which raises the line, replaces it upstream and straightens it out. You also play fast and loose (the raising of the rod followed by lowering it again) to straighten the end of the line and the leader, particularly at the end of the drift (see diagram). The depth at which the fly drifts depends on the size of the hook.

* *Low water. Calms. Shallows.* In these you fish with a greased line. The fly should drift at about a foot beneath the surface. The line should be greased to within two or

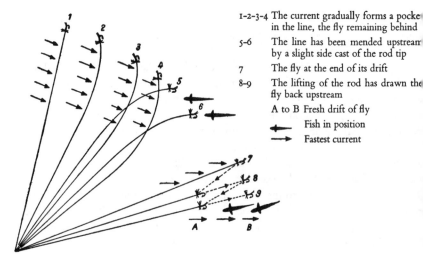

1-2-3-4 The current gradually forms a pocket in the line, the fly remaining behind

5-6 The line has been mended upstream by a slight side cast of the rod tip

7 The fly at the end of its drift

8-9 The lifting of the rod has drawn the fly back upstream

A to B Fresh drift of fly

← Fish in position

→ Fastest current

Fig 58 Mending the Line by moving the Rod Tip

three yards of its point and it is this ungreased part, the whole of the leader and the fly which must always be submerged. The fly sometimes has a tendency to come to the surface, but a horizontal, rapid and abrupt movement of the point of the rod will make it sink again. This method of fishing is very exciting from the fact that it resembles dry fly fishing and that one can see the fish take.

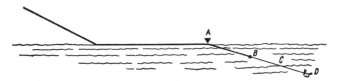

A The line is well greased up to about the foremost 3 yards of the front taper
B Junction of line taper with leader
C Leader
D Fly

Fig 59 Greased Line

* *Flies.* All the principal patterns for salmon or sea trout from 8 to 3/0. The smaller ones for the greased line. Colour: clear light, pale coloured flies; bad light, dark coloured flies. I have a weakness for the prawn fly whose supple hackle round the body often gives a semblance of life and on which I have caught all my fish with hooks No.2 (General Practitioner).

The sea trout of the Em systematically refuse the floating fly while, on the Laerdal in Norway, it is accepted when conditions are favourable.

In 1956, I had the privilege of being invited by the Duke of Roxburghe to fish his water on the Tweed during the spring run of salmon. After my experiences on the Em with the greased line, I was anxious to learn more about it, especially with low water flies. One thing the Duke taught me was how to strike for spring salmon (the Em sea trout take the fly much more frankly). You must hold one or two feet of slack line in hand and, when a fish takes, the slack must be immediately released to give the fish time to turn and obtain the best striking angle for the leader. Should you strike too soon, nine times out of ten the fly will be pulled out of the fish's mouth. Spring fishing on the Tweed is my favourite type of sport owing to the possibility of landing a salmon with trout tackle. One morning, in one-and-a-half hours, fishing one pool and using a 9½ ft. rod, I had the good luck to kill six nice fish.

I have copied, from the big book of fishing statistics kept by the Chevalier Ulfsparre, the results for the last twenty-five years and I think that it is of interest to publish them.

Sea trout and salmon taken on the Em from 1926 to 1952

	Spring	Autumn	Total
1926	434	28	462
1927	518	57	575
1928	510	66	576
1929	392	26	418
1930	264	57	321
1931	146	62	208
1932	465	49	514
1933	753	54	807
1934	827	93	920
1935	905	109	1,014
1936	802	77	879
1937	751	142	893
1938	659	106	765
1939	477	—	477
1940	333	44	377
1941	1,000	27	1,027
1942	734	39	773
1943	538	45	583

1944	478	38	516
1945	315	101	416
1946	358	105	463
1947	700	65	765
1948	434	74	508
1949	845	13	858
1950	367	27	394
1951	161	29	190
1952	802	—	802
	14,968	1,533	Total 16,501

Approximate average weight: Spring: between $6\frac{1}{2}$lb and $19\frac{1}{2}$lb.

Autumn: between $8\frac{1}{2}$lb and $26\frac{1}{2}$lb.

The best catch for one day: 6 fish, 113lb (sea trout – to one rod – and taken by a British fisherman).

Record: 32lb $5\frac{1}{2}$oz (sea trout).

Length of the principal fishing: 1 kilometre.

Norway

It is in Norway, that honest country, on the big steeple-chase course of the Aaro, that I have felt the greatest excitement and achieved for once the rewards of my perseverance.

Norway! The dream country of all anglers! The region of the Arctic circle, a wild Paradise! Fish and yet more fish and few anglers to disturb them: that is what most of us think when we glance at the map and see thousands of miles of river flowing into fjords, lakes and yet more lakes. One of my friends, who has cast his line in most of the fifteen hundred miles of water of the Viking country, when telling me of his journey, said: 'Finally, I was crossing the Arctic Circle by the Storsteinnes road to the Lyngen ferry, in search of a river in virgin country, when I saw a little track that would just about take a car. My map seemed to show that it led to a river flowing down from Lapland. I decided to try it. After six terrible miles I came to a dead end. I found a narrow path that I thought must lead to the river. At last, I was going to discover virgin water! My friend and I put on our boots and mounted our rods. After two hours' walking, we came to a little clearing on the bank of a river which was flowing crystal clear. On the right, upstream, rocks masked part of the reach. My heart was beating; I was in that state of ecstatic anticipation one feels when one has travelled over fifteen hundred miles to find ideal fishing. I selected a fly and set about offering it to several promising rises. Then, suddenly, I thought I must be dreaming! It was utterly impossible! I said to my companion: "Have you brought the little radio?"

' "No; I left it in the car."

'Was I the victim of an hallucination? I looked at my companion and saw that his face expressed bewilderment. I listened. There was no doubt of it, *The Third Man* seemed to be coming from beyond a big rock! I walked round the rock and found a boy of some ten years of age, sitting on the bank with a stick and a worm on the end of a string. Beside him on the moss were several red-flanked trout. He was waiting for a take and whistling the famous melody, learned, no doubt, from the radio during winter evenings!'

This warning had put me on my guard, but I always try, when about to travel to a new country, to make a triple check on all the information I receive. I knew that the date of the salmon's arrival varied from year to year, as well as the state of the water, and that on the average it was only in one year in three that there was a chance of really good fishing. It was therefore necessary to try to hire fishing on one of the rivers where success was most likely and to make sure of fishing it at the best period. If it could have a large pool, particularly a pool at the foot of a big waterfall, where the salmon are obliged to remain for some time, it would be ideal!

I had selected Malangfoss on the Malselv, a hundred miles north of Narvik. And I wanted to fish as late as possible to try to avoid rain and the spring spates. The further north you go, the later the salmon arrive, which was another reason for choosing Malangfoss. My friends, Gaillard and Elby, had come back full of enthusiasm for this splendid river and I had cross-questioned them about it. Elby told me that he had killed a lot of salmon, of which one was over thirty pounds, and Gaillard had caught ten in five days' fishing, one of over forty pounds on a fly! But, as I have always noticed, information given by fishermen tends to lack precision about certain very important details. In spite of considerable correspondence with the Norwegians, from which I derived but little information, I discovered when I got there that there were several important snags of which I knew nothing, and that I was in danger of being allowed to fish only every other day.

THE ARCTIC CIRCLE

I flew from Paris to Stockholm, and took the train from Stockholm to Narvik. The journey took two days with twelve hours' stop in Stockholm. My inseparable fishing companion, Jacques Chaume, who had never caught a salmon, was with me.

Narvik has been entirely rebuilt; brand new, it has a hotel, the Royal, which is ultra-modern and has over a hundred rooms. As soon as we arrived, we telephoned John Rovold, who owns the biggest tackle shop in the town. John is a big, dark, fine looking fellow who no more resembles a Norwegian than I do! If he bought his clothes in Savile Row, he could walk without question into the House of Lords! He is a delightful, modest fellow, a great fisherman and shot, and was extremely kind to us. He was to join us at Malangfoss about the 18th July, to accompany us to other rivers in the district between the 20th and 30th.

We left the next day at eleven o'clock in a hired car for Rundhaug, six miles from Malangfoss, where we arrived about three. The hotel lies on a great bend in the Malselv, in which we noticed many rises. A quick glance told us that they were grayling.

The rooms were very comfortable, with hot and cold running water, bathrooms close at hand, central heating, impeccable cleanliness and plenty of food.

My first night beneath the midnight sun. I slept very lightly!

THE GREAT AQUARIUM

At last the time had come! We got into the car with all our paraphernalia and, twenty minutes later, were at the Foshaug farm, lying three hundred yards from the river, which was invisible from it. After ten minutes walking through woods, in which the ground was carpeted with moss and fresh green grass, I saw the fishing hut perched on the edge of a slope fifteen yards above what seemed to be the rough waters of a little lake, till I saw a huge waterfall from which a mist was rising due to the violence of the river's fall. What a sight! What an enormous aquarium for salmon! Below was a big island, two hundred yards long, separating the river into two channels: one narrow and rapid, the other wide and fairly smooth. Salmon rising ever and again completed the enchantment for the angler. It was the giant pool of Malangfoss.

From the hut came two tall men, each well over six foot: the head of the clan, Konrad Foshaug, and his brother; they looked us up and down, and then shook us by the hand with a quiet dignity.

'Have you caught any salmon?'

'Yes. We took five during the night and lost one forty pounder, all with a spoon, flies are having no success. Luckily, I've got an assortment of ironmongery, as well as fly rods.'

Then he told me the good news.

The fishing rights belonged to the riparian farmers. The Foshaug family, on the right bank, and three other farmers on the left. They do not fish together during the same day, but in turn throughout the twenty-four hours. Each period begins at ten o'clock at night and sometimes until the same hour the following night. We therefore had only five days assured fishing and, by a piece of bad luck a Scotsman had arrived the day before and there would be but one boat between us. I noticed that there was another hut near the waterfall on the opposite bank.

'What about the left bank?'

'I don't know. There's already a Swede there who comes every year at this time. You must see the three farmers who have the right to fish every sixth day.'

After a good deal of discussion, I persuaded them to ask the relief that night if we could have a boat the following day. Fortunately, thanks to the assistance of Sandmo, the Rundhaug grocer, who had also forgotten to inform us, thinking that the Foshaugs would do all that was necessary, we only missed one day in ten, besides two owing to a spate which, luckily, rarely lasts in those parts for more than twenty-four hours. When the river is falling or, at least, not rising, the fish immediately become active.

On Foshaug's invitation, we put our rods together, while he watched us. When he saw our large spinning reels, he stared at them incredulously, and then proceeded to test our nylon, which he broke easily.

'You can't fish here with tackle like that!'

He showed me an old, shapeless greenheart rod with a fly-type reel and a devon. I tested his nylon: it was the same diameter and no stronger. To ram the point home, I told him that, with the very same tackle, I had taken sharks weighing two hundred pounds at Agadir, but I could see from his expression that he thought I was pulling his leg!

At last, we were ready, but the Norwegians had gone into the hut to join two others, who were also members of the numerous Foshaug family. They sat down at the table to eat and hold a council of war. It was impossible to guess what they were plotting but, given the slowness of the procedure, I began to realise that we should get no fishing till the moment seemed good to them, and that, at all costs, we must be patient. Moreover, since they fished all night, when the fish were taking, they were tired during the day and often rested. We had the right to fish continuously for twenty-four hours, but I had come to enjoy myself and had never been a supporter of mass-production fishing. I explained what was happening to Jacques, who was taken aback and prepared to tell them in his best English that at 50 kroner a day (£2.2.0) it was sheer robbery!

'Leave it to me', I said. 'With a little tact and kindness, I hope to be able to arrange things, but I feel sure that any attempt to hustle them will be fatal, because the Norwegians are a fine, independent people, but accustomed to live to a rhythm suited to their climate'

We thereupon sat down on a bench in front of the hut and smoked consoling pipes, while waiting for the council of war to come to an end! After a good half-hour, I heard: 'Let's go!'

We took the path leading to the boat. Jacques got into the stern and I amidships. There was a bright sun and it was beginning to get warm. It was eleven o'clock. We crossed the strong current under the bank which swept us downstream, but some vigorous rowing took us across on a slant and we entered the smooth waters by the upper end of the island on our way across to the left bank. When the water is normal, it is the best part of the pool. The boat was held at the speed of the current and our oarsman propelled it across the stream from right to left. We cast our lures, Jacques a spoon and I a devon, lent by Konrad. We were harling, making the lures zig-zag without using our reels. They moved only by the current. I then had the inspiration of a lifetime. To give Jacques the same chances, I suggested that we should take the fish in turn.

'If the two first take my devon, I'll hand you my rod with the second, and so on.'

He accepted, happily for me! I soon had a strong pull, but was unhooked. Shortly afterwards, Chaume cried: 'A fish!'

But it was the bottom! He had let out too much line! He cleared it and, a few seconds later, again raised my hopes. As for my devon, it continued to sulk.

Suddenly, Jacques' rod bent. A fine salmon jumped clear of the water some forty yards from us. He raised his rod and began reeling in, but the line began running out again. I shouted to him to put on the brake, but he dared not hold his rod with only one hand. He had turned pale! I leaned over and seized the brake lever. His rod was bending to the point of breaking, but Jacques clung on and so did the fish! Our ghillie was rowing as hard as he could, trying to get the boat away from the tail of the current where there were rock-strewn rapids.

'Gently, gently,' he said, 'give more line!'

He was afraid we would lose his fish, for we were fishing for him! Chaume began to weaken and could not maintain his gains of line. His fingers were turning white, and I had to adjust the brake again. Suddenly, I heard: 'Reel in quickly!'

The fish had jumped upstream and was swimming towards the boat. The reel was turning at full speed, then stopped suddenly: the rod tip almost touched the water! The fish began diving to the bottom, shaking its head violently. I encouraged Chaume and explained how to move the fish. At last, to my great relief, the salmon began to move and the reel to fill again. Jacques smiled, his eye was bright and lively and he was no longer trembling. To gaff it, we went towards the left bank, downstream of the hut, where there was a little beach. But we had not reached it yet! The boat stopped, the salmon had recovered and was trying to reach the current. Chaume's face manifested anxiety; he clung to the rod which was bending dangerously. The damned fish was still full of fight! Jacques' rod was almost horizontal. This was his first salmon, the fish one never forgets! I could see the moment coming when he would hand me the rod.

'Hold on, you'll get him! I can see him to the left, just under the surface. God, what a splendid fish! A monster!'

'Cling on!'

The boat touched ground, Konrad and I leapt ashore. Jacques, trembling again, got to his feet, tripped, just managed to recover himself, and stood in the water, bent as double as his rod. At that moment, the salmon came to the surface quite close to the boat and the line was in danger of passing beneath it. Foshaug was in a terrible state, and shouted: 'Look out!'

Fortunately, the fish stopped and Jacques succeeded in bringing it in. At last, it was at our feet, fighting as much as it could with its head, then slapping the surface of the water with its tail. It was utterly exhausted, and so was Jacques! The fish was gaffed. The blood flowed. A club descended on its head. There were thirty-five pounds of fresh run salmon, all blue and silver and still covered with sea lice, on the bank!

Chaume sat down on a rock, wiped his forehead, and took off his wind-cheater. I embraced him! We were both delighted! What a splendid fish! Long live Norway and Malangfoss! Jacques had caught his first salmon, having travelled very nearly two thousand miles to do so. And now, it was my turn! I would show the Norwegians how one caught fish with ultra-modern tackle.

My hopes and ambitions were premature!

To begin with our master-gaffer said: 'I think I'll now go and have a little rest'. Really, the fellow seemed to take great care of himself! He had rowed hard, it was true, but if he were already tired, our hours of fishing would be even more limited! We took the opportunity of watching the grayling, constantly taking the flies that I now saw for the first time; their bodies were like those in Austria, but their wings were much larger; they looked like little sails the shape of an upturned pear. We decided to bring our little dry fly rods the next day. The rises were mostly rapid and often ended in a splash; the hatch was at its height; it was like a regatta of tiny sailing yachts, disappearing suddenly, one after the other, in a minute whirlpool lasting a fraction of a second. But the rest period went on! At last, I took my courage in both hands and gave Konrad to understand that, after so long a journey, I very much wished to take my first salmon on the Malselv.

'Don't be in a hurry! You'll take your salmon and many more when the moment comes!'

He returned to contemplating the river. At last, I heard him say: 'Let's go!'

He rose to his feet and started slowly in the direction of the boat. We jumped quickly into it. I had replaced my devon with a spoon. We went into action again! Chaume's rod suddenly bent promisingly, but Konrad said: 'The bottom! Bring it in!'

I was beginning to think that Jacques was getting hooked too often! I cast again and let my spoon hang about thirty yards from the boat. We were zig-zagging again. Out of the corner of my eye, I was watching my companion's rod, when I suddenly saw it bend. He cried: 'A salmon!'

He held on to it all right, and it was another fine one. But I remembered our agreement, and, handing my rod to Konrad to place in the bows, I took Jacques's.

'Look out Charles! He's fighting very hard and he's very strong.'

'So am I. And I'll have him out for you in a couple of ticks.'

He was the devil of a brute. The reel was rapidly emptying, but I hurriedly put on the brake and, taking the bull by the horns, exerted all my strength.

'Gently, gently!' Konrad continued counselling.

To cap it all, Chaume also began giving me advice.

'Charles, you're mad! You'll break everything! Take your brake off.'

But I knew what I was about. I knew my tackle. I had used greater force on the Moroccan sharks and I began pulling like a galley slave. The salmon was fighting hard but I refused to yield it a yard of line, and my rod remained bent double. Our oarsman, who had at last understood that I would go my own way, decided to make for the bank as quickly as possible, and I began dragging the wretched salmon after us; it must have wondered what was happening to it, as it began quickly exhausting itself by making the wildest efforts! We touched ground. I leapt out of the boat – with the suppleness of a telegraph pole – and exerted all my strength to bring it in. The pitiless gaff once more fulfilled its executioner's role: twenty-three pounds, a good weight! I had shown them what a Swiss was capable of! But I heard Konrad say: 'You must go at it more slowly, or you'll lose a lot of salmon'.

He showed me the treble hook of which one branch was bent open.

'And now, a rest', said our oarsman. 'It's lunch time.'

When we returned to the right bank the fish were being very active. And, what was more, Mr Stephen, the Scotsman, who had the advantage of a much more energetic oarsman than ours, was having continuous success. He already had four salmon!

We hurried over luncheon, but it did us no good since it was only an hour later that the, by now traditional, 'Let's go!' was heard. I had been told by Sandmo that it was between eleven and four o'clock at the latest that the salmon would take. The notes in my fishing diary confirm this information precisely. I put on a big curved spoon on which I had changed the split rings, replaced the lower hook by a stronger one and added a smaller hook to the top ring. Stephen was now resting and we had the whole of the best part of the pool to ourselves. I thought I held all the trumps.

'A salmon!' Chaume shouted once more.

But the fish became unhooked at once, which restored me to hopefulness. It should now have been my turn, for I was counting on the law of averages that should by now be in my favour. But not at all. It was my companion who once again placed his spoon in the right place. His line began to run out, with a fish that went off like a torpedo.

'Give me your rod!'

'No! It's my turn, the last one doesn't count, he got off the hook.'

There was no more to be said. He was within his rights and I had to content myself with looking on. It was all over very soon, and we had another fish of twenty-two pounds. Then, rest again. I was exasperated but there was nothing to be done about it but light another pipe and mobilise all my reserves of patience.

At last we began fishing again. In spite of my numerous changes of spoon, I had no success at all. Evidently, I had missed the boat in every possible sense and the Scotsman, who was fishing with two rods, had ended by revealing to the salmon the shortcomings of ironmongery as food!

After twenty minutes of failure, Konrad decided that we should try the counter current on the left bank which flowed towards the waterfall, and in which the fish had not been alarmed that day.

Jacques' hooking another fish showed me that I had let out too much line. I put this right and felt the vibrations of my lure which was now working perfectly. I regained my courage, the great moment must be at hand! As if the dream were coming true, two salmon broke the surface a few yards from us. I quickly drew in my line and tried to place my lure near them. I turned the reel as fast as I could, all my nerves were tense, my heart was beating fast! I thought I'd got it! I had it! It was my hour! I felt the joy of life again! But it was only a flash in the pan.

And now, Chaume, with the calm superiority of an old hand, was saying, without turning a hair: 'A salmon! Bring him in quick, Charles, he's a big one and very wild!'

I was flabbergasted! Foshaug, who had not forgiven my remark about the sharks of Agadir, said: 'Very good, Mr Chaume!'

233

And I remembered that, according to our agreement, it was my turn. I took the rod, but it went against the grain, as I'd been deprived of the satisfaction of hooking my own salmon! Jacques quickly yielded his place, and I had the impression that he was beginning to be sorry for me and to understand the pitiful grotesqueness of my position. He could not, however, help telling me that the spoon should be kept near the bottom, that he had weighted it in order to be able to fish with a shorter line and, what was more, that the fish was then more effectively hooked. This was a good lesson to bring me back to reality. When fishing, modesty is rule number one.

Clearly, all the salmon in the world were in league against me. But I was going to have my revenge. In spite of the continual advice to go gently and give more line from Konrad, I did my best to break the lot! Disgusted, deprived of all satisfaction in taking the salmon, I brought in Chaume's twenty-nine pounder in record time!

On the following days, it was the same story. The final results of our seven days' fishing at Malangfoss were: eleven salmon caught by me, and seven lost. While Chaume had lost six and taken fifteen. Of my eleven, five had been hooked by my generous and understanding companion.

On the sixth day, Stephens having left, we had two boats. Dr Hastings of Quebec arrived for two days, without tackle and without having reserved a boat. I invited him to come in my boat and lent him tackle. Twenty minutes after our spoons were in the water Hastings brought his first Norwegian salmon to the gaff: thirty-one pounds of fresh run fish; then another of eighteen pounds, while I had to be content with one of twelve pounds!

On the 19th July, our last day, some Americans arrived at the hotel. Dr Carnes Weeks, of New York, came up and spoke to me in the hall.

'You are Ritz? I've heard you spoken of at the Anglers' Club. I have with me a lady of sixty years of age who has already done some big game fishing, but has never fished for salmon. She's only with us for two days and I wonder if it would be asking too much of you to fish with us tomorrow and help her catch her first salmon?'

Chaume must have told him of my gifts as a mascot! However, it was better than nothing and who could tell what might not happen. I accepted. The next day, after fishing for ten minutes, this charming, sporting lady caught her first salmon, and after a great deal of excitement, Foshaug, the executioner, announced: 'Twenty-two pounds'. As for me, I had the consolation of acquiring a remarkable dexterity in the art of taking in my line at full speed and seizing my neighbour's rod within a second of time!

That very evening, returning from Malangfoss, I was giving the grayling a trial in front of the hotel, when I saw a big Cadillac draw up in the yard. It had a Vaudois number. Swiss! Fellow countrymen! I went along to introduce myself, and found Popol, my friend Paul Bernes.

'Popol! What a surprise!'

'Not for me, Charles, I knew you were here! I've come to spend two or three days with you! Nicolas Denissoff, his wife and daughter are with me; they are on their way to make a cruise to the North Cape.'

I was astonished. Denissoff! The Aaro! The Terrific! I was introduced to a delightful old gentleman of seventy-four years of age, but as lively and alert as a young roedeer, and to a delightful woman, very French in her manner. I immediately talked to him about rods, knowing the reputation this great fisherman had for casting. An hour later, I had got him to try all my salmon rods. There were eight of them. And, what was more, he tested them for an hour in the rain. His style is impeccable and so supple that the length of the casts he achieves is hardly credible. His verdict filled me with joy: perfect, even the fourteen and a half foot rods, but too weak and too short for his river. His river! I had dreamed of it! But I did not dare embark on that much too delicate subject!

That evening after dinner, Popol, that charming Popol, the best of friends, who became for Jacques and me during the second part of our journey a veritable saviour, said: 'You'll fish the Aaro, I know Denissoff will invite you'.

I felt a new surge of hope. All disappointment vanished.

The next morning, before the Cadillac left for Tromsoe, where the Denissoffs were to embark on the ship for the North Cape, I heard these exciting words: 'Paul Bernes will drive you over to us in five days' time, and you'll be our guest for two day's. That night, I did not sleep a wink.

THE GREAT AARO STEEPLECHASE-COURSE

Having been joined by our hosts, who had returned from the North Cape, at the station at Otta, three hours' drive brought us to the Lake of Hafslo, which pours its waters into the Aaro by a succession of waterfalls, descending more than six hundred feet in less than one and a half miles. The road then follows a gorge, a chaos of broken water, and suddenly the fantastic Aaro appears, hidden away at the bottom of a tiny valley which runs down to Sognfjord. The hills on either side are in reality small, steep, green mountains covered with the stunted birch trees of Norway. Big sheep feed freely on them almost in a wild state.

The car stopped on the bridge which leads to the left bank, where the house and farm are situated. At the bottom of the valley, near the waterfall, there are three more houses and the turbine building. The house stands some thirty feet above the river and is opposite the principal pool. Here nature reveals all the splendour of these northern countries and one has the impression of being cut off from the rest of the world. From the wooden terrace that surrounds the house, one can see part of the fjord, immediately below the river's mouth. The latter makes a great S-bend some one thousand, five hundred yards long and about sixty wide, an uninterrupted succession of currents with white broken water, ending in a last great rapid which falls boiling some ninety feet in two hundred yards to reach the level of the Sognfjord. This S contains platforms, artificial plank weirs, bridges, great rocks, in all some twenty obstacles. Moreover, the big stones and rocks bordering the river, combined with the speed of the current, make the pursuit of a fish more than perilous, unless one is young and very active. Wading is very dangerous. It might be the grand steeplechase course at Auteuil! Thanks to these great works, the fishing has been enriched with numerous artificial pools and resting and spawning places for the salmon, which the waterfall above the turbine prevents going further upstream.

It was eight o'clock at night. It was still light, but we were to start fishing only next morning. After dinner, our friend baptised us: Charles became Sacha and Jacques Jascha. Then he showed me his tackle. He has been broken so often that he attaches great importance to the solidity of his knots which are all reinforced with aluminium cellulose varnish. He only fishes with a fly or a prawn. And one should see the care with which he mounts his tackle. Every weak point is verified, the leader, of three twisted

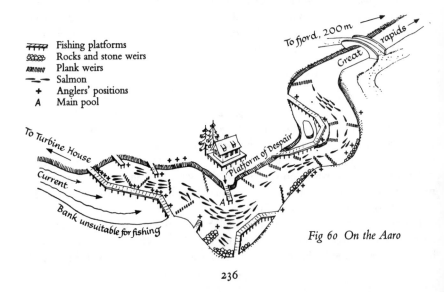

Fig 60 *On the Aaro*

236

strands of nylon, is tested, the points of the hooks sharpened, etc. Paul Bernes, who the previous year had succeeded in landing a fifty-five pounder with a fixed-spool reel and gaffed it on his own, explained to me that, on the Aaro, owing to the speed of the currents and the power of the fish, you must endeavour to stop them whatever the cost at their first run, even if it breaks you.

On the wall of the dining-room, I saw a drawing of the biggest: seventy-six pounds in weight, 4 feet 8 inches in length! This monster is on view in the Bergen Museum. It was taken on a prawn in the Tender Pool on the 31st July, 1921. In the fishing-room, I found on a table a pile of more than twenty drawings of fish over fifty pounds.

The next morning there was bright sunshine. The river was still low, but had risen a little. During the whole month of July, Denissoff and Popol had not taken a salmon. They were refusing to take and were very late owing to the lack of water coming from the lake of Hafslo.

Our host decided that it would be wiser to wait for the late afternoon. The fish were wary and it would be better when the light grew dimmer. We took the opportunity of fishing the estuary in the fjord to see if the sea trout had arrived.

At last, the great moment came. It was six-thirty when Jacques Chaume threw his spoon into the Solkin pool, which, with the Prawn Pool, is the best place on the river. At the fourth cast, he hooked a salmon. I went off to the platform on which he was standing. He was bending double and straightening up again but could not succeed in stopping the fish which was fighting like mad. Suddenly, the rod went straight. Broken! The nylon of ·027 in. had been cut through on a rock.

As for me, I had been fishing for twenty minutes without result, until dinner-time in fact. As soon as I had drunk my coffee, I left Jacques to play *belote* with Denissoff, and went to the platform. There was still half an hour of daylight. Perhaps I might have luck!

And, indeed, at my third cast, I felt an appalling tug which nearly made me lose my balance. I resisted the fish's jerks with all my strength. The rod bent to breaking point. I was trying vainly to get in line, when suddenly my rod tip straightened up, so suddenly that I very nearly fell over backwards. I was broken! Broken on nylon line of ·027 in., which had been carefully checked and tested! I was disconcerted, but had no regrets. To be defeated by such an adversary was honourable enough.

There is no point in relating in detail all the incidents of the next few days. It suffices to say that, during this first stay on the Aaro, I was subject to the greatest and most splendid emotions that an angler can hope for. I knew great hopes, mad excitements and bitter disappointments! Pursued by continuous bad luck, I succes-

237

sively lost the nine salmon that I had the joy of striking and holding. My companions were more fortunate. Our host landed four salmon out of five and Jacques Chaume two out of four. But I left with a feeling of enthusiasm and gratitude, having practised, in a unique setting, the greatest sport imaginable.

If I was full of gratitude towards my host, I had nevertheless a revenge to take on the Norwegian salmon!

During our journey back, Popol informed me that Nicholas was to stay on the river until the end of September. I was to join my Zürich friends on the Traun at the end of August, but I should be back in Paris in the first days of September, and free once more. I was haunted by one idea: to see the Aaro again.

As soon as I had got back from Austria, I wired Nicolas: 'Can you have me for a week?' And forty-eight hours later a Sogndal hired car dropped me on the bridge over the river at ten o'clock in the morning. In a few minutes, I reached the house where I saw my friends playing *belote* on the terrace. They greeted me with open arms and at once put me at my ease. I was very embarrassed, fearing that I had abused their kindness. But one must recognise that the Russians of the *ancien régime* are *seigneurs*!

There was one question I was longing to ask, and I couldn't wait to enquire of Nicolas: 'Have you taken any salmon on the fly since I left, and are they still coming up the river?'

I learned that in August, Nicolas had once again hooked a huge fish which had finally succeeded in passing through a dam which was short of two planks, but that, since that particular adventure, not a fish had taken the lure. As for sea trout, there were some, but the big run had not yet taken place. In 1950, the total catch had reached about two thousand. We would try, nevertheless, to take a few breeding fish for Nicolas, but we would spend most of our time at the mouth of the river in the fjord and concentrate our efforts on the sea trout.

The afternoon and the evening rise were without results in spite of a few salmon behaving like porpoises in the Prawn and Solkin Pools.

The following morning, I mounted my fixed spool reel with a ·010 in. monofilament line and a little Carrère spoon on a very light 7 ft. spinning rod. I also took a Master fly rod, and both dry and wet flies. When we arrived at the river mouth, Nicolas decided to fish with my 14 ft. rod and little wet flies with double hooks. He advised me to take the boat with Anton, and try my luck in the lower currents opposite the boat-house. Casting lightly, I took several fish and saw several rises at the end of the smooth water, downstream of the point on the left bank. Moving out into the stream, to a place where a current divided into two parts, I noticed that there were rises along both currents. I presented a floating Cahill towards the left bank, where

*After an hour's fly fishing on the Em: two
sea-trout weighing 20 and 13 pounds.*

The Malselv above Malangfoss

Miss Sweden 1952: a 21-pound sea trout from the Em

there was least depth, and quickly took two fish of about a pound each, but was surprised to see that they were trout. I then tried on the right, and took three sea trout of the same size. The hatch lasted about forty minutes and I had a catch of fifteen fish. On the left, I was taking trout, on the right sea trout. Anton, who had never seen dry fly, watched me with great interest and said that he would much like to try it. I went back to the bank, where several fish were still active close in and in a very short while my ghillie, who was an excellent salmon caster, had grasped the technique and caught three fish.

We had been keeping our eyes on Nicolas who now signalled to us to join him. He was wearing bathing shorts, had had a swim, and had also taken several fish though he had lost a very big one. He had unfortunately sprained his wrist, owing to wearing boots without nails, and in spite of many warnings!

As we had only been fishing with the fly, I thought there was a chance of trying spinning before luncheon. The tide was beginning to go out. It was noon. I went to the second platform to get as close as possible to the opposite bank where there was some good, deep water. I might perhaps find a good fish! I sent my ·353 ounces Carrère, weighted under the swivel, across the river and brought it slowly back so that it should work along the bottom. After several casts without result, I left the platform and waded out into the current which soon stopped me. My lure went out and sank two yards from the opposite bank, and I saw a monster leap out of the water and fall back with an enormous splash! Nicolas shouted: 'Charles! A huge sea trout!'

I had but one idea: to cast again at once and try and place my spoon over the fish. I started reeling in quickly, but a powerful tug bent my rod in two. Good God, I had it on! I was certain that it was a salmon, it was too big for a sea trout. What was I to do? My line was running out at full speed. Everything would break! And I remembered all my misfortunes in July! Another jump! On ·010 in.! I had merely to resign myself to waiting for the end! This was it! I was broken! I turned the reel and the line came in. How very strong the current must have been! For I felt much more than the normal pull. Incredible! I still had my fish and he was coming slowly but surely in! I regained courage. After all, I was quite close to the fjord and in a position to follow my fish wherever he might go, particularly since the boat was not far away. I called to Anton: 'Be prepared! Bring the boat over!'

I was terrified. I had had the most extraordinary luck at the two first jumps, the fish's tail had not touched my line. If it did so, I should see it no more! Then, I raised my little 7 ft. rod above my head, having put on my brake practically to its utmost extent, so as only to work on the reel. The salmon was still coming toward me. It was incredible! It was going down the current towards the fjord. I understood. It did

239

Aaro: Four giant salmon from Denissoff's collection:
Weights 53, 54, 54 and 58 pounds
Lengths: 4½ to 4¾ft. (coloured outlines on cardboard)

not know what had happened to it. It could feel neither my rod nor my reel and was allowing itself to go with the current! I would try Nicolas' trick. I began going slowly backwards downstream, regulating my speed in accordance with the fish, in such a way as to maintain only a light and uniform tension and let it fight only against the spoon of which it was trying to rid itself. I tried not to let it feel that it was held on a lead. Backwards! Forwards! Stop! Then it began all over again and, incredulously, I began to realise that the fish had completely lost its head and was still going down the current, from time to time making a momentary halt, followed by a move towards the centre, each time with less decision. It was now just below the surface. Its dangerous tail was close to my line; I was trying to hold the line so that it was not in alignment with the fish's body when it came to the surface. What a dance! It went right, left, backwards and forwards; and I kept a smooth, uniform tension, increasing it almost imperceptibly when I felt that the fish was beginning to slow down. This manœuvre seemed to be succeeding, for we were approaching the end of the current and entering the fjord. But I was in the water up to the top of my boots. Luckily Anton had come up, and I got into the boat in order to reach the gravel bank from which I could get to the little false arm beside the boat house, the perfect place for the finish, if my great day had come! Anton manœuvred the boat perfectly and the salmon was still following! I felt I was going to bring it to the gaff. And now we had reached the gravel bank. I disembarked just in time, for a new rush obliged me to hurry to the centre. But it was only a short alarm. The fish stopped once more; and then the performance began all over again. It was continuously coming towards me; my reel was almost full. Then it came to the surface again! I could see it! Over twenty pounds! It shook its head and jumped out of the water but I was just behind it, watching out for my line. I moved quickly to the right and avoided the danger. Finally the fish stopped and remained motionless, letting itself be led on like a dog on a lead! I went back, and then back again, ten, twenty, thirty yards, and drew near to the boathouse. I was now on the great expanse of smooth water with a depth of two feet at the most. I went backwards again. There was now no more than about twenty inches of water and my fish, realising the trap into which it had fallen, became desperate and tried to escape, but it no longer could. It no longer had the strength to make a rush and only succeeded in floundering on the surface, almost touching my line, which I managed to keep out of its way by raising my arms as high as I could, though they were already tired from holding this position, for which I had not taken the precaution of training myself!

It was over! Here was the fish belly upwards. It was unbelievable! Nicolas, who was with me, gave me a last piece of advice: 'Charles, go to the narrow end of the current and bring him on to the stones, but only when you have got him completely exhausted'.

I asked him to get the gaff ready, but we only had the little stick with the cod hook, which Antoine used for sea trout! This was the climax! I went backwards and dragged my fish till it touched the bank. Nicolas gaffed it and pulled it towards him. The stick broke, but Anton was there and, lifting the fish on to the bank with a kick, fell on it and managed to hold it. For the first time, I heard: 'Bravo, Charles!'

We had no need to be concerned. The fish was completely exhausted and was not even flapping its tail. It was a splendid female still in perfect condition, its belly full of eggs.

I shall not try to say what I felt at that moment. I turned to Nicolas and saw his expression. It was certainly one of the most splendid moments of my life as a fisherman. My stop-watch showed fifty-five minutes; and on the scales my fish marked twenty-five pounds! Two days later, at the same time and place, I got another salmon with my first cast, and though exactly the same procedure followed, I was really able this time to savour each moment of the wonderful fight against an adversary which defended itself with the fury of a wild beast to preserve its liberty. Forty-five minutes later, a twenty-seven pounder received in its flank the little hook which had been mounted on a new stick. We had never imagined that the same thing could happen twice.

Since that day, Nicolas no longer insults my ironmongery, though I know that he still has reservations. Basically, he is right, for the fly will always be the only lure for self-respecting fishermen. But, half a loaf. . . And then, after all, I have an excuse, for it was certainly none of my doing that these two wretched fish should let themselves be taken so stupidly! I thought of the coloured boy on the Beaverkill who said: 'Perhaps God has told these poor fish to be kind to this foolish Swiss fisherman!'

I was perfectly aware, during this struggle, that the jerk of each turn of the reel instantly incited the fish to fight. One had to give the fish the impression that it was the current which was carrying it along, and this sometimes persuaded it to let itself go. It is for this reason that one can succeed sometimes, when the river conditions permit, in mastering a big fish fairly quickly with an ultra-light rod. The fish then fights only against the hook which it wants to get rid of at all costs, instead of trying to regain its liberty. After repeated failures, it begins to get hysterical and fights without method, dashing off on exhausting rushes, instead of using the tension of the line as a fulcrum.

The river of despair

I asked my dear friend, Sam Field, who leased the River Aäro for many years, to record his most thrilling experience. This is his story.

Fishing for Aäro salmon is not the kind of sport one usually associates with any other river, be it in Scotland, Norway, Iceland or Canada. This fierce stream – an unbelievably fast and dangerous water – is only half a mile long and the current is such that its salmon are exceptionally broad, heavy and powerful. They provide the most exciting sport imaginable.

Most of the river's eight or nine pools have been made by driving huge wooden piles into the bed. These break the flow to some extent and it is here that the salmon lie. Wading is out of the question and one fishes from the shore except at those pools where platforms have been erected.

When a salmon is hooked it is imperative that maximum pressure be applied to lift its head and prevent the fish from moving into the main stream. Long and powerful double-handed rods are advisable, for if one should fail to gain control at the first encounter, all is lost.

The river was controlled by Nicholas Denissoff who, for many years, bought up the netting rights in neighbouring fjords and kept the water well stocked from his private hatchery. It is interesting to note that many fish from the Aäro hatchery, used to stock the rivers of other countries, returned to this river.

The Aäro holds the world record for the largest salmon taken with fly: weight, 76 lbs; length, 4 ft. 8 in. The fish was set up and is now in the Bergen Museum. Mr Denissoff killed several in excess of 60 lbs and has lost fish that must have exceeded 70 lbs.

The tackle commonly used gives some idea of the enormous power of the current and the strength of the fish encountered. Our rods were of split cane with steel centres, 15 ft. long. We used the heaviest of lines and double-hook flies ranging from 4/0 to 7/0. A special machine was made to twist three strands of 25 lb test nylon into a 75 lb test leader and all knots were sealed with a fast-drying varnish. Our 300 yards of backing was invariably between 75 lb and 100 lb test.

Nicholas Denissoff was a small man, a banker who had left Russia for Great Britain before the revolution. He had lost so many salmon that his insistence on super-strong tackle was almost obsessional.

We never did find a reel adequate for the job. We even tried saltwater big game reels, but despite such powerful tackle we were well beaten whenever a fish made its way into the main stream.

On my last day on the Aäro, Nicholas suggested that we fish each pool twice. First, I would try the fly. If unsuccessful, he would use the spoon, though he rarely fished with anything other than a fly.

At Pool No.1, the Home Pool, I cast a large fly for some fifteen minutes without raising a fish. Nicholas took over, moving a few yards at a time until he had covered the furthermost reaches of the water. No luck; but at the bottom of this pool there is a submerged rock and it seemed that on his last cast he had fouled the spoon on this boulder. After tugging and pulling for several minutes the hook failed to come free. I took the rod, determined to free the line or break, and found that I could do neither one thing nor the other.

We decided to move downriver to Pool No.2, instructing our ghillie to try his strength and, if necessary, to cut the line and join us below. As we walked down we were astonished to hear a wild shriek and turned to see Anton, our guide, racing along the bank, sometimes falling or tripping, sometimes dropping the rod; bloody knees and hands, and a mad look in his eyes as he did his utmost to prevent the fish from reaching the main stream.

There was no stopping that monster. It jumped once or twice, a massive, silvery giant, then headed for the fjord. Both line and rod broke and another huge fish had escaped. Nicholas estimated its weight at 70 lbs-plus. Why not? Nicholas never exaggerated.

I need hardly say that the spoon had not snagged the boulder. The salmon had taken the lure as it passed the rock and held it absolutely immovable. Our ghillie had been on the point of cutting the line when the fish swam downstream.

No fisherman worthy of the name will need me to record our feelings or the conversation which followed. Thank God, our wives had remained in the house. We fished no more that day: Nicolas, Anton and I went home and with the utmost solemnity consumed one bottle of vodka.

Coco Chanel

That great dressmaker, Coco Chanel, lived at the Ritz for more than thirty-five years. Her suite in the Cambom building was just opposite mine. On one occasion, knowing that she had been fishing the Alta with His Grace the Duke of Westminster, I asked: 'Mademoiselle Chanel, did you enjoy the salmon fishing in Norway?'

She told me of her concern when the Duke invited her to join his party.

'Never having fished before, I was most anxious. After all, who would want to make a poor showing at such a time?'

She need not have worried. One of the Duke's friends who always joined him on the Alta, was a famous fly-fisher. Coco explained her problems to him and received the soundest possible advice.

'Mademoiselle, in fishing we try to lure the salmon with an artificial fly. Casting is a simple matter, but when the fly is in the air the fish cannot see it. Your best chance of success is to keep your fly constantly on the water.'

He added that she need have no qualms about choosing the right pattern, nor waste her time changing flies. 'Just look at the sky . . . When it's clear and bright, tie on a Silver Doctor. When dark and overcast, use a Black Doctor. Nothing could be simpler.'

Being of a very practical nature, Coco followed his advice. As a result, on several occasions she landed more salmon than His Grace.

Fly-fishing for salmon on the Alta

I hope I shall be pardoned if in this chapter I devote myself to the technical problems of fishing with the fly for that royal creature, the salmon, and leave the description of the landscape to my illustrations.

The principal theme of this book being dry fly fishing for trout and grayling, I propose to limit my observations and conclusions, in regard to the salmon, to the results of my experiences during a five weeks fishing holiday on the Alta, though I make no pretence of writing as an expert on this subject.

Our party consisted of ten fishermen who killed over 400 salmon during this period, and what I have to say about this fish and the manner of catching it is based on the observations of myself and my friends during the course of this visit. The problem of the salmon and of salmon flies has been so comprehensively dealt with by writers who have penetrated the arcana of the subject that it is scarcely possible for me to contribute anything new to it.

As a specialist in dry fly fishing, I am more concerned to describe fishing for salmon with the fly sufficiently intelligibly, accurately and vividly to enable brother fishermen, who have never had the luck to experience this peculiar and highly specialised branch of fly-fishing, to grasp and appreciate the essential points of the sport. I would like to introduce them to the general context of the subject, present its principal problems to them and make them as familiar with the realities of modern salmon fishing, as if they had been fishing with me on the Alta. At the same time, I hope to enable them to draw comparisons between dry fly fishing for trout and grayling and wet fly fishing for salmon.

My modest belief is that the heart of the most hard-boiled fisherman beats faster with excitement on the capture of his first salmon, but that to take a trout or a grayling with his first cast represents the real acme of the angler's skill. All the same, should an opportunity for salmon fishing offer itself, grasp it with a glad heart. Salmon fishing presents a splendid contrast to the refined art of the dry fly fisherman.

A fighting fish provides a splendid spectacle and a dead one a vision of proud beauty.

Before I start talking about the Alta, I should like to describe, if in summary fashion only, the two most burning problems that disturb the peace of the sporting salmon: netting and poaching. I propose quoting from a pamphlet entitled *Salmon fishing in Norway*, which I received from the Norwegian Travel Agency in London, an unimpeachable source of precise information. This reads: 'The netting of salmon in the sea is injurious to river fishing. Netting in rivers is diminishing gradually in extent, but the same cannot be said of sea-netting. The old complaint of excessive netting in the fjords is still being voiced as loudly as ever it was. Certain narrow fjords, running deeply into the land, are virtually barricaded with nets, so that the salmon making their way to the rivers where they spawn have to negotiate almost impenetrable obstacles. It is reckoned that not more than one or two of every ten salmon succeed in finding their way into the rivers, the remaining eight or nine being caught in the nets. It is obvious that this practice is gravely prejudicial to river fishing and that it affects future generations of salmon, since relatively few mature fish ever reach their hereditary spawning grounds.

'The Norwegian authorities are fully aware of the importance of this difficult problem and are doing their best to control the practice of netting. The law lays it down that no salmon nets may be set between 6 p.m. on Fridays and 6 p.m. on Mondays. A clever salmon therefore will presumably make for the river of his choice only at week-ends. In Finland, where most of the rivers and lakes are state-owned, netting may be practised only with special permission from the authorities and this permission is rarely granted.'

With reference to the inspection of fishing and control of poaching, the pamphlet goes on to say 'the serious increase in illegal fishing is a matter of general knowledge. In this country of great distances an effective supervision of fishing waters is not only difficult but very costly. And, what is worse, it has transpired that the inspecting personnel and the members of local fishery commissions have on occasion made common cause with poachers.'

Government inspectors are now using new tactics to catch poachers in the act. At the weekend, when netting is forbidden, they fly along the coast in small aircraft and take a series of photographs showing the positions of the nets. These photographs reveal clearly whether a net has been left open in violation of the law. If it has, the owner of the net is prosecuted. This form of supervision was introduced in 1947 and has led, especially in North Norway, to remarkable results. On one inspection flight, in 1947, fifty nets were photographed. Only one of these was closed as the law prescribes. Forty-nine net-owners were prosecuted.

Magnus Berg, the Fisheries Inspector for North Norway, reports a case where the net-owner pleaded in defence that the photograph showed a net belonging to another fisherman. However, the Inspector, using a magnifying glass, was able to prove from the photograph that the defendant himself was standing on the bank by the net, which was incontestably open. The penalty was inflicted without further argument.

Olaf Gregerson, an Assistant-Inspector for North Norway, once checked thirteen nets in the course of a Monday morning. Nine of these were open and contained about 120lb weight of salmon. The fish were released and the net-owners punished.

Control of fishing from the air has no doubt come to stay; its effectiveness has been proved. Every poacher on the coast feels apprehensive when he hears the sound of an aircraft.

A good deal of poaching takes place even on the Alta. The Union of Owners of Fishing Rights appoints ten overseers, whose duty it is to watch the river day and night during the season when the salmon come up the river. The usual apparatus employed by poachers is a round tin of the sort in general used for green peas or other vegetables. To it, a handle is fixed. A line of nylon thread is wound round the tin. For bait, the poacher uses a heavy crocodile spoon bristling with hooks. The spoon is thrown by hand while the poacher holds the tin in his other hand, using it as a stationary drum reel. If he sees a danger of being caught, he lets the cheap device fall into the river and quickly makes off. In one month, I saw three of them at work.

* *The product of these salmon waters.* It is interesting to compare the weight of salmon taken in the Alta with that taken in the Laerdal, for instance, as these two rivers are of strongly contrasted types.

The Alta is a broad, powerful river with brown water. It is fished from a boat.

The Laerdal is a middle-sized river, which is fished from the bank. Its water is perfectly clear and swiftly running.

Alta:		1946	1947	1948	1949	1950
Weight of rod-caught fish..	Pounds	17,160	17,754	10,714	8,800	8,800
Percentage of total catch ..	..	57%	78%	70%	85%	100%
Total catch (rod and net) ..	Pounds	29,920	22,814	15,334	10,340	8,800

95% of rod-caught fish were caught from boats. There was an average of 4 to 8 rods on the 20-27 miles of river.

Tana:		1946	1947	1948	1949	1950
Weight of rod-caught fish..	Pounds	5,940	8,800	9,240	6,820	4,400
Percentage of total catch ..	..	7%	11%	13%	9%	6%
Total catch (rod and net) ..	Pounds	78,093	79,200	70,400	72,600	74,000

Laerdal:		1946	1947	1948	1949	1950
Weight of rod-caught fish..	Pounds	17,160	11,440	18,700	18,920	16,500
Percentage of total catch ..	..	97%	93%	94%	96%	92%

Net-fishing insignificant. Rod-fishing exclusively from the bank. An average of 30 to 40 rods on the 16-20 miles of river. These figures show that the Laerdal produces the greatest number of rod-caught fish, but the average weight per head of salmon caught is smaller.

* *Details of Interest.* The biggest salmon ever caught in the Tana was captured by Postmaster H. Henrikson. It weighed 79lbs.

The record for the Alta was a 60lb fish caught in 1951 by Lord Dudley.

The Alta produces the most consistent results for fly-fishers. The average weight is about 23lbs, but fish weighing 40lbs are not uncommon.

The record catch for a day was made by Roar Jöraholmen with 44 salmon in 24 hours.

The Duke of Roxburghe caught 39 salmon and grilse in one day in 1860.

Mr Harewood caught 26 salmon in one day in 1876.

Major Trotter (a one-armed man) caught 29 salmon weighing 615lbs in 8 hours in 1925.

The Duke of Westminster caught 33 salmon weighing 792lbs in one day in 1926.

The Alta is not fed by glacier water and its temperature is higher than that of the sea. The success of the artificial fly in this river is probably due to this fact.

In the year 1953 my friend Herbert Pulitzer, a great sportsman and a generous host, told me that he had rented the Alta River and invited me to fish with him there from 26th June, 1954. This was an unexpected piece of luck. For years, it had been impossible to obtain access to this outstanding salmon-river.

For nearly a hundred years the Alta had been rented to British sportsmen. In 1862 the Duke of Roxburghe had signed the first lease with the Union of Owners of Fishing Rights on the Alta. He was succeeded by the Duke of Westminster, who held the lease until his death in 1953.

This mighty river is divided into five beats stretching from the mouth to Topper, the highest of the great pools. Above Topper the river is not fishable as it rushes through a narrow gorge. Any angler who wants to fish above Topper has to be a first-class climber.

Two rods are allowed on each of the five beats. The current is so strong that it is impossible to row against it and the boat has to be held in position by two boatmen with long poles; or by steady rowing against the current while drifting slowly downstream.

Consequently, it is only possible to fish downstream. The boat must be controlled so that it moves less quickly than the current. When it reaches the lower end of the beat it is pulled ashore and taken back on a truck; that, at least, is the practice on the lower beats. On the two upper beats, in the neighbourhood of Sandia, a couple of boats with outboard motors are used and on the top beat, near Sautso, the boats are often moored. As the road stops a mile or two below Sandia, trucks cannot be used above a certain point. Today (1958) outboard motors are used exclusively.

The Alta produces remarkably fine fish. Reckoned over the whole season, the average weight is from 24 to 25lbs. During the first fortnight of the season (26th June-10th July) a still higher average is attained. Forty pounds are not uncommon. Although we caught eleven fish above this weight, 1954 was merely a good average year.

More fish are caught with the fly on the Alta and the Laerdal than on any other Norwegian river. I gained the impression that rod-fishers on the other rivers made a preponderance of their catches with a spoon or with prawns.

Fly-fishing for salmon is indisputably less difficult than the art of deluding trout and grayling with a dry fly. In salmon-fishing one has no need to deal with tricky situations by clever casting. Sureness of aim, the ability to make up your mind quickly and the perfect presentation of the fly play a less important role. Generally speaking, the angler's task is to cover by long casting and the correct steering of the wet fly the greatest possible surface of likely stretches of river or of pools. When a fish has missed his fly or when a fish he has spotted has refused it, the angler must cast again to the same spot, though of course the accuracy of his cast depends more on the skill of the boatman than on his own. Boatmen who know their business can usually manœuvre their craft in such a way that a fly thrown by even an inefficient caster will drift over the spot where the fish is lying.

Nevertheless, the good caster will catch more fish. Any fisherman who knows how to withdraw his fly in a single motion and plant it in the right place without preliminary brandishing, and who can lay it on the water so that it drifts in front of the leader, has substantially better prospects of success than a less skilful angler. A good caster, moreover, can throw to greater distances and consequently cover a greater area of water.

In my opinion, the skill of the boatmen and above all their knowledge of the art of rowing to suit the fisherman are the decisive factors in the angler's success. The manner of rowing is of the highest importance. Among the twenty boatmen whose services we could command one young man was outstanding for his oarsmanship, his short, light strokes causing the minimum of disturbance and noise in the water. I was continually amazed to see how effortlessly he appeared to be rowing, though always managing to keep the boat on a favourable patch of water and for longer than any of his comrades. His boat and that of Roar Jöraholmen were easily top of the list for catches during the month I was there. I attributed the success of young Jöraholmen largely to the invaluable support of his mate, a young and powerful lad, who was, incidentally, the local ski-jumping champion. Both these youngsters knew the river by heart, performed their job with zeal and enthusiasm and were able to foretell with remarkable accuracy the most likely places for fish according to the state of the water. Their competence was so great that more often than not they were able to predict exactly where and when the fish would take the fly. Whatever the conditions, good, bad or indifferent, they would never admit defeat and, by their example, inspired the angler to do his best and explore thoroughly any piece of water in which they were holding the boat against the current.

The differences between the various boats' crews were indeed striking, both in respect of their skill in manœuvre and the help they afforded the fisherman, including the gaffing of the fish. There was one man, a very good boatman, who, when nothing was doing, incessantly whistled a little tune on a very few notes, a practice that eventually got on the nerves of the most hardened angler. There were also lazy oarsmen and others who were simply not much good. One of the things to which I objected most was a general tendency to gaff the fish too early, too deep and with unnecessary brutality. This often entailed a risk of breaking the cast. The practice was probably not unconnected with the rule whereby boatmen receive half of the catch, which tempts them to kill the fish as soon as possible.

Even a bad caster can hope for success when fishing from a boat, while bank fishing puts a premium on skilful casting. It is true that the boat fisherman has the handicap of having to cast sitting down most of the time, which in a wind can be very awkward.

It is indispensable for the boat fisherman to be able to handle a two-handed rod in such a way that he can lead now with the right hand and now with the left, which enables him to fish on both sides of the boat. Moreover, in a wind there is a great danger of the fly blowing round the fisherman's head, if he casts beyond a certain distance. In my opinion, the two things in which it is most important that the fly fisher from a boat should be proficient are the following:

1. *Mending the line:* that is laying the line on the water after placing the fly and, as it drifts down, correcting its position by mending it upstream so that it describes a curve against the current, which the pressure of the stream will straighten without pulling

on the fly. The danger of dragging the fly will be thus diminished and at the same time the fisherman will ensure that the fly floats ahead of the leader.

2. *Fishing the cast out:* that is leaving the fly to drift until it describes a circle and comes finally to a standstill on the other side of the boat. At this point, you must check the fly for a moment and then pull in three or four times with the line-hand – slow, short pulls – before beginning a fresh cast. Tony Pulitzer and his sister-in-law have assured me that they have taken many fish by this procedure; and from the day I adopted it, my own results improved markedly.

OBSERVATIONS ON THE SUBJECT OF TACKLE

* *The hook.* In salmon fishing it is even more important than in trout or grayling fishing to make sure that the hook is constantly sharpened. The salmon often seems to leap at the fly and snap at it with sudden violence. It frequently happens that in doing so he misses the fly but touches the leader and gets foul-hooked. For this reason many fishermen prefer using double hooks and employ these especially when the salmon is snapping at the fly or is taking only middle-sized or small patterns of fly. Start sharpening the hook with a very fine watchmaker's file and finish the operation by polishing the point with an Arkansas stone.

* *The line.* You should never omit to test the tensile strength of the line before fishing. If it tears, you must tear off all the weak strands till there are none left. The end of the line must be at least ·04 or ·045 of an inch thick, otherwise there is danger of its breaking. A nylon line keeps the fly just under the surface, while a silk line allows it to sink deeper. By greasing it, you can keep a silk line from sinking too deep. In my opinion, when the water in the Alta is normal, you get more takes when using a nylon line. But, when the water is high, it is an advantage to use silk line, as it is in deep pools, whatever the state of the water.

* *The leader.* I prefer a nylon leader in one piece, of from ·016 to ·024 in. It should be relatively short, about 6 ft. long, to enable the fisherman to bring the fish up to the gaff without making it necessary to pull the knot uniting line and cast through the ring at the top-joint of the rod. It thus becomes possible to gaff a fish from the boat. Much time is lost if you have to go to the bank to get hold of your fish, and the time element is important in view of the short duration of the salmon-rise.

* *Backing.* For backing I use only the Tergal or Dacron line. They are both very resistant and do not stretch. These lines are so thin that you can take 150 yards or more under your ordinary line on the reel. They also enable you to use smaller reels and to fish with lighter rods. They wind closely round the reel and provide a strong and well-proportioned support for the casting line.

* *Splicing.* The junction between the casting-line and the backing must be effected in the most solid fashion possible. The splicing has to be able to resist not only a hard pull but also the friction caused by passing through the rings, as well as the effects of damp. It must be done by a specialist. Unfortunately, when you buy a complete salmon line you cannot, without further testing, be sure that the factory splicings will prove satisfactory. You should subject these splicings to a severe test before starting to fish.

I splice my own lines and, in doing so, adopt a procedure which is speedy and sure, if not particularly elegant, and which has fully proved its value. I fasten the end of the casting line to the beginning of the backing with two running knots, one at the end of each (as in the illustration) and then draw the knots tight leaving a space of ¾ in. between them. Then I put a whipping of Ashaway's Splicefloss over the junction of the lines, allowing the whipping to taper off at both ends. If this is done the knots will be covered. But whipping alone will not produce a smooth surface and for that reason I drench it with viscous collodium, which I beat with a hammer until it is round and smooth and finally overlay it with one or two more coats of collodium. Instead of collodium, you can use a solution of rubber, as in patching motor tyres. When it is thoroughly dry, you must make sure that the splicing runs easily through the top ring of the rod.

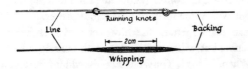

Fig 61 *Securing the line to the backing*

The result appears somewhat coarse and thick and makes you apprehensive of difficulties in casting, but a practice cast will soon dissipate all misgivings. It is invaluable to know that the splicing will not give way under any possible tension.

* *Length of Line.* I consider that about 200 yards is the ideal length for a salmon line (backing included). This thin backing has the additional advantage of exposing less surface to the pressure of the water. When a fish I am playing changes direction and causes the current to press against the resultant loop, I have less reason to fear a break than if I were using a thicker backing. One of the main reasons for my liking for this reserve of line is that I prefer to give a running salmon more time instead of holding him by force.

Never omit to test all old splicings carefully at the beginning of the season. It is more advisable still to cut them off and splice afresh. Old splicings often look solid enough, but break when you are fishing and that generally entails the loss of the largest fish, not to mention the leader.

* *Reels*. My reels have no adjustable brakes. It does not suit me to be continually adjusting the braking apparatus in order to suit it to the thickness of the line on the reel. When a fish has taken more than 50 yards of line, the diameter of the coil round the reel is considerably diminished. Any mechanical brake, however, works with greater force on a diminished coil than on a full one. No method of braking can compare for accuracy with that applied by the forefinger which avoids the errors of the mechanical brake.

I always brake with my forefinger. I use reels of which the two cross-plates both turn and are easily reached. I use the Hardy 'Perfect', which I prefer to any other. A good and *very strong* ratchet is obviously indispensable, because it must do most of the braking, the hand being used only in emergency.

For fastening the reel to the handle of the rod I consider two moveable holding-rings more serviceable than a screw reel-holder. With two movable rings the reel can be fitted to the spot most convenient for the fisherman, taking into account his greater or lesser length of arm, which in the case of two-handed rods is a significant factor. On the other hand, I recommend that the rings holding the reel to the handle should be made fast with some form of waterproof plaster.

The fisherman can then be certain that, however hard a fish fights, the reel will not twist round the handle but will remain in line with the rings of the rod.

* *Rods and reels*. When, in 1953, Tony Pulitzer visited his future beat on the Alta, he made detailed enquiries in regard to the most suitable gear and tackle. It was then explained to him that it was necessary above all to use powerful rods – fourteen and a half and fifteen and a half footers. The Duke of Roxburghe had used such rods with reels that, in addition to the ordinary casting line, could hold two hundred yards of flax backing. The Duke had got Hardy to make him special reels with a diameter of six inches. Pulitzer acquired several of them. Subsequently I had occasion to consult Captain Edwards, whom I regard as one of the best salmon-fishers in England. He was far from being definitely in favour of heavy rods. He considered we ought to be able to catch fish with rods and reels of standard size, that is to say rods of a maximum length of $14\frac{1}{2}$ feet and reels with a diameter of $4\frac{1}{2}$ inches. Nevertheless, to be on the safe side, he advised us to use the same tackle as the Duke and his friends had used. I had volunteered to procure the necessary gear and had been given a free hand to do so. I did not want to take any risks over tackle destined for Tony and his guests, but I did not hesitate to provide myself with some gear of medium weight and, above all, with lighter rods. I went so far as to acquire a one-handed rod for myself. I knew that, as soon as we began fishing, we should find out soon enough what was best.

Soon after our arrival on the Alta, I unpacked my rod-box and asked Jöraholmen and his son to look through the whole assortment. They, too, shared a preference for heavy tackle. When I showed them my light rods, their incredulous smiles warned me to talk about something else. Nevertheless, I would not allow myself to be diverted from my purpose and thought it worth while trying out the 14½, 13, 12 and 10½ ft. two-handed rods and even the 9½ ft. one-hander. I began with the 14½ ft. Parabolic and a 6 in. reel. After a night's fishing with this tackle the situation was clear to me. Before I had caught my first salmon, I changed my rod for the 13 ft. A few days later only one of our party was fishing with the traditional 14½ ft. rod. To fish with such a heavy implement, when casting constantly for six to eight hours, is indeed hard labour. It feels like handling a crane.

Some three weeks later, I fished a stretch of water near Sautso above some rapids. If you hook a fish there you have to hold him at all costs or he will run off into unnavigable water – nor can you follow him when fishing from the bank. As a precaution against accidents, I used a 14½ ft. rod and was almost immediately into a 24lb salmon. I put my crane in action, according to plan, and pulled with all my might. The poor salmon had no idea what had happened to him and decided to give up the struggle from the first moment. He had no chance of getting away and, within five minutes, was up against the side of the boat and let me hold his head above water. I felt as though I had been fishing with a heavy sea-rod. Of course, there are circumstances in which such heavy tackle seem appropriate, but I derive but little of the true pleasure of the sport from it.

The 13 ft. length proved completely sufficient for my needs. It was fully strong enough to deal with big fish and bring them safely to the gaff. I even look on its action as being too strong but it may be that this feeling is due to my pronounced preference for short rods. I have done excellently well with my short rods in places where long rods were considered indispensable – and so I gravitated from a 13 ft. to a 12 ft., then to a 10½ ft. and, finally, to my 9½ ft. one-hander. During the last days of my stay, I merely took my one-hander and, for eventualities, my 12 ft. two-hander, when I went fishing. This same tendency obtains, as a matter of fact, in the U.S.A. On the Restigouche, anglers use rods of from 11 to 13 feet. Unfortunately, American rods have a too pronounced top-joint action and consequently it is necessary to make a practice cast. In windy weather, they do not prove reliable. As a general conclusion, I would say that for most fishermen rods 13 to 14 feet long are indicated. They facilitate casting from a sitting position, when fishing from a boat, especially when there is a wind.

* *Flies.* We all know that salmon flies are purely fanciful creations. We have also some grounds for supposing that the salmon, during the spawning season, does not consider the fly as food, seeing that it fasts throughout its sojourn in fresh water. Why then does it go for the worm, the spoon or the prawn? Why does it take only at certain times? I cannot pretend to answer these questions, but one fact is certain: the salmon's first choice is the prawn, the second the spoon-bait and, after them, the fly alone. In Norway, generally speaking, the fly is the least productive form of lure, though in the Alta it is responsible for catching more fish than the spoon, the spinning-minnow or the prawn used only by the natives. This is no doubt due to the fact that most of the fly-fishing is done from boats, which facilitates the correct presentation of the lure, while the spoon is principally used by the natives who fish from the bank, before the opening of the fly-fishing season. However, in other waters, the superiority of the spoon cannot be challenged. It appears also that the best prospects for the fly on the Alta are in the early days of the spawning season. The more water there is in the river, the better are the chances for large flies, sizes 10/0 to 7/0. But as the season progresses and the water level falls, smaller fly-patterns, Nos.4 and, even, 1, are recommended. In Canada and Newfoundland fish are taken on the dry fly when the water is low and clear. I never heard of this happening on a European river. Of course, to achieve such a result, you must have seen the fish and know exactly where it is lying, for you have to offer it the fly repeatedly before it will decide to take it.

The choice of wet fly patterns for salmon is almost as great as it is for trout. The boatmen on the Alta and the old fishermen select their fly according to the time of day, the state of the water and the light, with an expertness which easily surpasses my own capacity. I have fished altogether with ten different boatmen. There was no uniformity in their views about flies. Each had his favourites and his individual notions, as every fisherman has. They took into account the weather and the light, fingered about in my heterogeneous collection of flies and seemed finally to base their choice on a mysterious instinct. Generally, these preliminaries involved a waste of valuable time. When the salmon are taking, every second is precious. Time is wasted also on the knots fastening the fly to the cast. The complicated knots used by the Alta boatmen, when changing a fly after a fish has missed or refused, take a long time to tie. The fresh fly should undoubtedly be offered to the fish with the least possible delay and for that reason I use for salmon flies the same simple and quickly tied knot as I do for trout flies. The fly does not perhaps stand out quite so prettily, but the knot holds and saves valuable time.

I keep asking myself how a salmon can detect the slight variations between the different classic types of fly without a thorough knowledge of the whole collection

Catching a 38½ pound salmon

above: The author with his favourite Alta guide, 1959
below: The Bradstrom pool on the Alta

The prize salmon from the Alta for 1954–5: 49 pounds

evolved by the united efforts of manufacturers, dealers and fishermen over a period longer than a century. But one thing has struck me forcibly and that is the fact that our boatmen usually selected one of the best known and most popular patterns such as Jock Scott, Thunder and Lightning, Mar Lodge, Black Doctor, Silver Doctor and so on. This is probably because they have become familiar with these flies which, due to their popularity, if not necessarily to their effectiveness, are to be found in every salmon fisherman's fly-box. I admit I am no expert in these matters, but I am all for simplicity. On the Alta, I recalled my success with sea-trout on the Em where, the very first day, I had noticed in the fishing-room the rod of Prince Wilhelm of Sweden, an experienced fisherman of the highest class, which carried a prawn-fly dangling at the end of the leader. I followed the example of this master and was often too lazy to change the fly, which was admirably successful and enabled me to win the sweep for the biggest catch in the first week.

In the winter of 1954 during a visit to Farlow's in London I had laid in a stock of prawn-flies, General Practitioner, for use on the Alta and I subsequently used them on half my fishing days at least. The prawn-fly enabled me to catch my biggest fish and also helped my friends to land most of their largest salmon, weighing from 40lb to 49lb. To start with, my boatmen were very displeased with me for using this far from classic fly: but further shocks awaited them, for our two American Admirals had brought with them their Bucktails (Rusty Rat) made from the tail-hairs of the fallow deer, which were quite different from the classic English flies – indeed, some-one went so far even as to use a lure consisting of little brass balls strung together with hackles wound round them from back to front. This object, which was also called a 'fly', looked like a caterpillar two inches long and had a small hole drilled in its tail. All these unorthodox lures caught as many fish as the classic English types.

After a few days, reliance on the orthodox began to falter and finally our boatmen began to ask for our heretical flies. Neither numerous individual attempts to solve the problem nor the study of our statistics of fish caught produced any proof that the salmon themselves had a definite preference for particular flies. On the other hand, it seemed to be established beyond doubt that the salmon recognizes any fly offered him a second time and refuses it, if he was not tempted by it at the first presentation. In order to outwit it, you have usually to proceed according to the principle of opposites. This led me to a simple solution of the fly problem. I would choose two classic patterns, a bright one and a dark one, for example a Mar Lodge and a Black Doctor. Then, I would take a type with less pronounced colouring such as the Jock Scott and with it, by way of contrast, a prawn-fly. You can do a lot with these four types. I usually began with the prawn-fly or any other fly I fancied at the time and, if the

Preparing to transport the gear and haul the empty boats across the Sautso rapids.

fish would not take it, I changed to its opposite. As a tactical device this proved highly satisfactory. As far as the Alta was concerned, I had no use for any other theories. In Brittany, salmon specialists will not hear of any fly with a metallic sheen and on the Alta, too, glittering flies are not outstandingly successful.

In 1954 I limited myself to the following selection: Black Doctor, Mar Lodge, Jock Scott, prawn-fly and a few Bucktails of the Rusty Rat type.

According to my record, out of 277 salmon:

56 were caught with the Jock Scott (yellow-brown body),

42 with the Black Doctor (black with silver-ribbed body),

26 with the Mar Lodge (silver with black-ribbed body),

37 with the prawn-fly, among them most of the forty pounders, and

more than 20 with the American Bucktail (Rusty Rat) made of doe's hair with a body of orange silk and a black head with a white eye.

The Americans used the Bucktails more frequently than we did and were particularly successful in catching big fish with them. Other flies, with which a small number of fish were caught, were Durham Ranger, Silver Grey, Silver Rat, Thunder and Lightning and Black Dose; for no obvious reason these flies were mostly left in their cases and but seldom used for fishing.

The above figures do not cover all the fish we caught, as on several occasions I omitted to find out exactly what my companions had done. In any case, the 137 fish caught by the Americans on the beat starting at Sandia must be added to our total of 277, which brings the grand total to 414 salmon.

* *The Tubefly.* I first used tubeflies on the Alta in 1957 and was pleasantly surprised. Having missed two fish, fishing with a Jock Scott and then with a Thunder and Lightning on a short, medium-fast run of water, I changed to tubeflies given to me by my friend Babington Smith and tied by him.

On that occasion I took two salmon and lost two others which had accepted the fly. The fault was mine, as I discovered several years later: I had not pushed the eye of the treble hook into the plastic tube. The tube was thus free to slide up and down the cast or leader and the nylon tended to cut the tube open, making many changes of fly necessary. Having discovered that mistake I decided to give the tubefly a further trial on the Nausta and Jölstra rivers in 1968, 1969 and 1970.

Suddenly, the enormous possibilities of tubefly fishing and its great mechanical advantages dawned on me. Today, I use no other pattern and my observations and the results I obtained may be of interest.

But first, what is a tubefly?

The body of the fly is formed from a length of plastic tube, usually a ball-point pen refill, from three-quarters of an inch to one and a half inches long. I prefer one inch. A two inch fly does not sink well and is more difficult to cast in a wind.

Two tufts of hair, each comprising thirty hairs of polar bear or Arctic wolf fur, are tied at one end on either side of the tube. If you so wish, the hairs can be evenly spaced around the tube and their number increased to a total of 100. I favour a maximum of sixty because such à fly functions well when new and continues to do so after it has been in use for some time, even though it may then have lost up to a third of the original dressing.

Each hair is dyed; the point black, the upper part of the hair blue or yellow, or blue and white, red and yellow, etc.

Two hook sizes suffice; the smallest a No.1 treble, with No.4 the largest size used. The eye of the hook should be pear-shaped, making it an easy matter to force the plastic tube over the eye and so obtain a tight fit. A pair of small, flat pliers performs this operation more effectively than one's fingers, and with greater safety.

These trebles are so small that they weigh less than a standard single or double hook. They hold well, the point penetrating to the bend of the hook and making it impossible for it to be opened or straightened out in the fish's jaw. As a result, few fish mange to break free and my best salmon to date was a 35-pounder, taken on a No.3 treble.

Of all patterns of salmon fly, I am inclined to give the tubefly first choice. If we compare weight and volume, the tubefly is light and will react more readily to variations of current. There is the further point that the flow of water and oxygen through the tube may create a very lively effect and for this reason I never seal the upper end of the tube to prevent water penetration. It is, of coruse, impossible to know exactly why a salmon moves to one fly, but ignores another. When these fish enter freshwater they are excited, chock-full of love and anticipation of the wonders ahead of them – Spring madness, if you like. No human can ever have a complete understanding of the forces behind this great migration, but I have at least proved, many times, that salmon favour a tubefly of this type when other lures attract them not at all.

* *Conclusion.* Any angler who does not try the tubefly is, in my opinion and with respect to all concerned, more crazy than the fish. Experiment! You will find how easy it is to cast against the wind with these flies and how accurate one's casting can be. In addition, the tubefly has superb water penetration. As to its colour, the choice is yours: I am firmly convinced that the fly's action is the key factor. As proof of their effectiveness, in the last three years *using nothing but tubeflies* I have taken more than 150 fish and my close friends several hundred more.

The Alta compared with Canadian salmon-rivers on the Atlantic Coast. For the last 20 years, Tony Pulitzer's brother, Joseph Pulitzer, has fished the best Canadian salmon-river on the Atlantic coast, the Restigouche, and he has placed his records at my disposal.

In 1954, we caught 414 fish on 27 miles of the River Alta. This result compares not unfavourably with the figures of the Restigouche for 1953, though one must not over-look the fact that 1953 was a bad year on the Restigouche. On Pulitzer's 20 miles of water, which belongs to the Restigouche Salmon Club, 514 salmon were caught. As I have no information about the figures for the best years on the Alta I cannot unfortunately compare them with 1952, a good year on the Restigouche, when the total catch amounted to 1481 salmon.

One record of which the Alta should be proud was made by Jöraholmen Junior, who once fished the whole beat in twenty-four hours in his boat and caught 44 salmon.

Our best results for a single day were:

Mrs I. Pulitzer   8 salmon in one night.
Tony Pulitzer   7 salmon in one night.
Charles Ritz   6 salmon in one night.

In 1958, Sam Field took 17 fish in one night.

The average weight per fish on the Alta is about 23lbs, but on the Restigouche only 18lbs. On the Restigouche a 40lb salmon represents an exceptionally fine fish. During our season on the Alta we caught 11 salmon over 40lbs in weight. My heaviest fish weighed 49lbs.

Any report on salmon-fishing in Norway would be incomplete if it made no mention of the summer plague, mosquitoes. These insects are particularly in evidence during the light nights – the best time for catching salmon. Liquids like 'Off', Gard or '6-12' from the U.S.A. have, when properly applied, thoroughly proved their value. If you smear your face, neck and hands with this stuff, you will have peace for a couple of hours. I often counted over a hundred mosquitoes on my boatman's cap and one or another of these would from time to time make a recon-naissance flight round my nose, without, however, daring to settle on it. In such cir-cumstances the mosquito usually made an impromptu landing on my hat. They seem to prefer flat caps to hats, as providing more convenient surfaces for landing, resting and taking off. I was told of a peculiar native device for protecting oneself against mosquitoes when fishing from the bank of one of the countless lakes in Lapland. It consists in recruiting a couple of Lapp women between whom one stands, and who attract the insects, which have a preference for strong scents.

The sea coast round the mouth of the Alta is frequently visited by seals. It sometimes happens that seals find their way into the river. When this occurs the salmon become alarmed and cease to take. The Duke of Roxburghe once caught sight of a seal near Sautso eighteen miles upstream from the mouth of the river. It had forced its way through three rapids.

We caught a number of fish in the Alta that had been damaged by the nets in the fjord and a few with wounds caused by seals.

I should like in conclusion to give an account of the biggest fish I have caught in the Alta, which weighed 49lbs. I succeeded in tempting it with a prawn-fly after it had refused or missed a Mar Lodge. As soon as it was hooked, it ran downstream but let me lead it into calm water where, after a ten minute fight, I was able to bring it to the gaff and get it into the boat. As for several days previous to this I had been spending my evenings after fish weighing 30 pounds my powers of discrimination were so confused that on this occasion, although I knew I had caught a good fish, I could not believe it was anything extraordinary. As I was playing it, I experienced none of the exhilarating sensations one should have when one has hooked a monster, nor did I feel any pride in my achievement at the time of catching it. It was only when I had it on the scales that my heart began to beat faster.

On the other hand, there have been days when I was not entitled to fish the salmon pools but was free to go after sea-trout and grilse, days on which I have had much more thrilling moments. I shall never forget catching a salmon of 29lbs on a 9½ ft. one-handed rod while fishing for grilse. When I got home at three in the morning, I fortified myself with a cup of strong coffee and condensed milk followed by the customary aquavit, after which I wrote the following account of the proceedings to my friend Auguste Lambiotte, whom we used to think of daily while he, like a good husband and father, was spending his holidays with his family in Biarritz:

'Alta. 26th July 1954. 3 a.m.

My dear Auguste,

I have just come in from fishing and swallowed my supper. Today, I couldn't fish salmon water, having given my permit to Tony Pulitzer's brother, as it was his last day on the Alta. On all the rest of the river one is free to fish for grayling, sea-trout and grilse. At about 8 p.m., I began fishing from the bank with my 9½ ft. rod and soon landed a 3lb sea trout. Then a couple of grilse took my Black Doctor, but got away. After that, I got into the boat and made for a spot that looked good for grilse. It was just above some rapids. My very first cast produced a tremendous upheaval in the water. I had hooked a salmon. He started running upstream at a great pace and

259

made a big circle round the boat. My line ran out in a curve nearly 100 yards long. Part of the backing was already in the water. I was terrified that the pressure of the water would break me, as has happened to me before when I was into a big fish and the boatmen towed straight upstream instead of following the curve of the line and so reducing the pressure on it. Boatmen have, unfortunately, very little understanding of the relation between cause and effect, when a difficult fish is being played.

At last, I could see my unexpected adversary. I thought he had a very imposing appearance but did not look particularly large. He suddenly turned downstream towards the rapids. I tried to bring him to a halt by giving him some line and then exercising steady and gradually increasing pressure. The manœuvre succeeded and he stayed where he was, still fighting. I tried to draw him up slowly against the current but couldn't bring it off. After a tug-of-war that lasted several minutes he followed a sudden impulse and shot into the rapids. This athletic creature had still some surprises in store. We followed with the boat. The line and backing I had reeled out was already close on 150 yards long and the fish was moving ever more rapidly downstream. We could not follow him quickly enough for me to be able to shorten the line. The boat shipped some water and the seat of my trousers was soaked; otherwise everything was all right. After the first stretch of rapids there came another swifter bit. I asked the boatman if there were any rocks to run into and was relieved when he said there weren't.Meantime, the fish had gone down into the depths and carried on the fight from there. We finally got near him which enabled me to reel in some line, though part of the backing was still out. Luckily, I could trust my splicing which I had fixed up myself the previous evening.

The fight had already lasted more than half an hour when suddenly my fish ran off downstream again. He was a splendid fighter and missed no chances. He darted over the second lot of rapids with tremendous élan and my line ran out nearly to the danger-point. Finally I succeeded in stopping my salmon and steering the boat into smooth water once more. I was able to check him and reel him in with short vigorous jerks. But each time he got near the eddies on the edge of our quiet piece of water he started struggling with all his might and flung his head violently from side to side. I noticed several times one or two loose coils of line. It was probably when the cast, which had wound itself round the fish, got free. Suddenly the strain on the line ceased: had I lost him? No, he had only turned upstream. Then a violent tugging match began. Six times I pulled him out of the current and six times he hurled himself back into it. But his powers of resistance were gradually failing. He came up to the surface and tried to fight there. He was still more than 40 yards away from the boat and kept on needing more line. Finally, he became more amenable and let himself be pulled in. However, he remained deep in the water and began circling close round the boat and, during this manœuvre, I could neither lead him nor heave him up. He twice attempted to get away. My boatmen were tremendously excited and were prodding about with their gaffs. I ordered them to get me on shore, which they did unwillingly. I hate to see a good fighting fish finished off from the boat and I was afraid, on this occasion, that the boatmen, as is their wont, would make passes at the fish while he was still deep under water. On two previous occasions they had caught their beastly weapons in my nylon leader. On this occasion I was only using ·016 in. (about 14lb breaking strain) and was fishing with a one-handed rod, so I didn't want to run any risks.

When I reached the bank, I went back from the water almost without reeling in. A fish will generally be readier to allow you to pull him in, if he does not notice that you are pulling, as he does when you reel in. After a full hour of gallant fighting he finally surrendered and laid himself exhausted on his side, offering his gleaming flank to the gaff. Up to his last breath he had fought like a gladiator. A twenty-nine pounder! He was a salmon in perfect condition with a real crocodile's throat. I stroked his head in appreciation of his courage. And then, having uttered a loud cry of joy, I sat down exhausted on a stone and lit my pipe.

I would have given a lot to have had you at my side, dear Auguste, to share my hour of intense and thrilling experience. Tomorrow I'll take his portrait with my Rolliflex. You'll be interested to know that my backing was of Tergal Rhodia and couldn't have stood the strain better. The fly I used was a Black Doctor No.1. In friendship and with many greetings to all,

Charles.'

In conclusion, I should like to thank my luck for bringing me together with Tony Pulitzer and his charming friends. The privilege of enjoying their hospitality on the Alta was a true gift of the gods.

* *A final observation.* In fly-fishing for trout and grayling the climax of my enjoyment is contained in the interval between my preparing to cast and the moment of striking. Playing and landing make a comparatively commonplace conclusion. In salmon fishing, on the other hand, I experience the greatest pleasure and satisfaction from the moment I first feel my fish's fighting power, when I wonder if he is big, little, or medium-sized, if he is strong and cunning or merely a poor devil who loses his head from fear and flaps round in aimless confusion. If he fights well, I give him plenty of opportunity to defend himself and plenty of room to manœuvre in, as I play him gently and considerately. But if he is one of the clumsy or pusillanimous or dumb

ones, I try to finish with him as soon as may be. What thrills me most in salmon fishing are the short moments when one is faced with an adversary whose strength one cannot gauge but who one hopes will turn out to be a champion.

Oola on the Alta

I had taken bigger fish on the Alta, while fishing as Tony Pulitzer's guest on the Jöraholmen farm, but never under circumstances as bizarre as the day I found myself being ghillied by a girl.

This came about by chance, as it was my day to fish a very fine salmon pool, adjoining a great rocky point, which is ordinarily fished by boat. But I had offered my boat to a friend who was leaving for home that evening. His fishing had been unlucky and we all wanted to give him a last chance. My host concurred, and suggested that I try fishing the pool from the rocky promontory, as long as I would have no boat at my disposal until after 2 p.m. when the other guest would have to leave.

This was challenging, as if I did succeed in hooking a fish, casting from the rocks, the only possible gaffing place would be on the lower part of the rocky point, where the footing for gaffing is on a narrow ledge, about three feet wide and twelve feet long and some three feet above the water level.

I pondered the problem through a late breakfast and at 11 a.m. decided to go look at this difficult landing spot, to see if I could figure out a way to cope with a fish there with nobody around to gaff it for me.

The cook was busy in the kitchen, the Jöraholmen family was out on the farm, the chauffeur had left with Tony Pulitzer, and I was about to give up the idea when suddenly I remembered that in passing the house I had seen somebody hanging up the laundry out in back. That would be Oola, I realised, the young Lapp girl who had only a few days before begun working as kitchen helper and laundress.

Nobody knew much about Oola, who was short and stocky and very round, except that young as she was she already had several children, back in the village of Kaiteno, from lumberjacks, village boys and slate quarry workers. She had explained, in applying for the job, that she needed money to send back to the Lapp woman who was taking care of her kids, the result of her too great kindness to mankind. Oola was high in the front and low in the rear, with a very round face, dark but extremely smooth skin and Asiatic eyes. She was a very sweet girl, with a most comprehensive viewpoint, always looking at us men hungrily, I thought, and we all felt sorry for the poor creature.

'Hello Oola, how would you like to go fishing with me for an hour?'

She jumped up in the air saying, 'Yes, yes.'

I picked up my rod and the gaff and we started for the trail, of about half a mile, that led to the pool, Oola following along behind me until we reached the first barbed wire fence.

I snaked under it, as it was too high to climb over, and when I reached the other side Oola passed me the rod and the gaff and started to imitate me. She stopped with a yell, as the barbed wire caught in her skirt. I managed to get her loose and urged her on and just as she started to crawl again there was another, louder yell, reflecting a more serious problem. This time the wire was taut and stretching almost to the limit across that area of Oola which resembled two honeydew melons. After several failures I finally succeeded a second time in giving her full freedom of movement and Oola was at last able to pass and join me.

This she did, however, in such a confused and excited state that she threw her arms around me and I had to explain with many gestures that this was not part of salmon fishing and I almost told her I did not want to increase her little tribe. So off we went again towards the pool through the mossy grass and the birch trees.

When we reached the top of the rock, I decided to show Oola what I expected her to do and exactly how to use the gaff. She became more and more excited and I stepped away from her so as to keep clear of her weapon which she was waving frantically. We went to the rocky point and I started casting. 'Oola: all you have to do is to hold the gaff and keep away from my line while I am casting and always stay a reasonable distance behind me until I have the salmon at the foot of the rock, ready for gaffing. She was holding the gaff and started to dance around me, again waving her weapon dangerously. I somehow managed to calm her and get her back to normal. After a few minutes I located two salmon just where the slack and fast waters met. This was a very good sign. I decided to use a medium size Arctic wolf hair tubefly and started casting.

All of a sudden I thought my fly had caught in a tree and when I turned I noticed the leader wrapped around the gaff and Oola standing close behind me. I stared at her and said: 'Now Oola, come and sit on the rock and leave the gaff on the ground and if you don't obey, you will have to go back to your chores.'

On the third cast, I was into a good fish. He immediately jumped twice and made for deep water and then up again for another jump as he tried to reach the current and swim downstream. He succeeded in doing this and took out a lot of line. I had to follow him trying to prevent the line from breaking on the jagged edges of the rock. I finally managed to stop the fish, then heard some wild yells, just as I had a slack line and the fish turned upstream. Suddenly I saw Oola, gaff in hand, doing some kind of a wild Lapp dance. By that time, my nervous system had almost reached its peak and I had the hardest time to control myself, the fish and Oola. At the end, in despair, I threatened to throw Oola in the pool. She began to cry and, gaff still in hand, started to return to the camp.

'Oola, come back at once, otherwise I will have to send you home to Kaiteno.'

She stopped, came back and sat down on a big stone. I was then able to concentrate on the salmon. Three more runs then he started to show signs of fatigue and I began to think that my usual luck was back. The fish tried twice to swim downstream and reach the current, but without success. He was finally almost still. I could start to bring him close enough for the gaffing. Then the great tragedy of my fisherman's life happened. I had decided I could not trust Oola with the gaff and the only solution was to hand her the rod realising that any additional delay would increase the chances of the fly tearing loose. I could see it on the edge of the mouth. Now I explained to Oola how to handle the rod.

'Oola, here is the rod, hold it high with both hands, one on the reel and don't move. Remain as still as a statue!'

I took the gaff and immediately had it fast into the fish and lifted him out of the water, on to the rocky ledge. But the salmon was still lively and got off the gaff while I was trying to grab him with my hands. Oola then pulled on the rod with all her strength and broke the leader which had already been frayed on the rocks.

As I was scared of losing him, I did the only logical thing that came to my mind. I flopped down on the salmon. All of a sudden, I felt a tremendous weight on me. Oola was so excited and wanted to be so helpful that she lay on top of me. When the fish had quietened down and I managed to get Oola off me, I looked around for a stone to kill the poor salmon but not seeing one, I sent Oola to find a suitable stone. She soon returned with a rock of about 20 lbs which she wanted to drop on the salmon and probably on me also. I ordered her to lay it down and succeeded in making her understand the need to find a small stone. Soon she returned with a smaller stone, but still too heavy. On the third trip she brought the right sized stone. I killed the poor salmon and finally he was ours! We were both shaking and then looked at each other and I felt like giving her a brotherly kiss, but at the last moment I changed my mind because she was looking at me with such spawning eyes.

The salmon tipped the scales at 29 lbs. From that day on, every time I saw Oola she gave me such a hungry look that I always had to tell her to stick to her laundry and that I had a French Oola waiting for me in Paris.

Upon my return to Paris, Ludwig Bemelmens was staying with us at the Ritz and when I told him Oola's story, he said: 'Charles, if you write about it, I will gladly make a sketch for you,' which he very kindly did.

But all my friends could say was: 'Oola indeed. Ooh-la-la, you wicked old Frenchman!'

And what kind of remark is that to make to a Swiss?

One fly or two?

In my opinion, the greatest salmon fly-fisher in the world is Major The Hon. J. Ashley-Cooper. In all the years that he has fished for the silver king he has landed an estimated 10,000 salmon, an achievement reflecting his extraordinary skill and a record that can have been equalled by few other fishermen of any generation. At a luncheon he gave for me at The Guards Club, London, on July 2nd, 1971, I asked him to sum up those points he considers essential to successful fly-fishing.

He told me that fly-casting – knowing how to cast – is by far the most important factor. Next, he said, the fly must travel at the speed of the water: no faster, no slower.

When you are fishing slow water give the fly a slight additional movement once it has penetrated and starts to move with the stream. Avoid jerking the fly. The movement must be smooth and steady, sufficient to persuade your fish that this attractive titbit is about to escape. The situation can be likened to a dog with a bone between its paws. Pull on the bone or move it steadily in any direction and the animal reacts as though you intended to take the bone from him – he goes for it! Move it too quickly and he has no chance of regaining possession.

In fast water you have to watch your fly all the time. You must know what the fly is doing if you are to control it and, once in a while, animate it sufficiently to convey to the fish that all-important semblance of life.

One of the key tactics employed by this very experienced fisherman involves the use of two flies, one on a dropper. He uses a rather short nylon leader and a short dropper of the same thickness to avoid tangling.

I asked for his views on mending line and learned that this is something he seldom finds necessary. In his opinion, no one who knows how to cast, and who knows that the cast has been made correctly, should need to mend their line. Many of the great salmon fishers *do* mend line automatically; a case of making sure that the fly goes down first and that drag is reduced to an absolute minimum.

We discussed the tubeflies I now favour for salmon fishing, each fly up to one and a half inches long. Major Ashley-Cooper suggested that I could make the tubes still shorter and that by so doing better results would be obtained, the shorter tube making fast, accurate casting still easier.

I had always imagined that he uses a very long rod. 'I do at times,' he told me, 'but I usually select a rod which is in proportion to the type of water I am about to fish, its size and current.'

As to one's approach to the water, in his experience fish usually lie against the bank of the stream. Try this water first. (The point is well proven by the lady angler featured in the final chapter of this book.) If you fish a good beat, knowing that salmon are there and that the fish are ignoring flies presented on your Wetcel line, try them on the floating Aircel line, or vice versa. This often produces results and is well worth the effort involved.

Ashley-Cooper's emphasis on the use of two flies so intrigued me that I sought and was readily given his authority to reprint an article which first appeared in Farlow's catalogue. In this he explains in detail his method of fishing with a dropper and tail fly. Here it is . . .

ONE FLY OR TWO FOR SALMON
by Major The Hon. J. Ashley-Cooper

Droppers are not often used in river fishing for salmon. Are they an advantage; do they increase the bag? Or are they merely a cause of added irritation and tangles, and of fish unnecessarily lost? Such are the queries which immediately spring to mind.

Given suitable conditions (of which more hereafter) there is no doubt that the skilled use of a dropper fly adds greatly to the interest and excitement of fishing, and that further it does increase the bag.

Admittedly this latter point is arguable, but if 30% or more of one's fish are caught on the dropper (a figure readily achieved by a reasonably skilful performer) surely there are good grounds for believing that the catch is bigger than it would have been if only a single fly had been fished, even if it is not increased by a full 30%?

Certainly two flies on the cast, fished properly, must increase the amount of water covered at each cast, thus enabling the fisherman to progress more quickly and more thoroughly. This is a consideration of some importance on big pools such as those on Spey or Tweed. (Even three flies on the cast may be tried, but the resulting tangles will probably be found too formidable!)

Further there is a distinct likelihood that two flies passing in quick succession over a fish are more likely to rouse him into action than one single fly, he being 'maddened by the swarm', as a well known Irish ghillie used to put it! There is no space here to go further into this theory, but experienced fishermen will readily appreciate this possibility.

Also the ability to fish simultaneously flies of different sizes, types and patterns, varied at will, adds immensely to the interest and gives a wide field for experiment. For example, some anglers assert that the use of a fairly heavy tail fly as 'anchor' to a dropper bobbing along the surface is a deadly method, particularly in strong streams or in slack water with a good ripple. You doubt it? Why not experiment and see?

Certainly playing fish with two flies on the cast is always more exciting than with

one fly only, and one has hair-raising experiences from time to time, resulting sometimes in triumph and sometimes in disaster. But if sport is one's object, here is a
good way of finding it!

Of course there must be strict limitations on the use of droppers; for instance, if
there is any appreciable amount of weed or if snags are a problem, droppers are
'out'. The risk of the disengaged fly fouling obstructions and causing the loss of the
fish becomes too great. Also it is dangerous to use droppers in pools very heavily
stocked with fish. The chance of a disengaged fly foulhooking or being taken by a
second fish, in the course of play, is great; and if it occurs it will almost inevitably
lead to disaster. One is lucky in such a case to be left still attached to the original fish.

Another bugbear is the extra tangles which seem unavoidable with droppers. A
little increased care in casting does help, but one must all the time be on the watch
for embryo tangles in one's cast and undo them straightaway. Tangles naturally
occur more often on windy days, in fact if it is too windy the use of droppers
becomes inadvisable; but on normal days a little extra care keeps such tangles to a
minimum, certainly not enough to cause undue worry.

No doubt it will be realised that fishing with a dropper is essentially a warm
water method with medium or small sized flies and a floating line. Whether droppers
would be worth while in spring with a sunk line and bigger flies is doubtful, but
there is room for experiment here. One word of warning; do not use droppers
after dusk when you cannot see whether or not your cast is tangled. It simply isn't
worth while!

As regards the assembling of a nylon cast for use with a dropper, care and attention is essential, though the process is not difficult. The knot where the dropper
leader joins the main cast is all-important, and too much trouble can never be taken
to see that this knot is correctly tied in the first place and that it is not subsequently
weakened. After long trial and experiment I have found only one knot out of many
which is completely reliable for this purpose; so many knots normally used by trout
fishermen will not stand up to the extra strain of playing salmon. This knot is an
ordinary blood knot, tied at the point in the cast where it is desired to attach the
dropper leader and joining the upper part of the cast to both the dropper and tail
fly sections. Cut off enough nylon for the tail fly section, and a short piece for the
dropper (Fig. A); hold them with their 'upper' ends level and you are ready to tie

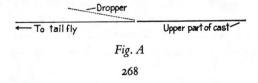

Fig. A

a blood knot (Fig. B) to join these two strands, treating them as one, to the upper part of the cast.

Fig. B

This blood knot should be drawn up slowly and neatly, with one or two extra turns of the single strand of the top section to make a balanced knot. It should be tested thoroughly after tying and after landing fish, both the dropper leader and the main cast being firmly pulled. If any weakness appears the knot should be completely retied.

It will be realised that this knot gives a straight pull, equally to both dropper and tail fly, through the medium of a blood knot which is the strongest form of join between two separate sections of nylon. Its only drawback, a small one beside the great advantages of strength and reliability, is that the dropper leader emerges flush alongside the main cast and does not stand out at right angles. An added refinement which remedies this drawback is to make a half hitch with the dropper leader round the tail fly section, immediately below the blood knot (Fig. C).

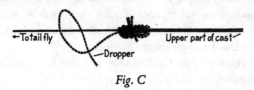

Fig. C

When this half hitch is pulled up reasonably tight, the dropper will stand out at right angles to the tail fly section. But, if a fish takes the dropper, the knot then 'hinges', so that the dropper falls into line with the upper part of the cast, and the tail fly section stands out at right angles. Whereas a thumb- or wind-knot causes weakness by cutting through itself, here one piece of nylon is looped round another with no ill effects. If a fish comes unhooked, it is easy to see which fly it took, as that fly will be in line with the upper part of the cast.

What should be the distance between the dropper and the tail fly, when the cast is assembled? This is important, and the best rule of thumb is to say that this distance should be the length of a good sized salmon. In this way there is a good chance that, with a fish hooked on the dropper, the loose tail fly will be 'masked' by the body of the fish and less likely to foul any outside obstruction; at the same time the dropper will be far enough distant from the tail fly to fish 'independently'. If the dropper is too far up the cast away from the tail fly, there is an ever increasing risk of the latter fouling some obstruction while a fish is being played on the dropper. If the tail fly and the dropper are placed too close together, the object of fishing two separate flies is largely lost. So when you assemble your cast make sure that the tail fly and dropper are correctly spaced. Vary the gap if you like, but on your own head be it if nemesis results from too wide a gap!

The length of the dropper leader should be about 4 to 6 inches. If this leader is too long it is apt to get twisted round the main cast and to form an unsightly tangle, enough to put any fish off; if too short, you cannot easily change the dropper fly.

The dropper fly itself can always be removed when a 'snaggy' pool is to be fished, and be replaced at any time later as required. The presence of the bare dropper leader higher up the cast will make no difference to the effectiveness of the tail fly when the dropper is removed, and there is no need to change the whole cast.

As regards the pattern and size of flies to be used as droppers there is plenty of room for experiment, as pointed out above. But on the whole the same rules apply as for the selection of a tail fly, fished singly. As to the best type of hook for dropper flies, the plain single is best for avoiding tangles; but, if you prefer doubles as being better holders of hooked fish, by all means use them. You may suffer a few extra tangles, but not enough to worry about. Trebles on the other hand are impossible for the dropper fly; they quickly lead to over-frequent tangles. Many people favour a tube fly on the tail, and a single on the dropper.

Finally a word about playing fish. As soon as a fish is hooked try to discover whether he is hooked on the tail fly or on the dropper, and in any case get him away and keep him away if you can from the neighbourhood of other fish. If he is hooked on the dropper take extra care, and try to keep him in fairly deep water away from snags for as long as possible. If at the end of the struggle you can wade in knee-deep to gaff him, so much the better; but keep him well away from your legs so that the loose tail fly does not foul them! You *can* beach him if you wish, but it is risky! You can also net him, but the tail fly must not foul the net before he is in it. In either case you should wait until the fish is well played out before you attempt anything.

The object of all these manoeuvres is of course to keep the loose tail fly from fouling anything. If it does it is odds on, though not a certainty, that you will lose your fish.

A huchen member of the salmon family (Hucho hucho) confined to the Danube system. They run up to 60 pounds and more, but only the smaller ones will occasionally take a fly.

A 48 pound huchen taken in Bavaria in July, 1957.

Monique – now Mme Ritz – with a fine catch of the "stupid salmon." With Ehrling on the Nausta, 1970

If the fish is hooked on the tail fly the hazards are not so great, but you must do your best to see that the dropper does not foul anything, such as rocks, boughs, weed, rushes, the bank, or your helper's clothing. So long as the fish does not run out a long line you should be able to keep the dropper clear without difficulty. It is easier than keeping a tail fly clear.

When your hooked fish has been either landed or lost, have a close inspection of *both* flies and of your cast. Discard anything that is doubtful. Incidentally you should make it a rule to do this also whenever you rise or pull a fish.

It is hoped that this short article may induce some readers to experiment with droppers to their own profit and amusement. Some disasters are bound to happen; but they should dwindle with practice and should soon be outweighed by the additional number of fish encountered and landed, and above all by the extra interest and sport obtained.

My second visit to the Alta

Whether one can really repeat an experience is a question I gladly leave to the philosophers. In any case, I felt the same joy when in 1955 I was able to make a second visit to the Alta, this time with my friend Dr Freddy Cavallasca. To our great regret, Tony Pulitzer was prevented by illness from joining us, but we had the satisfaction of meeting the Duke and Duchess of Roxburghe and their friends.

I have already confessed to the passionate interest I take in watching eminent fishermen at work and discussing their experiences with them. On this occasion, I got just what I wanted as the present Duke of Roxburghe is one of the best salmon-fishers in England and has caught something like 3,000 salmon with the fly. The views of such a distinguished expert were of the greatest interest to me, especially as I was able to observe how they worked out in practice on water with which I was familiar. I learnt much that year, fishing with him, and enjoyed his companionship – although when it comes to some fine points on tackle our views differ, especially on nylon, because he is a firm believer in gut, and, in all honesty, I must admit that his leaders were the strongest I have ever seen. They outlast my own nylon leaders. But my nylon leaders were so much cheaper, I could afford to put on a new one every day.

In England, Scotland and Ireland the gaff is seldom used to land a salmon because in those countries almost all the fish are sold and gaffing causes mutilation. A country in which the protection of animals is a national virtue objects to seeing stab-wounds on a dead salmon. In Norway, however, the Duke, like everyone else, used the gaff, but the one he employed, and had brought over with him, was a fine and delicate weapon of stainless steel, which left no conspicuous marks of damage on the fish.

The Duke's leaders are made of two or three strands of gut, not knotted together but wound round one another. The length of the leader corresponds to the length of the two upper joints of a three-jointed rod, so that the leader will never get involved in the top ring of the rod. For my part, I like renewing my leaders frequently and for this reason I hold that the nylon leader is more practical. Moreover, nylon, which is a homogeneous artificial fibre, is equally tough as well as being thinner than intertwined gut. It is also more supple which, in wet-fly fishing for salmon, gives it an advantage which should not be underrated.

The Duke uses a big six-inch reel on which he likes to have a good ratchet so that the boatman can hear at once when a salmon has taken the fly and know whether he is reeling in or letting out line. A quiet checking of the reel for the same purpose evokes the fisherman's well-known cry 'salmon', but this procedure involves the loss of valuable seconds in manœuvring the boat. Since one of the two boatmen always has his back turned to the fisherman, though they both must work together with absolute unanimity, the advantage of using a ratchet on one's reel in boat-fishing has become clear to me. Nevertheless, I prefer a lighter reel with a diameter of 4 to 4½ inches.

I consider the 16 ft. rod used by the Duke far too exhausting. When you are fishing six to ten hours a day for a fortnight, or more accurately speaking, nightly, the weight of the rod is no insignificant factor. I observed that one of the two ladies of our party contracted a violent pain in the right shoulder while the other often complained of exhaustion, though they were using only 14 and 14½ rods. The Duke had calluses on both hands. Towards the end of the time the other men were fishing at a slower tempo. However, Dr Cavallasca, a complete novice at salmon fishing, felt as little fatigue as I did. We were both of us able to use our 13 ft. Parabolics without blistering our hands. And in spite of frequent contrary winds, I was always able to keep my fly under control. It was only at the end of my second fishing trip in 1955 that I was able to establish to my satisfaction that I had succeeded in managing the 13 ft. salmon rod as efficiently as I could wield my Master P.P.P. of 8 ft. 3 in.

The length of the Duke's salmon rod had, in my judgment, the single advantage that one could cast greater distances, thereby substantially facilitating the business of mending the line and holding a greater length off the water to achieve a better presentation of the fly. But in my eyes that certainly did not outweigh the qualities of the 13 to 14 ft. rod which is handier and easier to manipulate quickly, especially when you are a small man.

Ashaway today makes multi-coloured salmon lines, the different sections being of various colours. This has the indisputable advantage of enabling the fisherman to judge before casting exactly what length of line corresponds to the distance to the spot to which he wants to cast. It gives special precision when you are making a short cast with a loose line. To avoid the necessity of cutting off a piece from the end of the line every day after fishing in order to replace the leader which has become shortened by the frequent change of flies (or, untying it, which weakens the point of the line), you should fit in between the line and the cast an intermediate piece of ·024 in. nylon, with a loop at either end. The upper loop fastens it firmly to the line while the lower one allows you to slip the cast on and off without difficulty. This device saves valuable line and valuable time as well when you have to change the cast while fishing.

Fig 62

This nylon link, ·024 in., between line and leader avoids cutting off pieces of line and saves time.

The Duke of Roxburghe finds that small flies, Nos. 2/0 to 4/0, are best in normal water conditions, while large ones are more attractive to the fish when the water is high or the current very swift. He is certainly right. With flies of medium size I appreciate the value of double hooks. On the other hand, a big salmon fly with a double hook seems to me to be too heavy.

When the sun's rays are shining upstream, there is a distinctly better chance of a fish taking the fly than if they are shining downstream. Does the sunlight in the latter case prevent the fish from seeing the fly or does it give him a too detailed, and therefore deterrent, view of it? However that may be, the salmon is loth to take the fly when the sun is in his eyes.

When a salmon rises to the fly without taking it properly, the Duke lifts the point of his rod slowly. If the fish decides to attack again, as is often the case, the fly moves only slowly out of his field of vision, which often tempts him to catch up with it at the last moment. And if he does not go for the fly immediately, he is at least not alarmed by its cautious withdrawal. Thus by presenting the fly two or three times to the fish one has a good chance of persuading him to take it at last. If this manœuvre does not succeed, the Duke advises a change of fly to one of a different colour or size.

In casting on to swiftly running water, you should hold the rod high on placing the fly on the desired spot, but lower the point as the fly floats away. By this means you ensure that the fly has less drag and sinks better, because the fast current has a shorter length of line on which to put pressure. On slowly moving water you should hold the rod more horizontally after placing the fly. In such cases, you should cast in such a way that the heavier part of the line, which is nearer the rod, reaches the water first and the lighter end of the line with the leader only rolls off afterwards. In this way you get the line out at full stretch, which makes it possible to lend a lively movement to the fly by raising and lowering the point of the rod. By slightly overcasting the heavier part of the line you can lay the line on the water in such a way that the fly is always ahead of the leader. The line should never be allowed to drift in a curve created by the pressure of the current, for in that case the fly does not float in a manner likely to deceive the fish. When casting, the Duke often mends the line in the air against the current before touching the water. As he fishes with a long line, he has thus less trouble in correcting it as it floats.

The question of the rise was also discussed. Observation over long periods shows that generally speaking salmon will take the fly at any time during the 24 hours of the day, but that before and after noon the fish often takes time off. Observation for shorter periods indicates that during certain hours the salmon is particularly active, but exact prediction is always difficult. Only one thing is certain. He who does not fish does not catch fish. A conscientiously kept fishing diary can offer valuable clues as I frequently observed when fishing with my friend Lambiotte. This provides at least a psychological factor, which, in a sport in which self-confidence plays a leading part, certainly amounts to something.

On the Alta the greased line seldom produced results.

One final conclusion that my fishing holiday on the Alta has enabled me to arrive at is the following.

As in trout-fishing so in salmon-fishing the practised and expert fisherman is in general more successful than the average fisherman. But not always . . .

Monique and the stupid salmon

Monique is a little blue-eyed girl, slightly built but very athletic; a girl with a great temperament and a zest for verbal battles and discussions. Her one regret is that she did not study Law. She is also a fine wing shot, but at the time of which I write all she knew about fishing had been gained from watching the *pêcheurs au coup* – the British term them coarse anglers – drifting red worms or maggots along the bed of the Seine, below the Eifel Tower. She always referred to my own efforts as 'fly swatting.'

For years I hoped, some day, to introduce Monique to *Salmo salar*. But in her view fly-fishing lacked action: it was a pastime for those incapable of more active pursuits. So it was that I gave up all thought of taking her to Norway *unless* I could find an aquarium pool – a tidal pool at the foot of a waterfall, as close as possible to the sea and stocked with fresh-run salmon ready to take a fly the moment it hit the water.

In the Spring of 1967, at the Normandy Hotel in Deauville (the Touque flows nearby, a stream with sea trout to 15 lbs in its lower reaches) we met Albert and his charming wife, Miette. Here was my man. He had fished most of Norway's finest rivers and employed a bevy of lawyers whose job it was to contact the Norwegian peasants who owned the fishing rights on streams flowing through their farms.

In July of that year Albert leased two rivers, about 100 miles from the famous Laerdal, and offered me a rod. His description of one part of the water matched the pool I dreamed of finding.

'One river,' he said, 'has a pool at the foot of the first waterfall, only a mile from the fjord. It's full of salmon and sea trout. The pool is tidal, of course, rising and falling twice every 24 hours. You can fish it at an ideal level for the fly four times a day – twice on the flood tide, twice on the ebb – and the fish are always active at those times. Fishing between 10 a.m. and 6 p.m., and without fishing hard, Miette and I usually take half a dozen from that spot. They're not big fish, but being fresh-run they are great fighters. And, Charles, you must bring Monique.'

This was my chance. Had I known the outcome I would have declined there and then, but not being clairvoyant I got no further than the thought that all fishermen exaggerate. (When sport is poor they explain it all quite happily by reasoning that the fish have not yet arrived or the water is coloured; it is too high or too low; the sun is too bright or a storm has been threatening for days. Alternatively, fish are scarce and few have been taken anywhere). But this time, Albert had to be right. There would be no second chance with Monique.

I accepted his invitation and faced the next hurdle. How could I persuade Monique to come with me? In the end we compromised: she promised to stay for three days and I guaranteed her at least two salmon.

There was one other problem. Monique had never cast with a salmon rod in her life and it was essential that she should learn to cast correctly before starting to fish. Thank Heaven, the pond of *Le Tir aux Pigeons* in the *Bois de Boulogne* was only a 10-minute ride from the Ritz. Pierre and I battled through six hours of practice, teaching her to throw a high back line until she became casting-conscious. Throughout that time I feared that Monique would quit at any moment.

Had I but known it – and all that was to transpire before this saga could end – I should have realised that this might well have been the best thing that could happen.

When we arrived at the Sunnfjord Hotel in Forde I started to unpack our luggage, only to find that the bag containing our fishing clothes – boots, waders, raincoats, etc. – was missing.

Monique was hopping mad. She hates rain, cold weather and discomfort in any form.

'Charles,' she said, in a manner that left me in no doubt that she was in earnest, 'this is ridiculous. I have no intention of fishing barefoot, the water here is too cold. Haven't I always told you to count the bags before you leave the airport? When is the next plane to Paris?'

In those few moments all my planning and conniving counted for nothing. I told her that there was no plane for two days, but that I would reserve a seat for her, immediately. And I did. I also cabled the Ritz, asking them to ship the missing bag with all speed. Monique could blame the airline, but I knew where it was: at the Ritz, Paris.

Luckily, Monique was allowed to spin from the bank, but the jinx that had travelled with us still exerted its baleful influence; the spinning reel developed clutch trouble. Monique was suddenly fast to a nice grilse – the first salmon she had ever contacted – but though she reeled in and in, the fish remained stationary.

It was a moment I shall long remember. Monique yelling that she had a big fish, a very big fish; reeling like mad and cursing the salmon because it moved not one inch towards her; ordering Ehrling, our ghillie, to wade into midstream and net her catch, without realising that he, poor man, only wore hip boots and that the water out there was exceptionally deep.

Thinking to ease the situation, I took hold of the line and handed it to her with the instruction that she should drop the rod, hold the line tight and walk up the bank. This simple and very practical manoeuvre met with unexpected opposition.

'I did not come here,' she said, and those blue eyes were positively icy, 'to hand-line fish like the mackerel catchers at Deauville.'

Somehow, that grilse was drawn into the shallows. Ehrling netted it, the sun shone and Monique was as happy as a small boy with his first gudgeon.

'Charles . . . Cancel my plane.'

I dare not look too happy. Casually, I told her that the missing bag would arrive next morning.

'Fine!' she exclaimed. 'I don't like this spoon fishing. Tomorrow we shall have waders and I can fish with the fly. I'll show you how to catch salmon'.

The following day the river was clear, but still a little too high. In order to make casting easier for her, I suggested that she should fish from the high rock beside the waterfall, a point from which even a badly cast line would soon straighten in the fast current.

'Nothing doing!' said Monique. 'You don't think I'm crazy enough to risk my life for one of these fish?'

I replied that I had a very strong rope and she would be perfectly safe. 'Darling Love, just tie the rope round your waist and I will stand behind you, holding it tight. My felt soles cannot possibly slip on the rock.'

During the discussion which followed, the rope, my felt shoes and my own ability to save her from a dreadful fate were all questioned and somehow survived. She finally agreed. But first, she said, we would try it without the encumbrance of rod and line. White with fear and convinced that she was risking her life, Monique edged forward on the big rock. And at that moment my luck changed: a salmon leapt into the air from the very heart of the water I wanted her to fish.

I do believe that her fears had vanished before the fish hit the surface. 'My God!' she exclaimed, 'did you see that fish jump? Quick, Charles, the rod. I must get him. And, please, lengthen this confounded rope.'

Her first cast was too short, too close to the rock.

'Monique, more line, please.'

Then the back-cast missed me by inches. I sat down, fast.

'Still more line, Monique. That's better: now let the line swing towards the rock.'

The tubefly hit the water in midstream and started to swing out of the main current.

'Charles! The line is pulling hard, very hard. I must have a fish. Oh, please, help me!'

There was a fifty yard run, a flash of silver as the fish jumped, then a slack line and Goodbye salmon. No cussing, no orders; just a poor little lady in tears.

For the next two days the salmon showed no interest in the fly. I asked Monique to concentrate on improving her casting and to master the high back line. She agreed and after an hour's practice she stopped looking forward and watching the line whip the water. Instead, she followed my advice and looked at the tip of her rod when it reached 12 o'clock. She noticed that the rod continued to move until it dropped to 3 o'clock. I helped her, holding the rod with her as she cast.

'Watch the rod, nothing else, and don't worry about how the line falls on the water. Try to stop the rod before it reaches 1 o'clock – that's absolutely vital.'

I took my hand from the rod and to my great satisfaction both the rod tip and the line stayed up.

'Well done,' I told her. 'Now, please try another twenty casts, and look up every time.'

Her technique was excellent. When I allowed her to look forward again Monique was casting a superbly straight line and her immediate comment reflected the boundless enthusiasm so typical of her.

'Charles, I have it. Oh, how wonderful. Look . . . I can cast exactly as you wanted me to.'

A fish broke water and she was fast to a small salmon.

'What shall I do?' she called. 'He's pulling so hard, I can't hold him.'

I told her to press with the index finger of her left hand against the inside face of the reel. Not too much pressure. Let the fish run whenever it seems to pull too hard. And when it stops, pump it towards the bank by lifting and lowering the rod, winding line on to the reel as the rod goes down.

Fortunately, the fish soon weakened and Monique, bubbling with energy, was once more in command.

'Ehrling, get the net. Hurry now: if I lose this fish I shall hate you.'

Ehrling had no intention of being hated by anyone. A few minutes later the fish was on the bank and Monique stood there admiring the first silver king she had ever caught with a fly.

This, she said, was the greatest moment in her life. She was so happy, so thrilled. But why had the fish stopped fighting so soon?

'I want another one. Perhaps I should change the fly?'

I persuaded her to leave the fly where it was and move with me to what I knew to be the best part of the pool – a small hole or pocket in the centre of the main current, not deep but a fine resting place for salmon and one used by all the fish going upstream towards the big waterfall. In fact, that fall is too high for them. After many unsuccessful attempts to negotiate it, the fish drop back and eventually find the smaller waterfall behind the island, a natural fish ladder.

The hole we made for has a nice swirl of water and when the current is not too fast it is possible to sink a tubefly vertically below the surface. There it remains stationary or moving gently with the water for a full second before the line pulls it away. In brief, ideal conditions in which to induce My Lord Salmon to take a fly without having to rush after it.

I confess that I was anxious that Monique should catch another fish or two. Other considerations apart, it would remove all risk of our speedy return to Paris. I cast twice to find out how quickly the fly would start to drag and had I been lucky I would have handed her the rod.

Those two casts revealed that the position was OK for an experienced fisherman, but not for a tenderfoot, not even for one with a high back-cast. It was a matter of line speed and the fact that the fly must hit the water first. This could only be done with a perfectly executed and very fast, very high forward-cast, raising the rod point at the last moment to speed the fly's penetration of the surface layer.

My suggestion that she should wait until the current slowed a little was greeted with the utmost suspicion and contempt. I had, of course, seen a fish and wanted to take it myself. I was, she said, an old fox, but not cunning enough by half.

The Old Fox, who had seen nothing whatever, invited her to go ahead. Fifteen minutes later, no results. I moved away. Fishing some fifty yards downstream, I caught two salmon.

'Charles . . . Let me have your place.'

We changed over and I give my word that I fished only the edges of the pool, taking great care not to spoil it for her. Yet I was lucky enough to land a good fish while Monique's best casting produced nothing at all.

Again came the request to change places, and again I agreed.

It so happens that, when hunting, Monique always shoulders her gun as she walks. She did the same thing with her salmon rod on this occasion, wading slowly upstream with a few yards of line trailing behind her. As I walked down I heard a splash, a fish took her fly and that quiet pool echoed with the song of a reel.

'Ehrling! Ehrling, I have one; get the net. Charles! Help me!'

It was a brute of a fish, a salmon that stopped dead when it reached the slow water opposite the bench where we used to sit and watch when fish were not taking. Minutes later it was on the bank, a 15-pounder, and Monique was jumping to conclusions that I found quite shattering.

'There it is, Charles; a bigger fish than any of yours. Could you ask for more definite proof that all your talk of tactics is so much nonsense? These salmon are stupid. All you have to do is drop the line in the water and walk upstream.'

What could I say? That was exactly what she had done. I knew better, of course, but deep down I began to wonder. And what would I have to endure when fishermen and their wives met at future cocktail parties?

With the passing of time, Monique's account of that day's fishing has become a masterpiece. It includes a reference to the fact that though I said a change of fly was unnecessary she decided otherwise and picked out a pattern she knew the salmon would like – an old Jock Scott I had carelessly left in her fly box. She adds – so help me! – that she is now certain that female salmon prefer pastel shades and male fish the darker hues.

My one consolation is that after ten years I finally succeeded in landing *her*, hook, line and sinker. We were married last summer. I am still wondering who was the most stupid: Monique, me or the salmon!

Conclusion

Dear Friends . . . all who have succumbed to the gentle art of fly-fishing . . . you have reached the end of my book. I hope it has proved entertaining and perhaps enabled you to form your own conclusions concerning some of the more important aspects.

To write yet another book on fly-fishing would have been a tough assignment. I confess that I did not have the courage to face it at my age. Indeed, had it not been for the encouragement and friendship of Arnold Gingrich, from the earliest days of our acquaintance, this final edition of *A Fly Fisher's Life* might never have been written.

Fly-fishing enjoys ever-increasing popularity, but many thousands of fishermen remain unaware of the knowledge needed to transform them into skilled exponents of this most delightful sport. To enjoy it to the full one must be well-informed; one must start the right way. Just as the man wise enough to choose the ideal wife will be happy all his life, so it is with fly-fishing.

I have done my best to convey that knowledge, both in the pages of this book and through personal contact with anglers in many parts of the world. It can be summarised as an appreciation of the mechanics of fly casting and the use of properly balanced tackle; a determination to practice the technique I refer to as 'High Speed, High Line' until a satisfactory standard is achieved, and the realisation that brute force is totally unnecessary.

Many people comment on the ease with which a top-class fly-fisher moves his rod, line and leader. If I have done no more than persuade you that by cultivating a relaxed but controlled style of casting your enjoyment will be increased many times over, then the writing of this book – and especially of this final edition – will have been worth while.

When you get to Heaven, as I have no doubt you will, look me up. Given enough time, I shall know where the best trout are lying. Even there, knowledge of the water and correct presentation of the fly should prove the all-important factors. Come prepared!

CHARLES RITZ